Montessori
from the Start

PAULA
POLK
LILLARD
AND
LYNN
LILLARD
JESSEN

Montessori from the Start

The Child at Home,
from Birth to Age Three

SCHOCKEN BOOKS, NEW YORK

All rights reserved under International and Pan-American Copyright Conventions. Published in the United States by Schocken Books, a division of Random House, Inc., New York, and simultaneously in Canada by Random House of Canada Limited, Toronto. Distributed by Pantheon Books, a division of Random House, Inc., New York.

Schocken and colophon are registered trademarks of Random House, Inc.

Library of Congress Cataloging-in-Publication Data

Lillard, Paula Polk.
    Montessori from the start : the child at home from birth to age three / Paula Polk Lillard and Lynn Lillard Jessen.
        p. cm.
    Includes bibliographical references and index.
    ISBN 0-8052-1112-8
        1. Montessori method of education.   2. Education, Preschool—Parent participation.   3. Child development. I. Jessen, Lynn Lillard.   II. Title.

LB1029.M75 L55 2003   371.39—dc21   2002191214

www.schocken.com

Book design by M. Kristen Bearse

Printed in the United States of America
First Edition
25 24 23 22 21 20 19 18 17

To John Lillard and Ned Jessen,
the best of "Montessori husbands"
for their wise counsel and unending
support, patience, and humor

Contents

Preface

Every morning when they come to school, we greet the children and their parents in the hallway. One spring morning a young mother said goodbye to her two older children at their classroom doors. She then stopped to tell us how much she was enjoying her third baby, born just a few weeks earlier. "I want to thank you for what you have done [in a course we teach for parents]. When you start off with that first baby, you're scared. You have made being a mom fun instead of scary." She paused and looked pensive for a moment, then continued, "Not just 'fun'; more interesting and rewarding. You have given me the self-confidence to do this job. I get teary just talking about it." She turned away then, but as she started down the hall, she added in a soft voice, "You showed me what to do." Moments like this, and similar ones with other parents who have taken our parent child course, inspired this book.

We are two women, each from a different generation: a mother, Paula Lillard, and a daughter, Lynn Jessen. Yet, we share a common mission in life: to understand childhood and its purpose, and to share this knowledge with parents so that they can help their children reach childhood's goals. We are both Montessori primary school teachers, certified to teach children from ages three through six years by the Association Montessori Internationale (AMI), headquartered in Amsterdam, the Netherlands. Additionally, Lynn is an AMI-certified Assistant-to-Infancy teacher, trained to aid the development of children from birth to three years old. Paula holds a Master of Arts degree in Montessori education from Xavier University in Cincinnati, Ohio, and has written three earlier books on Montessori education: *Montessori: A Modern Approach* (Schocken Books, 1972, highlighting education for children three to six years), *Montessori in the Classroom* (Schocken Books, 1980, presenting Montessori principles applied to a kindergarten classroom), and *Montessori Today* (Schocken Books, 1996, describing the Montessori program for elementary education).

Together with Jane Linari, a former colleague of Paula's from Lake Forest Country Day School, we cofounded Forest Bluff School in 1982. Forest Bluff is a Montessori elementary and secondary school for children from eighteen months to fourteen years. Additionally, for the past six years we have co-taught a parent child course at Forest Bluff that focuses on the developmental needs of children from birth to age three. It is this course that the mother was referring to in the hallway that spring day.

Each of us came to Montessori by a different path and at a different time in our lives. To give you further insight into the experiences that led us to Montessori, we would like to share briefly our personal histories. Paula, a mother of five daughters, now a grandmother of eight grandchildren, ranging in age from newborn to twenty-one years, tells her story:

I married soon after graduation from Smith College and raised my children in the 1950s and 1960s. In those days before Betty Friedan's *The Feminist Mystique,* women aspired to be at home as full-time wives and mothers. My generation did undertake significant volunteer work, however, and it was in this capacity that I first became interested in Montessori education. The elementary school that Lynn, age six, and her older sister, Lisa, age eight, attended was beginning a Montessori preschool class. I was skep-

tical about this "old-new" educational approach with its emphasis on "freedom" for children. When the school's principal asked
my husband and me to enroll our third child, Pamela, who was
then three years old, in the class, I volunteered to be the Montessori teacher's assistant. I was uncertain about my daughter's
response to this very different type of education, and my being in
the classroom would give me a chance to know firsthand how she
was faring. I also wanted to see for myself how it was possible for
children as young as three years old to handle "freedom" in a
Montessori classroom. I was a former public school teacher and
nothing in my previous experience indicated that young children
should be left "free" to direct their own education.

In the following months, I discovered that Montessori education is about much more than freedom for children. It requires a
prepared teacher who understands how children develop and
who is experienced in establishing a structured environment
that meets their needs at each successive age. The children are
not "free to do as they like," as I had assumed. Instead, they are
free to "work": to engage in sustained and productive activity
while, at the same time, learning how to behave in a community
of others.*

Gradually, I began to realize something that I had only sus-
pected might be true when I had my first baby at age twenty-
two; there is more to being a mother than just feeding, bathing,
dressing, playing with, and loving babies and little children.
These little ones under six years old are not miniature beings
simply growing larger, as a seed grows into a full flowering plant.
They are in the process of forming themselves into new beings
through a series of predictable planes of development. For me,

---

*For a more detailed description of this first experience in a Mon-
tessori classroom, see Paula Polk Lillard, *Montessori: A Modern
Approach*, pp. viii–xi.

being a mother was transformed from largely custodial, albeit loving, care into a stimulating, productive discovery of a new being
in formation and how I might aid that process. I was engaged in
an intellectual and scientific task of the most immense proportions and significance.

In the ensuing years, modern science has verified that indeed
the infant brain is engaged in an extraordinary feat of formation
and that the outer environment in large measure determines
what that formation will be. This is heartening news. Parents
now know that their role is not just important; it is the decisive
factor for their child's future. However, there is a dark side to this
realization, and we come now to the reason why I am so determined to convey the information in this book to others. Whereas
my generation had only one child care book—the original edition of Dr. Benjamin Spock's *Common Sense Book of Baby and
Child Care*—telling us what to do (and to be honest, we felt free
to ignore much of it, having absorbed the wisdom and experience of our own mothers and grandmothers), today's mothers are
inundated with thousands of books on child rearing by psychologists and others. This plethora of books, representing so many
people with differing backgrounds and experience, gives contra-
dictory advice and too often leads mothers to find themselves in
conflicting roles. Add to the confusion over what advice to follow,
the guilt so frequently experienced by mothers who work outside
the home, and the task of raising children is transformed from a
joyful, if challenging, journey of discovery to a tedious and arduous experience.

What to do? In this book, we go back to the discoveries made
at the turn of the twentieth century by a young medical doctor and pioneer educator, Maria Montessori. Her observations
and "discovery of the child" build upon the wisdom of the past
but carry us forward, too, to the twenty-first century. Today's
research and technology are corroborating every one of her rec-

ommendations for the education of children beginning with the newborn.*

Before we give an overview of the chapters to follow on Montessori's discoveries, let Lynn, a mother of three children ages ten, fifteen, and nineteen years, explain her path to Montessori:

The first thing that I remember about Montessori is the Sandpaper Letters. I was in the first grade and my little sister was in a Montessori preschool class. I remember thinking that those letters were magical. "Just by tracing them," I thought, "they could get inside your mind!" From the beginning, then, there was something unique and mysterious about Montessori for me. Yet, it was based on a practical experience of reality: something you saw and felt.

My next memory was of shopping with my mother who was helping to establish three Montessori Head Start classrooms in public housing projects and one elementary school class in an inner-city public school. I was eleven years old and I remember thinking that this was a way out of poverty for these children, a way to get out of the housing projects and gain a foothold in the larger society. The Montessori classrooms were beautiful, orderly places and were laid out with extraordinary care. Each bucket or brush or broom was thoughtfully chosen and placed in the room with such deliberation. The mothers in the housing projects prepared their children to enter these classrooms with great care and respect, too. The children were perfectly dressed

---

*Angeline Lillard, *Montessori: The Science Behind the Genius* (New York: Oxford University Press, forthcoming). Angeline Lillard, Ph.D., is professor of psychology at the University of Virginia and fourth daughter of Paula, sister of Lynn.

with tiny braids and ribbons in their hair or with shirts tucked in and pants ironed. The love of these mothers for their children and the belief they had in education made a great impression on me. One day I was a "helper," taking some of the children to a farm for a day's outing. All these little five-year-olds were sitting in the back seat, singing "Mr. Mixed Up, Who Do You Think You Are?" (a popular song from the '6os). Their openness, energy, and obvious enthusiasm for life made a lasting impression on me.

When I was a teenager, I drove my youngest sister to and from her Montessori school each day. At the end of the day, I would go into the classroom to get her. I was impressed by the peacefulness there. Even at sixteen, I knew it was unusual for young children in a large gathering to be so calm and relaxed. The teacher, Sister Anna (a young Catholic nun, in those days still in her black veil and habit), showed the greatest respect for her twenty-eight children; but it was their positive attitude toward her that most intrigued me.

When I was a freshman at Smith College, my mother began teaching in a kindergarten classroom based on Montessori principles in a suburban elementary school. Again I was impressed by the careful preparation of the classroom. I could see that each item was chosen for a distinct purpose and placed in a specific spot in the room. Nothing was there just for entertainment or for a frivolous reason. One day when I was home for spring vacation, I went into the classroom to take photographs for my mother's second book. The peaceful atmosphere of this Montessori classroom intrigued me, just as my little sister's Montessori classroom had when I was a teenager. My mother treated the children with respect, and they responded with a poised togetherness and self-respect in return. It was not what I expected from five- and six-year-old children in their kindergarten classroom.

About this time I also began to notice that my youngest sister who had had the longest exposure to Montessori, a total of five years, always kept herself busy in productive ways. She would sit for hours on end writing and illustrating stories at the kitchen table. She had an ability to choose her activities for herself, but it was her capacity for staying so focused for long periods of time—the discipline that such concentration requires—that impressed me most.

During this period, I also worked at a day camp for several summers. This experience confirmed in my own mind how differently children behave in an environment that is not suited to their needs. The children raced from one activity to another every thirty to forty minutes. Such a schedule and pace kept the children stirred up all day long. We counselors had to keep them moving from one end of camp to the other: from arts and crafts to swimming to tennis to archery, and so forth. If an activity required a change of clothes, they often had to miss it because the allotted thirty minutes did not allow for ten minutes to walk there and ten minutes to change clothes and ten minutes to walk back, plus time for the activity itself. It was ludicrous.

During none of this time did I consider becoming a Montessori teacher. I was majoring in studio art at Smith College and expected to be an artist for my professional career. After graduation, I began interviewing for available jobs for studio art majors and soon became doubtful about my options. For one thing, I discovered that nothing that I could do as an artist was going to have much positive impact on the lives of others. I wanted to make the world a better place, yet advertising was the obvious commercial career. I did not want to spend my life convincing people to buy things they did not need. I was at a loss.

At this point, my mother suggested that I go to Washington, D.C., for a year to take the AMI Montessori Primary Course. I thought, "Whether I become a teacher or not, I hope to have children someday and this training will be useful." I stepped into the course then with an open mind. After the first day of lectures by Margaret Stephenson, the AMI director of training chosen by Montessori's grandson, Mario Montessori, to reintroduce Montessori training to the United States in 1968, I was "hooked." I remember coming home each day and being so excited. I thought, "This could change the world. Each child represents a new opportunity, a new generation." In college, sociology was my only course to have the potential for a positive impact on the world, yet, I found it discouraging: with adults the problems are already there. But if you caught children at the beginning of their lives, maybe then it would be possible to start them on the journey to becoming productive citizens, capable of contributing to society.

Something came together for me at this point. I thought about my childhood experiences with Montessori: the beautiful environments of the innercity classes; Sister Anna's respectful manner with the children; and the calm, relaxed atmosphere of my mother's classroom. I realized that all along I had been thinking it took a unique person to teach in this way. Taking the Montessori course showed me that it was something that anyone could learn to do. Even I could do this, once I had the training. My path was set.

I taught for three years in two Montessori schools before becoming the founding teacher for the first primary school classroom at Forest Bluff School. My first child was born the following year, and it was through her that I expanded my interest in Montessori, first to the Assistant-to-Infancy level and later to the elementary and secondary levels. I went to Houston, Texas, in 1985 to take the AMI Infancy Course with Judi Orion and Silvana Montanaro, M.D., an AMI Montessori trainer from Rome, Italy. Two things had happened. First, pretty much everything was going wrong with Margaret, my two-year-old child. And, second, I realized that I knew nothing about the child under the age of three years. I knew how to give freedom to a two-year-old, but

I had no idea how to teach her to conform to any kind of limit. I knew how to give her things to explore and develop her intelligence, but I did not know how to help her develop inner discipline so that she could conform to the demands of civilization. I had gotten bits and pieces of information about preparing an environment for infants when Judi and Dr. Montanaro helped me set up a demonstration nursery at an international Montessori conference at Lake Forest College near my house just after Margaret was born. I subsequently set up a child-bed on the floor so that Margaret would have the freedom of getting in and out and moving about her bedroom. I involved her in household activities as I worked around the house. I realize now that I had the outline of what to do. I did not, however, have the all-important details to support the main concepts. It was a classic example of a little knowledge being a dangerous thing.

During the two summers that I was in Houston for the Infancy course, I followed Dr. Montanaro constantly, asking her questions and watching her interact with children. Unlike those of the students who had not yet had children, I knew what questions to ask. Yet, my frustration continued. In spite of my close and loving relationship with Margaret, I still did not really know how to help her with her behavior. Finally one day, Dr. Montanaro turned and glared at me. "No one is going to like this child!" she said. All along, she had been telling me that I had to teach Margaret to live in a world where she was not the center and that everything was not always going to go her own way. Yet, it was at this moment that the full impact of Dr. Montanaro's words hit me and I finally had the motivation necessary to act fully on her advice.

Two stories illustrate this point and help to give a picture of the problems I faced. At two years old, Margaret was used to being carried everywhere. I was her "human horse." Dr. Montanaro observed Margaret straddled on my hip, being carried to and from the parking lot each day, looking like she owned her mother and the world. By the third day, she had witnessed this behavior on five occasions. Now she said to me, "Put her down and let her walk." I said, "That doesn't work. She won't come." Dr. Montanaro said, "Put her down. I will watch her. You walk straight to the car and have a nice conversation with your friend Carol. You can encourage her to follow but you have to keep going." Off we started. Margaret looked at her mother in complete disbelief at this new behavior. She threw herself on the ground, then looked up and saw that I was continuing without her. She stood up, ran five or six feet, then threw herself on the ground again and looked up to see me walking on. This action continued three or four times before Margaret ran the rest of the way and arrived at the car, her little face all tearstained. Dr. Montanaro said to me, "You are never to carry her again. She has her own two legs to walk." For my part, I was amazed at how quickly Margaret learned to walk along beside me. The two problems for her, of course, had been that I carried her in and out of the parking lot every time, not just occasionally, and that it was always her decision, not her mother's.

The second story involves dinnertime. Margaret would eat dinner only when she was sitting in my lap. Dr. Montanaro said, "Don't let her sit in your lap." I protested, "She'll scream through the whole meal. It isn't fair to my roommates." Dr. Montanaro replied, "All of you need to pretend you are listening to a Beethoven symphony and go on with your meal. Include Margaret in your conversation. Don't just pretend she isn't there but don't let the screaming affect you." Just as in the first instance, when I had given her no choice but to do as I asked, Margaret gave up within a few days. Again I realized that she was not as determined about having her own way as I had thought. For her part, I think Margaret sensed in me a new aura of authority. It was as if she was saying, "Oh, this is the person in charge." As a result, she relaxed and began to follow my lead.

For the rest of the Assistant-to-Infancy Course, I gradually began to fill in those essential details. My strongest impression was of how much and how rapidly babies change and therefore how much the adult has to change in order to provide help all along the way. These changes involve a myriad of details from the newborn learning to scoot, to the crawling baby, and finally to the walking child. Each of these stages involves a very different being with very different needs. Therefore, the details of the environment must change in order to provide for these successive needs. When the course was finally over, the aspect that excited me most was the many different ways babies could be helped as they went from one stage to the next.

My education on instituting limits, of course, was not actually a part of the course. It was my "side course" with Dr. Montanaro. Just as AMI-certified teachers at all levels are required to take a refresher course every three years to maintain their certification, I believe the continuing education of parents as they work with their own children is the best guarantee of successful Montessori practice. The information given in the AMI Montessori courses is a priceless heritage. You can only know what questions to ask, however, if you then build on this knowledge by being "in the trenches" with children on a daily basis, whether in the home or in the classroom. It is for this reason that I co-teach the parent child course at Forest Bluff today and do regular home visit consultations for parents as part of this course. Understanding human childhood and how to help individual children meet its goals is a lifelong process that no one can ever fully comprehend. What I can do is continue to ask new questions and share the knowledge gained with others.

In the following chapters we present the stimulating and intellectually challenging approach to parenthood implicit in Montessori education. The Introduction begins with a brief description of Montessori's approach to children and why we believe that she succeeded, where others had failed, in the "discovery of the child." Her concept of the infant as an incomplete being, following specific planes of development in a process of self-formation, and her revolutionary definition of education are explained. Chapter 1, The Completion of the Human Being, espouses the theory behind the practical detail of the chapters that form the body of this book. The process of the child's completion of self and how we aid this self-formation of coordinated movement, independence, language, and the will, through encouraging specific universal human behaviors, are described. Chapter 2, Welcoming the Newborn, presents a detailed plan for the infant's nursery and the advantages of this plan for both the parents and the infant. Chapter 3, Discovering the World, discusses the infant as explorer, the means that she possesses for taking in her world, and the child's "work" as it relates to self-formation. Chapter 4, The Hand and the Brain, and Chapter 5, Crawling to Coordination, are parallel chapters detailing the development of coordination of the hands and the equilibrium of the body. A pictorial Time Line depicting the optimal environment to aid this crucial development follows this preface (see pp. xxii–xxix). Chapter 6, Practical Life, suggests activities to engage this newly walking child who now uses two hands in eager exploration of everywhere and everything, in a sustained and concentrated "cycle of activity." Chapter 7, Personal Care, explains how to aid the child's newly developing independence and use it to build the child's confidence in her emerging abilities. Chapter 8, Language and Intelligence, traces the infant's development of order and intelligence as they relate to the uniquely human gift of language. Chapter 9, The Developing Will, describes how to aid that most elusive of human capacities, the will. Montessori's insights concerning the child's development will give much-needed guidance to parents as they seek to balance freedom with

responsibility and help their child achieve the discipline necessary for a life of fulfillment and happiness. In Chapter 10, we
conclude with a description of the desired results of Montessori
education: young adults who know themselves well—including
their strengths and weaknesses—so they are comfortable within
themselves and eager to continue learning and striving for a better world throughout their lives.

if the baby is given freedom from birth, s/he will begin to slither

SUPINE

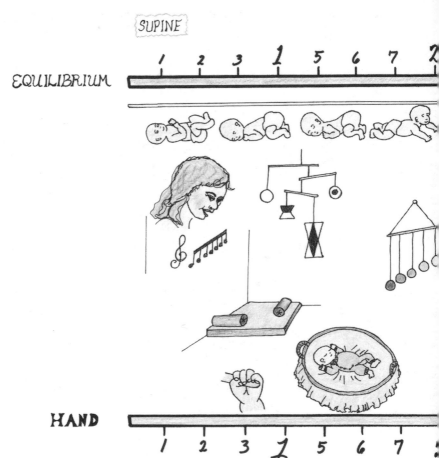

EQUILIBRIUM

1   2   3   4   5   6   7   8

HAND

1   2   3   4   5   6   7

instinctive prehension

PSYCHO-MOTOR DEVELOPMENT

control of the head
has been mastered

turns from
front to back

scooting

begins to
observe hands

prehension becomes purposeful

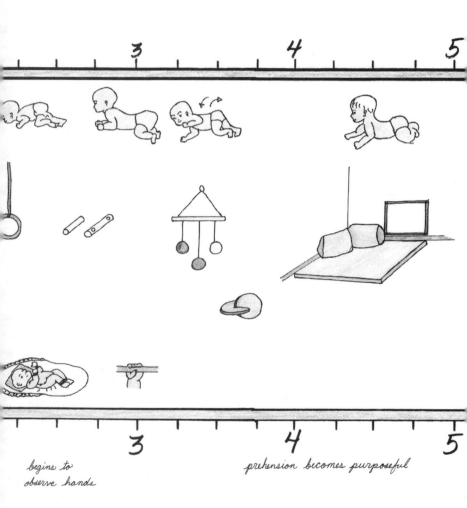

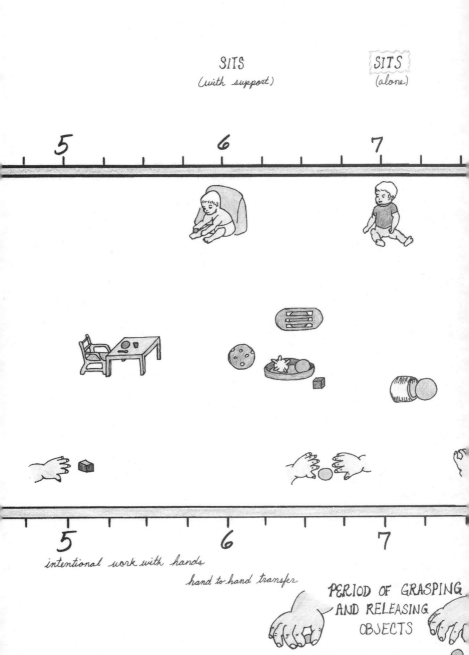

SITS
(with support)

SITS
(alone)

5   6   7

intentional work with hands

hand to hand transfer

PERIOD OF GRASPING
AND RELEASING
OBJECTS

5   6   7

pulls self to standing position

walks on tip-toes
holding on

8   9   10

8   9   10

holds objects
with arms

trol of fingers

prehension of very small objects
with pincer grasp

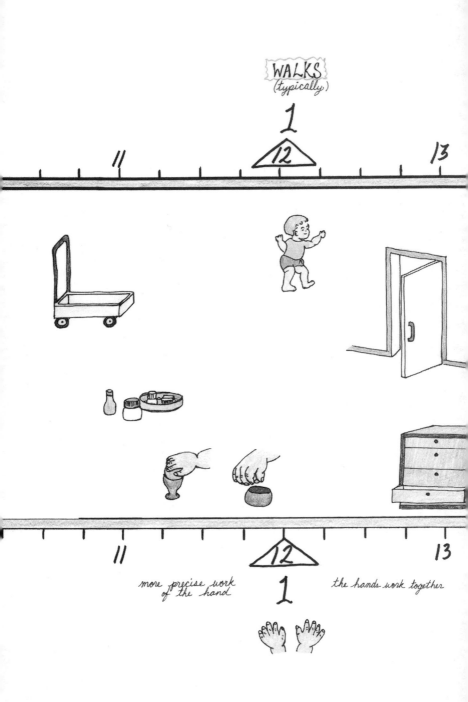

maximum effort: walks with heavy objects
climbs stairs holding objects

14   15   16

activities of the hand
directed toward work

14   15   16

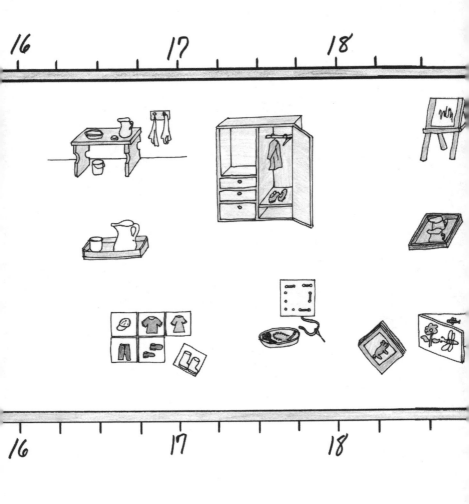

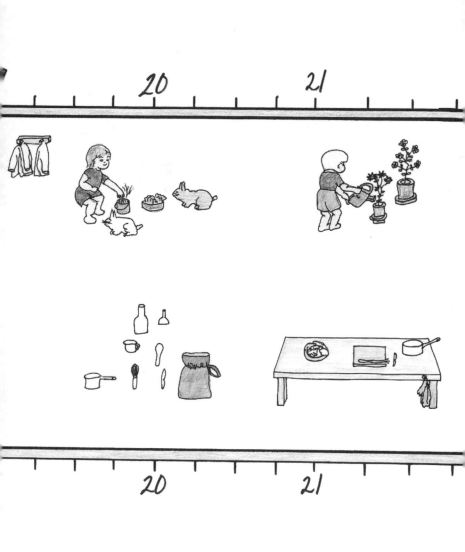

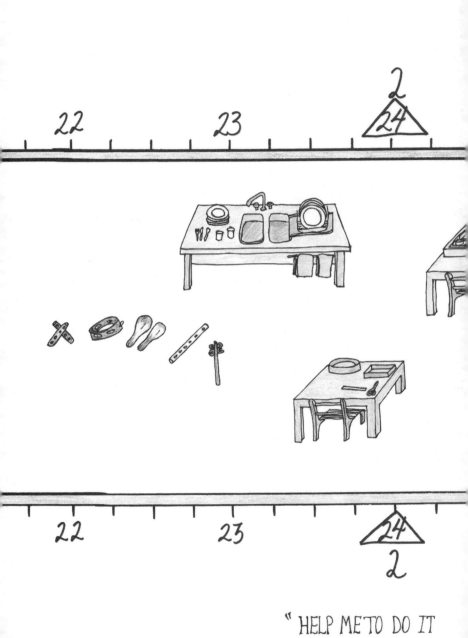

" HELP ME TO DO IT

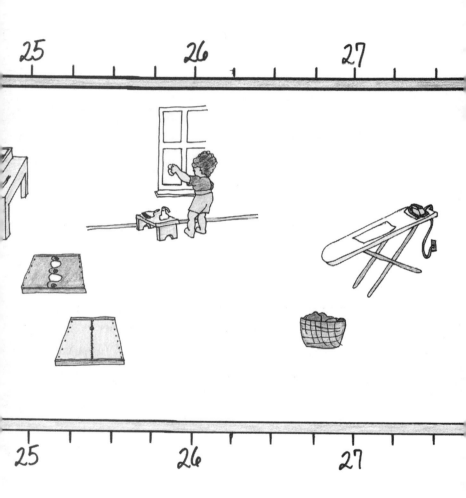

BY MYSELF "

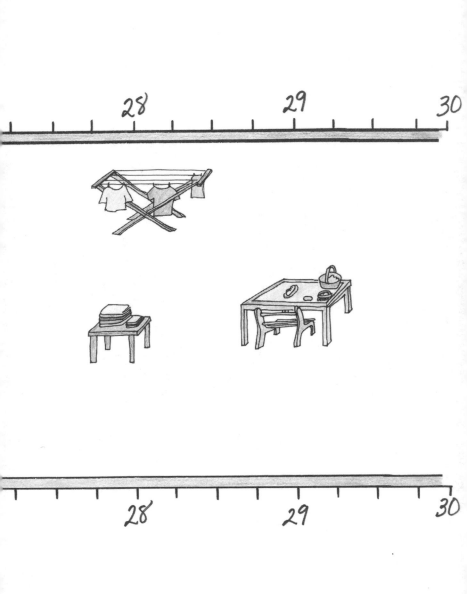

Montessori
from the Start

Introduction

In the early 1900s, Maria Montessori, practicing physician, and professor of anthropology at the University of Rome, presented a startling idea to the academic world. She asserted that the human infant is born an incomplete being whose unique task is to finish its own formation. The constructing of one's own self lasts for the whole period of childhood into young adulthood: from birth to twenty-four years old. This was a revolutionary concept that led inevitably to a second surprising conclusion. Education must begin at the child's birth. More than this, education itself must be reenvisioned. It could no longer be focused on the pouring of knowledge into a child with a "ready-made" brain. The mind was not ready-made at all. Education must help children to construct their own brains and to keep on constructing them until maturity was reached at twenty-four years of age.

For all the previous centuries, educators had deemed the child an essentially formed being and thus a vehicle ready to receive knowledge previously discovered and digested by others. How did Montessori come to the opposite conclusion: that the child is no miniature production of the adult but a fundamentally different being? What enabled her then to capitalize on this unique difference for the child's benefit, developing an entirely new approach to education?

Montessori was a woman of great intelligence and energy who exhibited a courageous and resilient spirit throughout a turbulent life of world wars and revolutions. However, her defining personal characteristic was her compassion for all forms of life. Her sensitivity to human need led her to choose medicine for her career in spite of an early aptitude for mathematics. Montessori's compassion for human life and background in medicine and its practice meant that her mind was well prepared for the observation of children and the discoveries that these observations led to.

These capacities cannot account, however, for the whole of Montessori's contribution to human progress. To understand the breadth of her discoveries and their meaning for our future, we must look to her lifelong search for the human spirit within the child. We can best illustrate this point by describing an encounter with children early in her medical career. Montessori was a young medical doctor in Rome when she was given responsibility for the health of the unfortunate children in the city asylums. In her writing, Montessori referred to these children as "mental defectives" because they appeared retarded. In truth they represented every definition of misfortune, from being orphans or simply not wanted, to being deaf or blind, to being physically or mentally handicapped. Housed as they were in inhuman conditions for children, they behaved more like animals than human beings.

Visiting them each week, this compassionate young doctor sought clues to humanness in their behavior, and hence a way to reach these children. She describes visiting an asylum one day and seeing the children groveling on the floor after crumbs from their meal. The woman who was in charge saw only greediness in the children. Montessori realized, however, that these children who had nothing in their environment to handle or explore were not eating the crumbs. They were manipulating them with their hands and fingers. Montessori asked herself, why? what human need was such action fulfilling? After much observation and study, she began gradually to understand how, as human beings, we develop our intelligence by learning through our five senses, and particularly through the relationship between the hand and the brain. In recognition of the building of the intelligence through this feedback loop of information from the hand to brain and back again, Montessori stated that nothing should be given to the brain that is not first given to the hand. By this she meant that abstract ideas and information of every possible kind should be given to the young child first in concrete form to be held, discovered, and explored. From this initial insight into the development of intelligence in young children, based on practical experience with children in extreme conditions, came all the Montessori materials so widely acclaimed today.

When Montessori began her work with children in the first years of the twentieth century, the prevailing attitude was that children had an "evil nature" which needed "correction." From the viewpoint of the twenty-first century this seems an odd conclusion. A lingering acceptance and belief in magical powers and superstition from earlier centuries may have accounted for this belief. During the intervening years, our culture has swung to the opposite extreme, regarding children as good by nature.° As a scientist, Montessori was objective about the nature of the child. Her emphasis was on the child as an unformed being, albeit a human and spiritual being. This neutral view of the child's "goodness" or "badness" left Montessori free to observe children's behavior without value judgments.

As a result, in succeeding years during her search for the human spirit within each child, Montessori gradually discovered the stages of development that all children and young adults follow—the specific powers that nature provides to help them reach their goals in each formative stage—and she developed

---

°For a clear and thoughtful historical account of this shift, see James Davison Hunter, *The Death of Character* (Basic Books, 2000).

specific approaches and methods to aid them in their journey to adulthood. When she observed that young children under age six were clearly self-centered and egocentric in action and attitude, she saw it as a phenomenon the purpose of which needed to be understood to know how to help them. Eventually, she realized that this natural drive of young children provided the focus and energy for their self-development. Rather than deserving condemnation and correction, it made possible, with proper aid by the adult, the development of the young child in the first six years of life into a strong individual capable of independent action, language, self-discipline, and basic academic skills of writing, reading, and mathematics: in other words, someone for the first time able to make a real contribution to others.

She noted other characteristics of children under the age of six. They go through very specific and well-defined periods of interest in certain areas of their development. For example, there is a period of intense absorption with order, another for language, and another for learning to walk. During each of these time frames, varying in duration from months to years, the child is so focused on the particular development that he will ignore other phenomena previously of great interest to him. His energy level and dedication to his single-minded task are extraordinary but terminate just as abruptly as they began. Montessori called these intervals Sensitive Periods.

Another phenomenon of the child under six years old observed by Montessori involves the child's mental capacities. If the child's mind is unformed at birth, how is he to learn about the world around him? How is he to take in the sensorial impressions from his environment and create knowledge from them? Clearly, the child has to have some ability to learn without the developed brain of a more mature being, with its already formed neural structures and synapses. In response to this dilemma, Montessori noted that the child seems to have a capacity for taking in the whole of his environment just by existing within it. It is an absorptive ability that is not yet based on selectivity; whatever is available to the child for sensorial exploration registers in his as-yet-unformed brain. This capacity for absorbing from the environment like a sponge soaking up moisture from its surroundings, which Montessori referred to as the "absorbent mind," is a phenomenon of the child's first six years. Like the Sensitive Periods, the absorbent mind disappears, and a new way of learning takes its place. Because of the natural emphasis on the child's development as an individual in the first six years and the unique capacity during the Sensitive Periods by the absorbent mind to aid this process, Montessori designated these beginning years as the child's first plane of development.

Similarly, when children after the age of six began to exhibit very different characteristics and mental abilities from younger children, Montessori did not try to change their behavior but to understand it. What she noted is that elementary school children between the ages of six and twelve years become interested in their peers, not from the self-centered viewpoint of younger children, but from a genuine curiosity and desire to understand on a deeper level the thoughts and activities of others. Rather than being focused primarily on a sensorial exploration of the factual world about them, they now want to devote the main thrust of their energies to getting along with others and doing things together. They are transformed from essentially "sensorial explorers" to "social explorers." This is an extraordinary shift in attention.

In addition, the elementary school child's mind is now beginning to reason, albeit on a child's level, and he is capable of distinguishing the real from the unreal—not based on the knowledge of others but on his own powers of reason and imagination. There is no parallel to the Sensitive Periods of the first plane in this second stage of formation, but there are definite interest traits that help the child with development as a social being. Montessori called these social interests of the elementary child "psychological characteristics." They include an intense absorption with issues of good and evil, justice and injustice, loyalty and disloyalty, and the rules and rituals of the group. The child has extraordinary energy and is physically healthier than in the earlier period. With his immense curiosity about all of life and his newly formed powers of reason, the child at this stage is in his most intense period of learning. In fact, Montessori called it the "Intellectual Period." Because of his consistent physical and mental strength, his great interest in life, and his grasp of abstract ideas, the child is an easy and pleasant companion for his parents during this period.

Montessori called the years from ages six to twelve the "second plane of development." Because children are no longer so self-absorbed but are now genuinely interested in the ideas and contributions of others, and because they are capable of abstract and imaginative thought, she created an entirely different educational approach from that of her plan for children in the first plane. In the first plane she designed materials primarily for individual use by the child. The children work near each other, and talk freely, often spontaneously helping younger children when they need it. In other words, they learn how to behave respectfully in a group. Montessori's plan for the second plane, on the other hand, emphasizes the child's newfound interest in others and aids his ability to work constructively with several of his classmates at a time in accomplishing a specific project or goal. Montessori designed her elementary school curriculum to enhance this objective. In addition, she based her elementary school plan on imaginative stories that introduce the underlying framework and unity of all knowledge. From this all-inclusive base, the children pursue ever-more-detailed knowledge through ongoing research in specific areas of interest. To assist them in their discoveries, Montessori created elementary materials to lead the children, now working primarily in small groups, from concrete representations of knowledge to abstract concepts. She did so with the same genius and practicality that she exhibited in creating materials for individual use for the younger children.

Because her primary concern was the human spirit within each child, it is worth noting that Montessori included music and art materials as integral parts of the classroom environment. They are freely available to the children at all times, and never relegated to a separate room and a "specialist" teacher down the hall from the regular classroom. The message to the children is that these expressions of the human spirit are not esoteric activities for the talented few but activities to be understood and engaged in by all. The beauty and naturalness with which Montessori elementary school students illustrate each piece of their work is ample testimony to this process of combining artistic expression with academic work.

The first and second planes of development, covering the first twelve years of life, complete the years of childhood. At their end, the human being has exhausted the opportunities to develop into a completely formed child. Now an entirely new formation begins. In order to make room for it, disintegration in the former construction of self as child must take place. Therefore, this period, particularly in the first three years, or subplane, involves a paradox. On the one hand, great new strengths and capacities appear in the form of more complex and energizing psychological characteristics. On the other, there is a great vulnerability and fragility, similar to that found in the child in the first three years after birth. Thus twelve-to-fifteen-year-olds are suddenly, and seemingly inexplicably, very self-centered and self-absorbed once again. They think everyone is noticing each small detail about them and that whatever happens to be going wrong (or even right) is because of their actions or lack of them.

As in the years from birth to age three, they are undergoing intensive physical growth and changes in mental capacities. They are prone to physical illness and have heightened needs for special nutrition, more sleep, and a balanced day with plenty of time for reflection and self-expression.

Perhaps most important of all, young adolescents have great need of close, one-to-one adult attention, just as in the first three years of life. The difference this time is that these adults cannot be only their parents, or even primarily their parents, because the adolescent already knows what his family stands for and what it believes in. That knowledge was absorbed in forming his self into a complete child. The psychological characteristics of adolescents are geared to helping them determine how the members of other societies of the globe live and fulfill their human needs. For such an exploration they want mentors outside their immediate families. At the same time, just because they are so vulnerable and weakened compared to the preceding plane, they need the comfort and companionship of intimate, supportive peer groups to dispel their loneliness and provide a haven of security and acceptance of their ideas.

Through all of these changes, the child is disappearing and the adult is gradually emerging. Thus Montessori identified the years from age twelve to eighteen as the third plane of development, and noted its similarities to the first half of childhood. The final plane, the years from eighteen to twenty-four, mirrors the stability and intellectual expansion of the second half of childhood, the Intellectual Period of the child. This fourth plane of development completes the two planes of adulthood. At its conclusion the adult is fully formed. If all has gone well, he is a mature being, ready to live wisely and responsibly and to fulfill his part in serving humanity.

In view of her discoveries of the planes of development and the child's self-formation, Montessori set a new goal for education as a process of aiding "the development of a complete human being, oriented to the environment [that is, aware of his place in the natural creation of the universe] and adapted to his time, place and culture [prepared to meet the challenges of a specific historical period]." Whether born in the Stone Age or the modern technological world, children have had the same needs in the spiritual realm to survive and contribute to the human group of their era and place. The only reason that each of us is here on this earth is our ability as human beings to meet these needs of the human spirit: needs of art, music, religion, and all other areas of self-expression and love for creation and humanity. It is by these means that we contribute to our particular culture and social group, and can change them for the better. We are indeed both a spiritual and a social species.

Montessori's definition of education then expands beyond the parental goal of the child's personal happiness to include the child's role in human destiny. Montessori regarded human beings as change agents in evolution. We have changed the face of the earth, creating and altering the direction of plant and animal life, transcending physical limitations of communication, and traveling into the cosmos, and now we peer into the human mind itself. Montessori believed that each child has a part to play in the continuing story of the human understanding and transformation of the universe. She called this individual responsibility the child's "cosmic task." The plane of development when the child becomes fascinated with this concept encompasses elementary school when the child is between the ages of six and twelve years. It therefore belongs primarily to the second plane.

As part of recognizing their personal role in human life, Montessori understood the importance of elementary school children realizing that the quality of their present lives is directly dependent upon the gifts of past generations. In her elementary curriculum she introduced the accomplishments of human beings throughout the ages and emphasized gratitude to them for their contribution. Elementary school children, especially, need heroes from the past and to recognize that they are part of the grandeur that is the pageant of human civilization. It is in the second plane, then, that the seeds of respect for human progress and the permanence of human civilization must be sown. This is very difficult to accomplish, however, if the work of the first plane in building a strong individual child has not been success-fully completed. The crucial first plane of development is, then, the focus of this book, and specifically its sub-plane, the first three years of life.

ONE

The Completion
of the Human Being

Before we begin the chapters of practical detail that form the body of this book, it is important to visit two more areas of thought about the formation of human beings. If we are going to help the human infant in the monumental task of self-completion, we need to understand where the energy for self-construction and positive response to life comes from in human beings. How do we encourage enthusiasm and interaction with the environment? How are they discouraged? Secondly, if we are going to define the human infant as incomplete at birth, we need to outline the specific formation that is necessary for the child to become a complete human being. Both of these topics come to light through an awareness of the differences between human beings and all other species.

We have said that the human infant is incomplete at birth. It is our role as adults to assist our children in the formidable task of finishing their own formation as human beings. Only in this way can our children become fully formed adults and reach the potential which they are capable of from birth. The degree of this challenge for both the adult human being and the human child sets humans apart from all other species. It is true that the young of some animals, specifically mammals, are born in an immature state. However, their task is largely pre-programmed by their genes, and their instincts follow a narrowly limited path of development. Given the care required by creation's plan for their species, they only need time to grow bigger and mature into adulthood. They pay a price for the predetermined nature of their existence, however. They have limited versatility in their adaptation to their environment. For example, the foal and calf are destined to eat grasses and grains; the tiger and lion cub, small mammals. The ways in which they meet other challenges of existence are programmed as well: their fur keeps them warm, horns and sharp teeth defend them, swift legs carry them from danger, and so forth.

The human child, on the other hand, is born with no set pattern of instinctive behavior to meet its fundamental needs for survival; its options are limitless. No predetermined response limits our possibilities in devising the means for meeting our fundamental needs for food, shelter, clothing, transportation, and defense. Instead of the specific instructions of instincts, we are given propensities to certain actions. Although we are born naked and defenseless without a means for shelter and with no instinctual knowledge of what is safe for us to eat, through these propensities we have more than survived; our behavioral tendencies account for the development of all the varied civilizations throughout the ages from prehistoric peoples to the modern era of telecommunications. Montessori offered a description of these propensities to help us understand how children respond to the environment in which they are born. She did not intend for any list of behaviors to be limited or necessarily definitive. Each of us could no doubt come up with a different list of our own. Nevertheless, the following ideas can serve as a general guide. For better comprehension and recall, we have combined them into four groupings.

The first grouping involves answering the question, what is out there? It includes exploration, orientation, and order. Human beings set out to explore the surrounding environment and discover its possibilities. When we do this, however, we have to be able to find the way back to our starting place. Hence the human action of orientation and order is necessary. We need to build a mental map of our surroundings and an internal sense of direction, distance, time, and sequence. Our expression in language and organization in thought are based on this ability to recognize and use order in our lives. When these tendencies toward orientation and order are disrupted—as in changing geographic or emotional environments—we experience disorientation and stress. Similarly, if we are restrained from exploring our world either physically or intellectually, we tend to become bored, even depressed.

A second grouping helps us deal with the results of our explorations: what might I do with what is there? Our propensity to abstract thought and our imaginations allow us to make new creations from what we find and see around us. Everything that we have in our modern lives of comfort and ease, and every vision of nobility, courage, and love, came from our innate tendency to imagine what is not yet before us. Hence, early humans watched animals use their hooves to dig and their horns to protect, and they devised tools and weapons of defense for human use. Through the ages, acts of human bravery and sacrifice were recounted to the young, and new generations dreamed of the heroic deeds and accomplishments that they in turn would contribute to society.

The third grouping is the largest and involves the crucial transition from dream to reality: how can I carry out my abstract ideas? To make this leap, human beings are given five key behaviors: manipulation, exactness, repetition, control of error, and perfection. To make the clothing fit, the house shelter, the boat sail, and the space shuttle soar required every one of these human tendencies during its development. In the world of ideas, communism and fascism were tried through these behaviors, and their results found wanting, even as democracies with dreams of liberty and justice for all are now striven for in many parts of the world, and are continually evaluated.

The last grouping consists of a single tendency. However, it can fairly be called the key to all the rest, for it involves a spiritual gift: the gift of ourselves freely given to others. This behavior answers the question, how can I tell others about what I have done? We call it communication. Without it, each new generation would have to rediscover all knowledge and wisdom of the past. With it, we stand on the shoulders of giants and can go forward in each decade to new heights in every field of human endeavor.

Because of the new global world of telecommunications, the thoughts and accomplishments of all human beings, past and present, are accessible to a degree that no one could have envisioned in times past. The opportunities are vast. Yet, the challenges are exponentially greater as well. How can we still the constant prattle and noise that surround us in our technological world, and find time and opportunity for the most meaningful communication of all: the intimacy of love, understanding and respect of one human being for another in the home, the school, the workplace, in nature, our places of worship, and in our marriages.

All of these behavioral tendencies—exploration, orientation, order, abstraction, imagination, manipulation, exactness, repetition, control of error, perfection, and communication—operate throughout our lives. However, they manifest themselves differently as we grow older. Exploration for a seven-month-old baby, a seven-year-old child, a seventeen-year-old adolescent, and a seventy-year-old senior citizen is demonstrated through different expressions. The phenomenon of exploration itself, however, remains a constant human behavior if we live fully from birth to death. Because our behavioral tendencies operate throughout our lives, to the extent that they are valid and universal to the human experience, each of us will recognize them in ourselves. We need only to look for them in our daily behavior.

Human infants use the stages of their development, as referred to in the Introduction, to help them in their task of self-formation. Specifically, in the first plane of development, they make use of their absorbent minds to incorporate the environment around them and of the Sensitive Periods to develop specific abilities such as walking and talking. In later developmental stages, they respond based on certain psychological characteristics that help them to develop their capacities.

It is these behavioral tendencies—operative from birth and continuing into the later planes of formation, and forming a constant connection with the environment—that will enable the child to finally become a fully functioning adult human being. They supply the energy and enthusiasm for the essential, continuous relationship with the environment throughout our lives. When they are fully operative in our everyday activities, whatever our age, we experience joy and a sense of being fully alive. To the extent that they are missing from our daily lives, we feel listless and unenthusiastic.

The energy of our response to life is directly related, then, to how our environment encourages and allows for the human tendencies in our everyday life. It follows that children need more than opportunity to respond to the environment; they will need encouragement. In the following chapters, we discuss ways to design the home environment for the child so that the human tendencies are actively encouraged. You will note that our suggestions are often at odds with the current fad or media hype. For example, psychologists today discuss the need for "stimulation" in the child's environment. The problem with this term is that it is vague. With the best of intentions, parents respond in excess and children are harmed more than they are helped. As you will see in later chapters, a simple but well-thought-out plan, geared to specific formation of the child at designated age levels, is the most helpful approach.

Nor should we forget that the mission of human development is also the basis for creating homes for adults, too. In order to develop our humanity, we must nurture the human tendencies in all of us. Our homes also should reflect adult needs for exploration, orientation, order, imagination, exactness, repetition, control of error, manipulation, perfection, and communication. All of these behavioral tendencies are clearly visible through, for example, music, art, and other forms of spiritual expression, which indicate that their rightful place is in our homes. The mission of developing the home environment has belonged primarily to women in past civilizations. Whoever may now assume this responsibility, the role of homemaker remains essential to human destiny. Today, although some of us enjoy the greatest affluence the world has ever known, we find that developing a home environment that serves the human spirit, a home of beauty, order, and simplicity, remains a very challenging task.

We now turn to the child we have referred to as "incomplete" at birth. In some ways, this lack of completion is shared with other mammals when they are born. In varying degrees, they also require adult-nurturing for a period of time before they become fully functioning adults. None, however, need the assistance of adults in their group for nearly a quarter of a century. This is the span of time Montessori identified as necessary for complete adult formation in the human being. Her conclusion is supported by recent scientific research demonstrating that the foundational neural structures in the frontal lobes of the human brain are not completed until approximately age twenty-four. It is in the frontal lobes that our most advanced reasoning and knowledge reside, including wisdom.

What must the human child achieve in order to become a complete human being? The development of the brain through sensorial awareness and interaction with the immediate environment is the beginning of the child's journey. This development is individual to each child; no two brains are alike. In this sense, we are all "originals." In fact, the brain that each human being builds is so different, it is amazing that we can understand and communicate with each other at all. We do, however—against huge statistical odds.*

The outward manifestations of brain development are the child's self-formation as an individual of growing independence, coordinated movement, language, and a developed will. In order to become a complete human being, the child has to advance in all of these areas beginning with the first days of life.

For the young of the animal species, independence as soon as possible is essential as a matter of physical survival. For the human child, independence, the ability to do things on one's own, is most important for its psychological component; it is the path to confidence and self-assurance. The infant is born as one who must be served. Gradually, the child is helped to take care of basic actions independently and, finally, to serve others. To grow in confidence in this process of forming independence, the adult has to prepare just the right amount of challenge for the child to face. Even adults lose confidence when they find themselves overwhelmed by situations where they have no chance of success. Yet, we routinely put children in this position by not thinking through simple acts of everyday life and then finding the best means for a child of that age to do them independently.

Everything we will describe to you in subsequent chapters will help the child to ever-increasing independence of action and therefore to the ability to help others who are less capable because they are either younger or otherwise less developed. Montessori outlined environments leading to the child's independent functioning at school as well as at home, thereby preparing the child for growing intellectual independence as well. The comfortable self-possession of students from a quality Montessori school is the attribute most often remarked upon in their assessment by other educators and professionals.

---

*See Lise Eliot, *What's Going On In There?* (Bantam Books, 1999).

The significance of independence for the human child then is the view that it gives of the self. In Montessori education, self-evaluation is a function of realistic achievement through independent action. Adults cannot give children confidence and self-regard through external praise and evaluation; those come as the result of the child's own efforts. An infant first explores an object, perhaps a carrot, with the senses of touch, sight, and smell. If the environment is properly prepared for her, at fifteen months of age, she can wash it with a small vegetable brush. By eighteen months, a child can use a vegetable peeler to peel one slice of carrot skin at a time and then discard it in a dish. She can use a small cleaver, with a filed blade so that it is not overly sharp, to cut pieces of the peeled carrot for eating or serving at family dinner. By five years old, a child can prepare her own lunch for school from preselected items and with a minimum of adult assistance. From such independent accomplishments come the child's sense of self-mastery and resulting self-confidence. (*Cautionary note:* Adults must always be in constant attendance or monitor closely when such objects are used.)

This independence in the child is not to help make life easier for the adult. In fact, at least initially, helping children to establish independence requires a great deal of effort and thought on the adults' part. Montessori encourages us to go to this trouble for children so that they will experience the confidence that comes from not having to wait for someone else to do what is needed. It is not to help adults, then, that we help children to become independent in daily acts; it is to help children.

The slow development of coordinated movement in human infants is one of the clearest signals that they are still in an embryonic state at birth. The length of time during which they lack coordinated movement is unique among the animal species. The young foal rises to its feet immediately upon birth, albeit in a wobbly state, and within hours is running by the mare's side.

The priority of safety undoubtedly plays a part in this early mobility. The foal's earliest movements are guided by instinct, however, and not by thought. The human infant, on the other hand, needs to develop purposeful movement guided by the mind. Such a development of movement depends upon mental formation that can only take place over time and in direct interaction with the environment.

It is the unique role of human beings as change agents in the universe that requires us to think before acting. If we are to help infants to healthy development of coordinated movement, we have to keep the goal of responsibility in action foremost in our minds. This means that we need to prepare an environment for the infant that will encourage action with purpose and with the possibility of consequences. We will discuss in later chapters what such an environment might be. Here we might simply say that the present practice of confining babies and young children in cribs, playpens, jumpy seats, swings, and so forth, hinders their early experiences in movement and exploration of their environment. Further, pediatricians are now advising that babies be put to sleep on their backs for reasons of physical safety. Unless parents make a conscious effort to put their babies on their stomachs when they are awake, babies do not spend sufficient time in this position to develop the necessary arm strength to get up on their knees, crawl, and then walk, at the natural times to do so. This delay in coordinated movement may have consequences for the child's future development that are not yet fully understood.

Our goal is to help the infant to meet each time frame in the development of movement from scooting to crawling to walking, from the use of one hand in grasping and releasing, to two hands working together, to the refinement of the pincer grip of forefinger and thumb working in opposition. On the perfecting of these two areas of movement, the body and the hand, rest the great accomplishments of human beings in response to their environment. No other species enjoys such a range of movement: from the disciplined grace and control of the ballet dancer and the skilled athlete, to the intricate, delicate, and precise hand movements of the surgeon in the operating room, the scientist in the laboratory, and the astronaut in the space shuttle. All of these productive movements are guided by the intellect. It is this union of coordinated movement and human intelligence that we seek to facilitate from the infant's birth.

The basis of language is communication. Certainly animals are capable of communicating with each other and this communication often begins at birth. Paula remembers vividly the whinny of a mare to her first foal immediately upon its emergence, one cold spring night many years ago. It sounded so encouraging, and indeed the little filly did struggle gamely to her legs and within minutes she was nursing from her mother. What surprised Paula most was the air of recognition about the mare, as if she had expected just this particular filly all along. Was there an instinctive communication between them while it was still within the womb? While there may be communication between mare and foal, it differs greatly from human language, with its unique relationship to abstract thought. Our language both written and spoken is a way to communicate our ideas to others: to know and be known by them through an abstract realm.

The word "infant" comes from the Latin word *infans,* which in translation means "incapable of speech." Although they are indeed incapable of speech at birth, human babies are programmed for language in their genetic structure. They have a brain that recognizes the basic sound units, or phonemes, for all human languages from the moment they are born. Such consistency is strong evidence of the deeply biological basis of the human infant's potential for language.

Of the first three areas of infant self-formation—independence, coordinated movement, language—language is the key to the child's intelligence. Intelligent thought depends upon language. We think in words and symbolic representations. Language allows us to have something in our minds, to manipulate it, and to create something new with it. We are able to hold a thought, enabling even the young child, through her developing language, to follow a simple command: "Bring me the red ball" or "Go get three spoons." One of the reasons we care so much about giving language to the young child is that this is a tool that the child is going to use to think and to build a mind. In a sense, then, our language is who we are.

The abstractions we create through language give us the capacity to elevate human actions to a higher plane, thus bringing meaning to an otherwise merely physical existence. Sexual behavior, merely an act of physical response in animals, is elevated through language to the deepest and most intimate expression of love and lifelong union between human beings. It is through this process of abstraction that the concepts of good and evil, and the virtues necessary for the struggle we face between them, arise. Art and religion, those uniquely human expressions, become possible, as do all the qualities that we associate with the spiritual and artistic: contemplation, solace, compassion, and appreciation of beauty whether of music, art, literature and poetry, or nature.

The development of the will completes the child's self-construction as a human being. Indeed, without a disciplined will, a human being cannot truthfully be called human at all. It is our ability to choose our behaviors, as opposed to control predetermined by instinct, which finally separates us from the animal kingdom. The squirrel hoards nuts for the winter, the rhinoceros uses its horn as a weapon, and the beaver uses its teeth as a tool to cut trees for the dam that will facilitate its shelter. None of these actions are by conscious decision. They are the result of an instinct for these adaptive behaviors. We choose our adaptation to the environment; animals do not.

Free to choose our own behavior, our first mission is the control of self. The child spends the first three years of life working toward a conscious control of the will. Unfortunately, the term "will" when it refers to children is often used inappropriately in our present culture. There are books that use the term "strong-willed" to discuss a child who cannot or will not cooperate with adults or family members—a child who, in fact, does not have a developed "will." In Montessori education, we focus instead on the development of the will as the positive force that enables us to learn from our environment and society and to make a contribution to them. How then do children develop this vital ability?

In the first weeks of life, the infant strives to maintain focus on a self-selected aspect of the environment. Eventually, sustained attention and repetition build neural structures within the brain that represent the knowledge gained. It is through this effort of concentration and control of attention that all learning takes place. All human invention and the ability to alter the world come from this ability to give focused attention to specific, chosen detail in our surroundings. Our capacity for concentration, then, is at the root of human progress. It is the best evidence we have that we are meant to be lifelong learners. Throughout our existence as a species, we have been continuously solving problems—from discovery of the productive uses of fire by early humans, to our understanding of biotechnology today and its potential uses for the benefit of humankind.

Over time the infant begins to develop the ability to inhibit her actions and by eighteen months is capable of a degree of self-awareness. It is not until approximately age three years, however, that the child begins to appreciate that her thoughts are different from those of others. During the period between eighteen months and three years, she must transform herself from a being that demands what she wants, when she wants it, where she wants it, into a child capable of complying with adult requests.

The child's freely given obedience is a necessary first step in adaptation to civilized behavior and to living responsibly in a community of others. We watch carefully as the child progresses from one who exhibits willful behavior to a child with a developed will: one who knows "I can focus my energies. I can restrain my actions. I can control my impulses." It is by no means certain that this transformation will take place. Just as with independence, coordinated movement, and language, we are not born with a disciplined will, only the potential to develop it. Children require very specific means to establish a conscious will by the end of their third year.

The purpose of the child's early birth is now clear. It allows for the development of independence, coordinated movement, language, and will, in relationship to an environment set in historical time. Adaptation to human circumstance and custom is therefore virtually limitless. The child is a spiritual being who asks, why am I here? what is my task, my responsibility? Adults need to recognize this search for purpose in life as they seek to aid the child in her completion as a human being.

The adults' role is to prepare an environment for the child, to guide her interaction with that environment and to give her freedom with responsibility. If they do so with knowledge, as well as love, the child is helped to grow to adulthood at twenty-four years as a lifelong learner who is ready to assume responsibility for others, to serve them, and, eventually, to become a parent herself. Thus, Montessori's educational formula is a simple one consisting of but three elements: the prepared adult, the prepared environment, and freedom with responsibility.

| # Welcoming the Newborn

For nine months the unborn child's environment is established for us. We have no role in its preparation beyond caring for the mother's well-being. As soon as the baby struggles from the mother's womb, however, we are faced with the task of preparing its second environment. This is our opportunity to consciously prepare for the infant's needs in self-formation. Because sustained attention and the will are central to every other aspect of self-construction, we must concentrate upon the development of these capabilities as soon as possible. The first weeks are a period of rapid and crucial development; we cannot wait while precious time passes. Our task is to give opportunities for concentration in the first weeks of life.

Let us consider, then, the newborn's bedroom. What do we typically find there? There is a crib, a changing table, perhaps a rocking chair for the adult. In effect, we are already saying, "This is a place where the baby is not awake." From the outset we take children to busy places in the house as soon as they awaken. They have almost no opportunity to be awake in their own rooms or to sustain their attention undistracted. We are going to discuss how to develop an environment where the baby can spend time alone in deep involvement, even on occasion for several hours.

For this deep engagement to occur, we must create an environment that brings the baby to the edge of his skill level. We have to find the right balance of challenge to the baby and support from the environment. We are able to do this by understanding and following the path of the child's development. At first glance, such a room for the baby looks plain and simple, especially when we compare it to the brightly colored and decorated nurseries that we commonly see. But this plainer nursery has an atmosphere of calm that is missing in busier environments for babies. It is soothing and beautiful in its simplicity.

Recently, we visited the home of parents who are expecting their first baby and have just completed our parent child course. Let us describe what the room prepared for their new baby looks like. The walls are a rich sky blue. They are bare except for a framed photograph of a landscape. It hangs next to a rocking chair where the infant can see it when she is on her parent's shoulder being patted and burped after feeding. There is a large window giving the room natural light, and there is a ceiling light that gives off a warm glow. A large, double-bed-size futon is in the corner of the room. Stiff, cream-colored bolster pillows line its edges next to the walls. The futon is covered with a clean, fitted sheet and on it there is a Moses Basket (a flexible sleeping and carrying basket, available in baby stores and catalogues), where the newborn will spend her first nights. There is a mirror attached to the wall at one end of the futon, and in the ceiling above it there is a hook for hanging mobiles. A low, wooden shelf holds a small basket and one tiny silver rattle. A childproof space heater in the corner (it is winter time) is set to maintain the desired room temperature. A colorful pile rug covers the wooden floor next to the futon.

One area of the room with the rocking chair is for nursing. There is a footstool and a small table for tissues, a small clock, and a glass of water for the mother. Another area is for changing the baby. This space has a small wooden armoire about three and a half feet high, just right for serving as a changing table. It has a white pad with a dozen reusable sheets of white rubberized flannel piled on top that the mother has found at a fabric store and cut to fit the "table." Next to the armoire is a simple trash can for soiled diapers. It has a foot lever for opening and closing the lid. There is a second smaller can for tiny washcloths and the rubberized sheets when they are soiled.

Inside the armoire is a neat pile of tiny cotton washcloths and a bowl for warm water to use for wipes, a stack of folded cloth diapers, newborn size, and other items for care (olive oil, nonpetroleum jelly and non-talc powder). There are three small drawers on the right for clothes and on the left, a tiny closet with a small basket for the baby's laundry. A two-by-three-foot piece of blue fabric with pockets hangs on the wall above the armoire. The pockets hold items to care for the baby: thermometer, cotton balls, nail clippers, hairbrush, and so forth.

The room is thus carefully, if minimally, furnished to address the four areas of necessity for the infant: an area for sleeping, for changing, for nursing, and for activity. Almost everything within the child's room is low to the ground and each item will adjust to her changing needs as she grows. The shelf is sturdy enough for her to use when first pulling herself up and learning to walk, and it will hold her toys. She will use the same armoire for dressing herself when she is old enough to do so.

For now, this environment gives the baby ample space both to lie down and to be active. Even as a newborn she can wriggle her body and move a short distance. When she is on her back, a hanging mobile allows her to practice focusing on and following the slow movement of its attractive objects. When she is on her stomach, she can work on lifting her head and see herself in the mirror placed in view on the wall by her futon. As she struggles to lift her head, she builds the strength to hold it up for longer periods of time, and will soon be able to view the whole room. From her stomach position she also works her legs and builds strength in her arms by repeatedly pushing up from the mattress. Finally one day, she will get her knees up under her and get across the room to something.

Following the information given in the parent child course, these parents will give rattles to her hand in logical progression, thus creating new challenges to the baby's grasp and discovery. By three months, they will hang an object just within her reach, allowing her to practice aiming her hand. Over and over she will try, finally managing to touch it. Eventually she will perfect her aim and will grasp the object, pulling it to her mouth for inspection. When she is old enough to sit, her parents will give her a wooden box with a hole in the top for a ball (large enough that she cannot swallow it) to go through. They will do this not to develop the skill of getting a ball through a hole but to give the child the right amount of challenge to develop her intelligence through sustained attention.

For this outcome, the task for the baby has to have just the right amount of challenge: not too easy, not too hard. J. McVicker Hunt, a prominent American psychologist of the 1950s and 1960s, called this "the problem of the match" and gave credit to Montessori for her unique solution to this dilemma. Montessori made the concentration that develops in the child through this "match" with the environment the cornerstone of her educational theory. Children in Montessori environments, whatever their age, concentrate deeply and are intensely focused because each material offers progressive levels of difficulty, thus ensuring that the child always has just the right level of challenge.

The awe that many visitors feel when they see children so entranced with their environment gives Montessori classrooms a spiritual quality. It is our capacity to become altered by sustained attention to our surroundings that is the most spiritual quality of human beings. We enter creation as a new species, we are made of dust just as all other species, yet we mold that dust into another being—each one an original. Our genes and our DNA do not make a human being. Our destiny is to construct our own personalities through a lifetime of learning and experience. If you doubt this mission of the human being, visit a Young

Children's Community of Montessori children between the ages of eighteen months and three years and watch their intense involvement in and absorption of their environment. They are working as hard as possible to further their self-formation into complete human beings capable of independence, coordinated movement, language, and will.

In creating an environment that encourages concentration, it is important to remember that if the child becomes conscious of anything other than the task at hand, his concentration is broken. By applauding, saying "wonderful," giving a kiss, or whatever, the well-meaning adult draws the child's attention to the adult and away from the task at hand. Too much such interference, and the child becomes self-conscious. When we are self-conscious, it is very hard to concentrate on the task at hand, whatever our age. To see this we have only to remember the problems we have in sports when we let our thoughts stray to the impression we are making on onlookers, or in giving a speech when we focus on our appearance instead of the audience and the message we want to give. When the child becomes deeply and constructively absorbed in a task, it is important to avoid drawing his attention to what the adults around him are thinking of what he is doing.

Our goal then is to build an environment for engagement for the infant, one that maintains a good balance of challenge and support, and where the adult is not overly involved. In creating the environment for your own child's room, you need to consider first where the child is to sleep, for where he sleeps will determine what he wakes up to. A crib, our conventional solution for the baby's bed, is not an inspiring place for an infant. What would be? Certainly allowing the child a view of the entire room from where he was placed would be helpful. A mirror on the wall next to him would add another way of seeing the room. A mobile hung from the ceiling eight to ten inches from his eyes and changed as he becomes familiarized with it, would give a focal point of interest in the earliest months. Allowing the possibility of movement into the entire room would open a whole world of interest. Thoughtfully chosen materials that follow the progressive development of the baby, placed in the room and always accessible, would guarantee that there was always a challenge for him. Finally, we need to allow the child to have time in his room and not thoughtlessly interrupt him.

Montessori designed such a bedroom for the young child, elegant in its simplicity, inexpensive to outfit, and easy to transform to meet the developing infant's needs. We have briefly described one couple's interpretation of the principles involved. Let us now review the principles of the four major areas—sleeping, changing, feeding, and being active—so that you can decide the best way to implement them for your own child.

The infant's bed is large and on the floor. A double-bed-size is best and the mattress must be only a few inches high.* Even a tiny baby, given this opportunity for unlimited movement, soon covers distance by pushing or pulling himself along. If he reaches the edge of the mattress, he tends to pull back. However, with only several inches to the floor, it is all right if he does not. For bedding, only the bottom sheet is used. A small blanket or comforter, similar to that used in a crib or baby carriage, covers the baby when sleeping. A small pad or sheet can be used on top of the full-size fitted sheet so that it is not soiled and does not have to be washed and replaced as often. No covers should ever be tucked in. In the beginning it is also possible to roll a small bumper of towels or fold wool blankets to place at the edges of the bed to ease the transition to the floor. The bed is placed in a

---

*A hide-away bed mattress or thin futon of no more than four inches is good—as in the selection made by the expectant parents described earlier. For older babies the mattress or futon can be somewhat higher.

corner of the room so that only two sides are exposed to the open room, thus limiting access to the floor. You can also run a crib bumper along the wall (or use stiff bolster pillows as in the example previously given). One mother told us that when her baby was four to six months old and really moving, she placed a soft rug next to his child-bed. In this way, he had a soft landing but could feel the dip during transition from bed to floor. Thus he learned about his bed's boundaries through a natural yet safe means.

The types of cribs which are widely used in America today were originally designed for the safety of children, to prevent them from getting into fireplaces or other household hazards. However, contemporary cribs can present a danger to young children. The most common accidents happen when the baby topples onto his neck and head, trying to climb over the sides of the crib. Some babies have sustained concussions and severe injuries to their back and spinal cord as a result. In addition, the period when children transfer from crib to bed can be difficult. They become accustomed to the order of going to sleep in a crib. They often resist the change to a bed, particularly if it coincides with giving up their crib for a new baby. The child also has no previous experience of sleeping without walls, so that falling from the new bed to the floor is an added concern. When the child begins life on a Montessori child-bed, he can make the change to a higher bed gradually by using a box spring and mattress between ages three and five years, and moving to a full-height, adult-size bed thereafter.

Because the child is sleeping on a floor bed, the room must be designed for his safety. This is done right from the beginning, so that no major changes are necessary later on. A secure gate is placed at the door, such as might be used at the top of a staircase. This is a precautionary measure while parents sleep in case the young child would attempt to come out of his room when it is not safe to do so. Thus the child is protected from harm but is not as restricted as he would be if he were enclosed in a crib. Examine every detail of the room carefully. Cover all exposed light sockets. If you use a lamp, secure the cord between the chest and wall so that the child cannot pull the lamp over or reach the socket. Windows need to be at a safe height. If they are not, bolt them closed or secure them by a grill or bars. Inspect the floor for small, loose items, and sweep and clean it daily. When proper care is taken, such a bedroom is the safest environment for the infant.

As in our example, a large square mirror, two to three feet in width and height and made of Plexiglas or thick safety glass, is bolted to the wall low enough so that the baby can see himself when he is able to lift his head up. In the meantime, the mirror extends his view of the room even from a completely prone position. A hook is placed in the ceiling over the bed so that mobiles can be hung and easily changed to keep the baby's interest. A simple chest holds the baby's clothes, diapers and supplies with its top serving as a changing area in the first months. The closet holds further supplies, clothing, and toys, and other materials for rotation as the child grows older and his needs change. A very low shelf has a single basket with one rattle in the beginning but gradually holds several more baskets, with cloth balls at first, then other age-appropriate materials as the baby develops. It is important that the bottom of both chest and shelf be low enough to the floor so that the baby cannot get wedged underneath when he eventually begins to go "out and about" in his room on his own.

In addition to preparing a good environment for the infant's powers of focus and attention to develop, parents have a role as protectors of their child's concentration once it begins. In order to do this, parents need to follow several principles. They must become observers of their child's subjective experience as opposed to his objective experience. In other words, they need to observe how their child is feeling about what he is doing. A child might do something very well and at the same time be bored by it. An older child who takes a test and does well but dislikes the whole process is an example. Outer actions do not always tell us what a child's subjective experience is; it is necessary to pay attention and be intuitive. In this way we can learn to recognize deep concentration in our children versus chaotic play. An eighteen-month-old saying "zoom, zoom" with his toy car as he plunges it over and over on the carpet is lost in meaningless and random activity. What we are hoping to encourage at this age is a focused attention on some aspect of reality so that learning occurs.

Adults have to be very alert to the child to notice when this sustained attention takes place. This is because we do not know what will really engage the child. A child of three years might become fascinated with moving the lid of a small bottle of polish off and on, over and over. He might never get to the polishing activity that it is part of. For this child, at this moment in his development, taking the lid off and putting it back on is a purposeful activity. He is perfecting the movement of wrist and fingers, working on understanding the lid mechanism, and especially focusing on hand aim. As adults, we have to try to understand what is a purposeful activity for the child at any given moment, and what is not. To do this effectively we have to develop our own latent powers of observation.

To help us better understand what the child is experiencing at times of intense concentration, we can consider our own moments of consuming engagement in an activity. For guidance we can turn to the work of Mihaly Csikszentmihalyi, Ph.D. Csikszentmihalyi characterizes these moments of intense absorption as "flow."* Montessori called such experiences in children "the child's work," because in this process she believed

---

*See Mihaly Csikszentmihalyi, *Flow, Finding Flow,* and *Becoming Adult.*

children were constructing themselves. On these occasions, we are deeply involved in the moment. We are clear and focused at the edge of our skill development. We do the activity for the rewards inherent within it (not for grades or salary, praise or recognition). It is always a highly focused, highly organized activity. We have an abiding interest in it and our motivation for it is sustained over time despite setbacks and failures. We persist and we work for perfection. Flow is experienced by the artist and the athlete, the scientist and the mathematician, the poet and the technologist, the student and the teacher.

Deep concentration is normal for human beings. Because it represents a normalized state, it results in relaxation and contentment in the individual. Montessori described children after periods of this type of work as peaceful, happy, even rested and refreshed, showing a marked generosity of spirit that was not apparent before.

In order to understand what it is that helps people to sustain flow in their lives, Csikszentmihalyi has conducted research studies involving creative, highly engaged people. He found that their common characteristic is that they have a certain psychological complexity. They go back and forth in their thinking from the intuitive to the rational. They do not try to stay in one mode. It appears then that there is a quality of playfulness to their thinking.

For this playful alteration to develop, children need both structure and support. We have discussed the physical components of the environment necessary for infants. Support comes from the emotional atmosphere of the home. A positive mood in the family allows children freedom from the distraction and stress of negative emotions. A negative atmosphere means that parents are not giving the support necessary for their children to develop a capacity for deep engagement and flow in their lives. The goal is to create a home life that is not overly serious and is filled with joyfulness and spontaneity. Parents must model these qualities and create flow in their own lives as much as possible. They need a balance between being too casual—not concentrating sufficiently on the challenges in their children's lives—and being too serious, intense, and goal-driven for them. Similarly, if children under three years old spend large blocks of time in a setting other than their own home, the adults caring for them there must establish a positive emotional atmosphere.

Another element to consider as we seek to understand the flow experience is the relationship of inhibition and repetition to the development of concentration. Montessori had an eminently practical answer to the duality of these needs. She engaged the whole child in the process of learning: the body and the mind, the hand and the brain. By keeping "doing and thinking" together, the child gradually develops the ability to inhibit all movements not conducive to the accomplishment of the task at hand. Furthermore, by encouraging repetition, Montessori guaranteed that the child would coordinate the movements for a task until they became permanent. Extraneous movements are pared off so it is not just a matter of fingers going over and over the same motions. The child is also canceling out unwanted ones. We now know what Montessori could only guess from outward observation: the child is building a more efficient brain by eliminating some neural possibilities through inactivation and strengthening desired neural pathways by repeated usage.

We know that there are many more children now who are handicapped by attention problems than in prior years. Our genes presumably have not changed, nor have our schools changed their teaching methods. So, to what can we attribute this new phenomenon other than to a new lifestyle for children? Yet, one wonders if the difficulty may have less to do with distractions in the environment as the child grows older, and more to do with a time period missed for developing focus earlier in the child's life and before school age. In other words, the problem may be a result of undeveloped concentration in infancy. We know that there is a Sensitive Period for language from the child's birth to approximately age six years. Is it possible that there is such a Sensitive Period for the development of sustained attention—a time period when the child should have developed concentration and not having done so is handicapped (as is the case with language) for the rest of his life?

Profound concentration isolates us from stimulation. We keep body and mind together in absorbed attention. Concentration protects the child from too much stimulation in his environment. For the mature mind of the adult, abstract learning is a viable process. We can learn by "sitting and listening," following outside assignments (homework), and taking tests on the knowledge prescribed for us. Regular schooling, in focusing on only half of the learning experience—the mind—does not enhance the child's concentration. The child is in a process of self-construction. Although children begin to reason and think abstractly by age six years, Montessori found that they still grasp concepts and develop their ability to think best when new ideas are presented to them through concrete representation—in other words, when mind and body are unified. She observed that it was not until the later elementary school years that children begin gradually, and on an individual timetable, to work entirely on an abstract basis. They do so voluntarily, at first still using materials to verify their already completed work and finally discarding them altogether. The intensive concentration of these Montessori students when they are ages twelve to fourteen years, now working in the abstract for three-hour-long uninterrupted study periods, is amazing to the adult.

The parents' challenge is to establish a home environment that encourages the development of concentration from the child's infancy and that supports flow experiences for all family members. Such a home reflects the complexity of life. Parents have to be both flexible and open-ended in their thinking and, at the same time, balance this environment of support with structure. Parents can protect their child's concentration by maintaining a positive mood and spontaneous quality to family life, by not overly indulging their children or overly restricting them. Overindulgence removes challenges; over-restriction inhibits activity and the opportunity to learn to control the self.*

Research has shown that when parents become rigid and too goal-oriented, there is an imbalance between challenge and support: support is too low, challenge too high. Parents and children alike become high achievers in such settings but there is no joy in their accomplishments. In homes where there is high support and low challenge, children do not develop focused attention. They are impulsive and, although they may appear to enjoy themselves, closer observation reveals that they are in fact unhappy and petulant. They have no goals and they do not develop control over their own wills. The most devastating of all are those homes where there is both low support and low challenge. These are homes where the needs of children for developing concentration are ignored entirely. Predictably, these children are best described as possessing a "chaotic attention."†

Parent protection and encouragement are necessary for an extended period for children to develop concentration in childhood. Children need challenges but they also need to live in a positive and secure environment. Such an environment allows them to focus their energies on their own development instead of physical and emotional survival. Childhood lays the foun-

---

*See Kevin Rathunde, "Montessori Education and Optimal Experience," *NAMTA Journal* 26, no. 1 (Winter 2001).
†Diana Baumrind, "Rearing Competent Children," in William Damon, ed., *Child Development Today and Tomorrow*, pp. 349–78.

dation for each individual's personality and response to life. Although human beings are in an unending state of development requiring them to be both flexible and adaptive throughout their lives, the development of concentration in infancy is an essential building block for future self-formation.

THREE

Discovering the World

Children under three years of age have different means from adults for sustaining their attention and thereby developing their minds. They are not capable of reason, abstract thinking, or imagination, so they cannot make conscious choices for their attention, based on intelligence. However, they have a unique ability to absorb the qualities of their environment just by being exposed to them. This "absorbent mind," as Montessori called it, is the basis of the universal adaptation of human beings. Because the infant absorbs every aspect of her environment, we need to be very careful about what we include in it. Certainly we want to build this environment on universal principles of beauty, simplicity, and order. Soothing as contrasted to strident colors and simple rather than complex patterns on the child's bedroom walls, for example, provide a beneficial backdrop. With less background distraction, objects specifically placed in the room more easily draw the baby's attention and encourage focus and exploration.

The infant has an absorbent mind with which to take in the general environment, but she also has a means for selected and precise exploration that leads her to sustained interest and focused attention, through each of the five senses. The baby explores from birth with the senses of touch, smell, and taste—all of which have to do with food and are the most developed at birth—but also with the senses of hearing and sight—the last two being the least developed initially. It is through exploration with the senses that the infant becomes habituated to a particular object. So rotation and new challenge are important as parents determine her environment on a weekly or monthly basis. Montessori called the child under six years old "a sensorial explorer" and based her educational approach for the child's early years upon the child's learning through the senses. Because she correctly identified the means whereby children under six years old learn best—that is with ease, absorption, and thoroughness—children in Montessori schools the world over typically become intensely interested in their environment and in learning itself.

What kind of tools then can we employ for the infant as a sensorial explorer with an absorbent mind? Clearly they must be concrete materials. Young children cannot use imagination or abstract thinking to learn about the world. Because they are not yet capable of abstract thought, they must know the concrete world first and thereby develop the tools that lead to abstract thought and the furthering of their own construction. Children need, then, concrete objects whose qualities they can absorb through their senses.

Most importantly, these materials must be of the real world. Because there is so much misunderstanding about fantasy in the young child's life, we repeat: everything that adults give to the young child for sensorial exploration should represent the real world. Young children's experiences with the real world become the basis for their imagination and creative thought in the elementary school years, when they no longer possess an absorbent mind but a reasoning mind. Sensations that give no knowledge of the world to young children are useless to them. Worse, they can give false information and therefore be far from harmless. Young children have hurt themselves, as well as other children, by jumping from windows, hitting with objects, choking other children, and even shooting at others with guns, because in their television cartoons and videos, they had seen these actions resulting repeatedly in none of the consequences of the real world.

The richness of the child's later imagination depends on the depth and extent of sensorial impressions in the earliest years. Children need so much in order to have this rich base. They need things that represent what is universally true and can be observed around our planet, whether in the Americas, Europe, Asia, or Africa. They need to experience what Earth is made of and what does not change: sand is sand, dirt is dirt, plants the world over function in similar ways and have similar properties. The needs of human beings are met in different ways in different places but, again, their fundamental needs for clothing, shelter, and food are universal. Nonsense songs, pictures, and stories that are the product of adult fantasy give no useful information about the world to the child under six years old.

On the other hand, being out-of-doors in natural settings gives infants and young children hands-on experiences that are concrete and reality based. The infant outside in a carriage for a morning nap wakes up to clouds moving across the blue sky, leaves rustling and waving in the breeze, wind on her face, the smell of tree bark in the hot sun. One day she will stand up and know the feel of cool green grass under her bare feet. These sensations are not just nice experiences. They are the basis of our recognition of our universality, perhaps even the realization of our spiritual being, which is our most abstract concept.

Infants begin their exploration of the world even before birth. Within the womb, they begin with no knowledge. Gradually, they progress to some taste, some sound, some differences in light and dark, the sensation of sucking their thumb, the feel of their own face with their hands, the touch of fluid against their body and its steady temperature. So infants do have a little knowledge of what is to come; birth is not a total shock. Most importantly, they will have acquired what is referred to in Montessori infancy training as "points of reference." They recognize their mother's heartbeat, her voice, and the rhythm of her movement. At birth, they already "know" their own mother.

After the baby's birth, we do not have to think about giving the sights, sounds, and smells of our homes to her. The baby absorbs them just by being surrounded by them. This absorption includes both the physical and emotional environment of our homes. This means that our conscious preparations for the infant have to take place before her birth. We cannot plan to paint or remodel the house or have trying relatives, even friends, to visit. We need to be able to give our full attention and energies to the new task at hand: assisting the development of a new self in the first days of life.

What do we consciously give to the newborn for developing her sensorial knowledge of the world, thus taking advantage of her unique ability to form herself after birth as a human being of her "time, place, and culture"? We want first to add to the child's visual impressions and opportunities for focusing her eyes and developing her sight. We have mentioned the child-bed on the floor which gives the baby more to see, versus the crib high in the air with a limited view. From the lower position of the child-bed, the child builds a visual map of her room before she begins to move about in it and take in even more. It takes time for the child to build this visual map. Repeated experiences are necessary for the visual cortex to lay down impressions in her brain. These experiences allow the child to add the necessary visual information to her internal map for movement in her room. They build a framework for her understanding of how distance is experienced between points in her map and the relationship of those points to speed and time through movement. Thus from the beginning, they build a sensorial foundation for physics. A child-bed prepares the baby to move about in her room just at the time that her brain is ready for more information to be absorbed through her senses. Thus she can provide for her own needs and continue her own learning. She is happy because her opportunities for learning match her abilities.

The mirror that we attach to the baby's wall next to the child-bed further enhances her sight by showing a different or "mirror" image of the room. The baby also sees her own image reflected and begins to connect her movements with the reflected movements of the child in the mirror. Thus she discovers that there are more faces to examine than just her mother's at feeding time. Eventually, she sees others reflected in the mirror as they enter the room to play or talk with her. Encouraging the newborn to spend waking time on her stomach so that she can practice lifting her head makes these first visual experiences with the wall mirror possible.

For the first few months, a mobile over the child-bed helps to develop the baby's abilities to explore the world visually. The baby gradually develops focus on a moving object, tracking of an object, and perception of color and depth. The mobile is changed every two weeks or so to accommodate the infant's habituation to that particular mobile and to match her progressive visual development. Hence, the first mobile portrays flat, black-and-white geometric shapes and reflected light from a glass sphere. Subsequent ones are introduced in ordered sequence: three octahedrons of colored metallic paper, ideally each in a primary color; five Styrofoam balls covered with embroidery thread in gradations of the same color and hung in ascending order from darkest to lightest; stylized paper figures of light metallic colored paper that move with the slightest current of air; and, finally, stylized wooden figures painted in pastel colors.

All this visual information about the world is picked up by the infant while she is "focusing and following" with her mobiles. It is essential to understand that these are highly selective and carefully designed mobiles. They present the infant with specific keys to her world in shape and color. They are not a bombard-ment of meaningless stimuli for entertainment or novelty's sake. There is a reason novelty occupies a baby, and all too often we ignore it and use novelty to keep babies busy so that they are not unhappy and bothering us. Babies seek novelty to learn some-thing previously not known by them about their world; as such it is a key characteristic and has a purpose. Too often, adults are completely thoughtless in what they give to infants, as if "any old thing" would do. If we want to give our babies an optimal envi-ronment, we need to think through the purpose of all that we give to them.

Mobiles are primarily useful to the infant only in the first few months. In the initial weeks, mobiles help develop her visual capacities for focus and tracking. After this period, she is ready for the next level of challenge. Now the mobile is hung at a height within the range of the infant's random arm movements. She is thus able to bat it with her hands, gradually realizing that her movements affect the mobile. She begins to try to make con-tact with the mobile on purpose, and her efforts result in deep-ened concentration and gradual control over her arms. Next, an object is hung by a piece of elastic. A wooden ring about three inches in diameter with a thickness of half an inch is ideal. The baby works to grasp it and, in one triumphant moment, brings it to her mouth. She is now ready to unify tactile exploration of objects with visual exploration. It is essential at this point that any object hung is suitable for this purpose. Therefore it must be durable, contain no rough edges, and be large enough to ensure that it cannot be swallowed.

The baby has entered a new arena of discovery: the relation-ship of sight and touch. Rattles are going to replace mobiles as the major tool for her ongoing sensorial exploration of the world. Through manipulation of rattles the infant discovers that the physical sensation in her hands relates to the shapes she is seeing. She gradually develops a coordination of sight with touch and sound. She sees and feels that the different movements she makes with her rattles create varying sounds: soft and loud, pleasant and unpleasant. She experiences differences in temperature and texture: wood and metal are smooth, and metal is cooler or warmer than objects around it. She discovers the relationship between size and weight: objects that are the same size but are made of different materials vary in weight, and so forth.

Eventually, the baby reaches a point where she has discovered the different capacities of her hands as they move over and around different shapes, grasping various shapes in different ways, and holding on to and letting go of objects at will. She now not only has the ability to take in information through her hands, but she is learning to use her hands to manipulate her environment. She arrives at a new level of challenge in the building of concentration and is ready to move on to the discovery of every-day objects of her environment.

The infant is ready to explore real objects around the home but cannot get to them yet on her own. While we are waiting for the infant to move on her own, we can collect baskets of common household objects that are safe for her exploration. Because she will become habituated to whatever we provide, we need to rotate the objects in these baskets every so often. When a familiar object is re-presented a few weeks later, the infant will look at it on a different level because her brain has progressed and she is ready to take in more information. In this way, the infant knows the objects more deeply each time they go away and come back. Repetition of the familiar is essential for developing focus and true knowledge at every stage of development. Infancy is no exception and is, in fact, the opportunity for laying a pattern of repetition in learning.

Later these same household objects can be collected again in baskets for use as language objects. We name the objects even for the infant: "measuring spoon," "spatula," "brush," etc. However, this is a casual mentioning for the absorbent mind. At a later stage, we use language consciously to deepen the child's knowledge of, and interest in, the object. We can further help with preparation for language development and the development of order by categorizing objects within the baskets. Doing so helps the child to understand that certain things go together in our world and what some of those things might be. One basket might have objects only found in the bathroom; another one, items from the bedroom; and a third, things from the kitchen; and so forth.

At last, the infant is off and crawling over the entire house and investigating everywhere on her own initiative. Children at this stage no longer need us consciously to bring objects to them. They discover for themselves what can be found in each room of their house. It is important now to take time to think about the organization of the home (or any other setting where a child of this age is to spend significant periods of time). Does it make sense? Is it ordered, simple, and functional? Is it beautiful? We want the baby to discover an orderly environment and thereby incorporate this order within her own mind. This is the opportunity to establish "a place for everything and everything in its place" before the baby is off and about, doing her own "rearranging." And we must be able to quickly and easily straighten and tidy rooms. It is also essential to check each cupboard, drawer, and closet from attic to cellar to be certain that items dangerous to a small child are removed or safely stored. Children under the age of six years, who have not therefore reached the age of reason, will eventually get into almost any item in the house, and they are often able to do so long before we realize that they can. Our goal from now on is to provide an opportunity for the child to discover an orderly home, in such a way that we can be certain that she is safe. (See Chapter 5, Crawling to Coordination.)

| The Hand and the Brain

Never give to the mind more than you give to the hand.
— MARIA MONTESSORI

Montessori's recognition of the role of the hand in developing human intelligence is unique. We know that we are the only species to possess the pincer grasp of thumb and forefinger. Yet, we seldom reflect that all human achievements, whether in medicine, science, technology, or art, are the result of the union of the human intellect and this unique grasp of the hand in the mature adult. In the child, it is the actions of the hand guided by the intellect that create a feedback loop of information: the hand reports to the brain, the brain guides the hand by this new information, the hand discovers more information by carrying out the new direction, and reports again to the brain. This process is a continuous action of learning and development. When the development of the child is allowed to proceed naturally in this way throughout the child's education—in other words, according to nature's plan that the mind and the hand operate in unity—the results are astonishing.

Montessori discovered the role of the child's hand in developing the intelligence by intuitive observation. She then took this discovery to its logical conclusion by emphasizing the importance of the hand as an educational tool. Although an increasing number of neurological studies now validate Montessori's conclusions about the role of the hand in developing intelligence, no other educational approach is based so much upon this key revelation. In this chapter, we trace the development of the hand in the child's first three years and outline Montessori's recommendations to parents for aiding that development.*

What is the human hand for? Of what use is it to the infant? At birth, the hand is an undeveloped tool. Therefore, the first job of the infant is to get the hand ready as a tool that he can direct. At the same time, the infant is gaining information through his hand. Already in the womb, the myelination of nerve fibers between the infant's hand and brain is completed for the skills of thumb-sucking and touching the face.†

As an undeveloped tool, the infant's hand at first can carry out only imprecise movements. These movements match approximately the level of information that the infant's brain is capable of taking in: at first, only the feel of texture and the sensation of his thumb in his mouth. Therefore, the level of muscular skill and coordination matches the level of mental development, and the hand and the brain are operating in sync. It is in this sensitive area of matching mental to environmental,

---

*We suggest that you follow the Time Line (see p. xxii) showing the infant's development of the hand and that of body equilibrium. Montessori developed this Time Line to show how the preparation of the body and hands proceeds in unison from the beginning of life, with development in one area complementing that in the other. By making clear the indirect preparation that precedes all outward signs of self-formation, the Time Line helps to allay parental anxieties about the moment a specific skill might appear.

†Myelination is a process whereby a protective sheath of insulation, consisting of a soft, white, somewhat fatty material, is formed around neuron fibers, allowing electrochemical messages to travel from the brain to muscles. Without the development of the myelin sheath (a gradual process that takes place on a different timetable for different parts of the body), the infant cannot activate the muscles.

however, that a problem can develop as the infant matures. If the brain gets ahead of the hand, a disunity results and the hand is no longer feeding the mind. In other words, when the skills of the hand and therefore information to the brain are not in a balanced relationship, the undeveloped hand holds the brain back. It is this dilemma that Montessori sought to avoid by emphasizing support for the development of the child's hand from the earliest years.

When the infant is born, he has a surprising reflexive grasp. If you stroke his palm gently, he will close tightly on your finger, sometimes with such strength that he can support his entire body weight. Because some animal babies cling tightly to their mothers' fur as a means of survival, it is possible that this remarkable reflexive action is part of our evolutionary history. In any case, it disappears entirely in the human infant within three to four months.

For our purposes, the most significant aspect of the infant's hand development in the first two months of his life is the lack of intentional grasp. The infant's arm and hand acts as a single unit in a scooping and sweeping motion. If this "arm-hand" unit interacts with an object, he can bring an object to his body. There is no intended purpose here, however, nor is the infant capable of bending his wrist. The "arm-hand" simply scoops and sweeps as one. At two months, the baby's reflexive grasp diminishes but an intentional grasp is not yet fully developed. The myelination of nerve fibers controlling the arm and hand is still incomplete, making an intentional grasp neurologically impossible. It is not until three to five months of age that the infant's prehension becomes purposeful: he now has the ability to intentionally reach and grasp. In addition, he can purposefully close his hands around an object to gain information about that object for his brain. The continuous feedback loop of hand-to-brain-to-hand can now be activated intentionally by the infant.

If the child has not developed purposeful reaching out to,

taking, and holding on to an object by age three to five months, he has to rely on someone else to put items in his hands. In this case, he may let go of the object before he is ready to—before he has gathered sufficient information from it. Similarly, if he has developed the ability to reach and grasp objects but is denied the opportunity to do so, he will be in an equally dependent state. Either situation presents strong implications for the infant's development of will and independence. The young child's mind is already absorbing messages from his environment: "I am capable" or "I am not so capable." The child is also not in a position to learn all he can from objects if he is not able to hold each one as long as necessary. Parents who inadvertently thrust one new object after another into an infant's hands create just such obstacles for their child.

As we mentioned in the previous chapter, it is at this point that the mobiles hung for the newborn to develop his visual system and ability to focus need to be changed. Because an infant of three to five months of age is able to reach and grasp, we are going to give him mobiles for batting, grasping, and holding. Again, these mobiles must be made of objects safe for the infant's mouth as this is where he will immediately place them. Most store-bought mobiles are appropriate only for much older children, usually three years old or older. They are far too elaborate and delicate for a baby to explore safely. And they are usually hung close to the ceiling, unfortunately far out of the newborn infant's sight and out of his reach if he is somewhat older. In addition, there are mobiles designed for infants, incorporating music boxes that the adult must wind up. The infant lies in the crib, looking at a mobile which he cannot see well, watching something go around too rapidly for his eyes to follow, and hears music. We look at such a sight and find it comforting and reassuring; somehow the baby looks so sweet and innocent. In reality, this may be a nearly useless experience to the child.

For the three-month-old infant, Montessori recommended

hanging a simple mobile for grasping, by attaching a durable object such as a wooden teething ring to a piece of elastic. The elastic is tied to the mobile hanger at the end of the string previously used for holding the newborn's mobiles. Attaching elastic to the mobile hanger allows for the give-and-take of the object. The infant grasps the object, brings it to his mouth, releases it, and the object springs back to its original position, ready to be grabbed and brought to his mouth again. Sometimes the infant overreaches for the object and sometimes he underreaches, giving him continuous experience with depth perception. In this process the infant also becomes gradually aware that his batting and hitting at the mobile object cause it to move and turn. He is the source of the movement—not an adult or a mechanical device—and thus he gains a sense of his emerging capacities. As a result of the thoughtfulness of adults in providing just the right aid to match his developing hands, the infant gains knowledge of himself and his environment.

At some point, as the infant bats and grasps a hanging object, his own hands cross their line of vision. Here is something even more interesting than the object for which he was reaching. He explores his own hands, finding his fingers, and accidentally interlocking them, then awkwardly jerking them apart. He has begun his discovery of the human hand with its amazing capacities as a tool and source of information about the world.

Because infants have different experiences with the same objects, depending upon age and ability, it is not essential to buy or make new ones as the baby progresses and develops (the exception being the initial introduction of mobiles for visual development in the early months). In fact, it is often beneficial to rotate and recycle the same items. At three months, the infant may simply hold an object. At four to five months, he may begin to manipulate the same item. Holding and manipulating give the baby two very different experiences, each building upon and reinforcing previous information and skill development. As mentioned earlier, habituation will occur, and reintroduction of an object after a time lapse may be necessary. In our culture we are far too prone to introduce one new object after another to the baby as soon as interest begins to lag in a specific item. Therefore we want to stress again: repetition is key to the learning process at all ages. Rotation, not substitution, is the answer to the process of habituation to objects.

At six months, the infant begins to examine objects through hand-to-hand transfer, purposefully moving an item from the right to left hand and left hand to right. He begins to realize that both hands are getting information. Through this transfer he has a different experience of the same object. Experience with hand-to-hand transfer of objects has implications for development of preferred handedness and the development of the right and left sides of the infant's brain.

During this first six-month period, the infant's type of grasp progresses. In the beginning, his grasp is similar to that of a monkey. He has no thumb use and can utilize only four fingers and the opposing palm. The thumb sticks straight up or it lies next to the hand. Gradually, through myelination of the nerve fibers and subsequent development between brain and muscle, the grasp changes and the infant uses four fingers with the opposable thumb. Now the baby has a pincer grip, but it is a flat pincer movement. A piece of Cheerios cereal can be grasped but the fingers are straight. With this flat pincer grip the infant rolls a Cheerio into his mouth. Neurologically the potential for a full pincer grasp now exists but the infant needs to refine this movement through repetition and practice. There is not much wrist development yet. The baby is still using a whole arm movement with the arm and hand acting as one instrument. He can shake and bang objects, but without wrist involvement. Many store-bought rattles do not take into account these limitations of the infant under six months. The rattles are too heavy, poorly shaped for grasping, and much too big for a baby's tiny hand. In addition, their design is awkward, making them impossible to shake with graceful movements.

We need to be constantly aware of the infant's capacities at each age and to think through the purpose for each object that we give to him. We want to give him only those items that are helping him and remove from the environment those objects that are not serving a purpose. Being thoughtful of our baby in this way is difficult. We are busy with so many of the demands and issues of our adult lives. Yet, the infant is totally dependent upon adults to meet his developmental needs in these early months. We need to slow down and think through our priorities. What could be more important in our lives than aiding the development of concentration and intelligence in our baby?

It is not until he reaches seven or eight months of age that myelination finally makes possible the baby's control of his fingers. His awkward grasp disappears and he begins his efforts to refine the movements of his fingers. By age nine to ten months, he has fingers that are truly useful, and he achieves a finger-thumb position that is capable of precise movements. This development of the hand from imprecise movements and awkward grasp to refinement of finger control has followed a logical path. The information that the hand is capable of gleaning is in continual balance with the capacity of the brain to receive that information. It takes many months of receiving general knowledge of the environment through the five senses before the baby is ready for the precise and detailed information delivered by the fully developed hand. A pincer grasp at three months of age, before the infant had a wider sensorial experience of the world, would have meant, in effect, jumping ahead of his mental capacities.

The necessity of building the infant's background of general knowledge before we expect him to understand specific details is a theme that is emphasized over and over throughout Montessori education. It is only when we—whether as adults or as children—can relate new information to past knowledge that we are capable of making discoveries with that new information. An educational emphasis on memorizing facts in isolation cannot lead students to understanding how to make use of those facts. Language development is a good example. Infants must be bathed in the sounds of human language from their birth. From this general background of a jumble of sounds, the baby selects certain ones and eventually puts these chosen sounds into a unit with specific meaning. To better understand the infant's experience of more general to specific knowledge through the gradual development of the hand, try holding your watch in your palm and transferring it from palm to palm. Now hold your watch by a pincer grip in one hand and transfer it by this grip from one hand to the other. Compare the information that you are receiving in weight, texture, and temperature. Close your eyes and repeat the process to heighten your experience.

Fortunately for our convenience, there are more useful objects commercially available to help the hand development of six-month-olds than there are for younger infants. One item that is readily purchased consists of a clear sphere with colored balls inside that rotate when the child spins the sphere. The sphere has a suction-cup base that is designed to attach to a table, holding it in place. The seated child reaches for the sphere, pulls, bats, and tries to grasp it, exploring the capacities of his hand and the movement of an object in space. A five- or six-month-old baby who has missed experience with grasping objects can use this toy for adjusting his movements in reaching and grasping a moving object. For all infants, this toy helps the child further develop hand movement guided by the intellect.

An example of a store-bought item that you can alter for a ten-month-to-one-year-old is a box with four balls to hammer through four holes. Put the hammer away and take out the rubber inset which makes it necessary to use real force to push the balls through the holes. Next, line the holes with a spongy material such as that used to line hangers. Now the holes will yield when the baby pushes the balls through with his fingers.

Best of all, Nienhuis, a manufacturer of Montessori materials, makes excellent wooden toys that aid the development of the hand for children of six months and older (Nienhuis, 320 Pioneer Way, Mountain View, CA 94041-1576, http://www.nienhuis.com/). You can purchase items such as a box with a hole on top for putting a ball through to a tray below, and a box with an incline and a hole for the ball to roll into a drawer. These items help the baby to develop eye-hand coordination and indirectly allow him to experience object permanence. They also give experience with a cause-and-effect situation and aid the infant in practicing movements guided by the intellect.

Although parents sometimes find good commercially produced articles, the best source of developmental aids for your baby is very often your own ingenuity. Not only do items that you put together yourself have the advantage of being less expensive, they also require you to give thought and attention to the specific needs of your individual child and how a particular activity is going to match those needs. For example, from the time that your baby is six months old you can take a wicker basket and put two or three favorite toys in it, such as a rattle, ball, and wooden ring. The basket should be approximately three inches high and eight inches in diameter. Place it near your child and let him do as he wishes: exploring the objects, and putting them in and out of the basket. Items are exchanged as interest wanes in the present ones. The purpose is to give the infant an opportunity for an "in and out" activity, to help him coordinate hand activity that is guided by the intellect and to give experience with limited choice so that repetition and thereby absorption of knowledge are guaranteed.

By eight or nine months, your baby can explore putting a wooden egg in a cup and a wooden cube in a box. The infant, holding the container in one hand and a wooden egg (or ovoid) in the other, puts the egg in and takes it out of the container. When he is proficient with the egg and cup, you can introduce the cube and box. This activity is more challenging for the baby because it is necessary to line up the corners of box and cube in order for the cube to fit within the box. You will want to be careful not to present this activity too soon, or your baby may become frustrated and perhaps use the items for throwing instead. If you have difficulty finding a cube and box that fit together, you can make them from cardboard and cover them with paper. The egg and cup should be approximately one and one-half inches high. The cube should be one and a half inches in width and height, and the box just big enough for the cube to fit easily. Both of these activities enhance eye-hand coordination and give the infant an opportunity for two hands to work together in a meaningful way.

One of the most effective items that we have seen was made by a mother for her fifteen-month-old. She took a cloth-covered cardboard box with a hinged lid, and put a slit in its top just large enough to accommodate a poker chip. Because the challenge-to-development match was balanced, her son enjoyed repeatedly putting the chips through the slit, retrieving them by opening the lid, and beginning the process all over again. In terms of development, he was learning to hold the chips very precisely with his thumb and forefinger in a proper pincer grip. His will and focus were concentrated on a repetitive task that was enhancing his eye-hand coordination and his understanding of object permanence (the chips disappeared into the box, only to be reclaimed from within it a moment later). Most important of all, he was learning something about the importance of struggle in life when it is matched to one's growing capacities and how it feels to succeed when one has achieved his goal by his own efforts.

By the time the child is fifteen months old, the early mission of hand and brain development is complete: the intellect, guided by information supplied by the hand, is developing, and the hand is now an effective tool. Providing all has gone well with opportunities to develop the pincer grasp and take in a wide array of general information of the world and its qualities through the human tendencies of exploration, manipulation, repetition, control of error, precision, and so forth, the child has readied himself for a new role.

Although the infant is hard at work with objects that help him develop himself in specific ways for the first fifteen months after birth, adults typically call this dedicated work of the child's "play." Yet, in this process of "play," the child has accomplished an extraordinary feat: he has gotten himself ready for activities directed toward work with structured materials—in other words, for human activity. This human activity has to do with meeting what have been the fundamental needs of human beings since time began: for food, shelter, and clothing. These fundamental needs are met primarily through the activities of adults in the home: preparing food, cooking, baking, gardening, arranging flowers, caring for plants, cleaning, dusting, sweeping, mopping, washing, drying, folding, sewing, and so forth. At age fifteen months, the child is ready and eager to copy these adult activities. He is in an upright position; his brain is ready; his hands are freed for work; his human tendencies are urging him to contribute to the life of his home and family. He wants nothing so much as to "work" alongside a loving adult in the home, or other appropriate setting, throughout the day, doing what Montessori called "the practical work of life."

Yet where is it that we find many of these willing "young workers" in today's society? Too often they are not in the home or a homelike setting at all. Instead, they are out and about most of the day, parked in the drop-in room at the health center while parents exercise, strapped into a stroller at the mall or grocery store, or confined to a car seat in transit while father, mother, or sitter is on the car speaker phone, making calls and planning the next scheduled events. When the child is at home, the television or VCR is often on, and he is surrounded by plastic toys and mechanical games in an environment of entertainment, rather than of collaboration with adults in their daily work.

And too often in the United States, another problem occurs for our fifteen-month-old children. Typically they are nowhere near their potential in development of the fine motor skills of the hand. Yet, these are the skills that prepare children for activities with structured materials and the simple work of daily life. As a culture, we have a psychological investment in our babies' learning to walk, to jump, to climb, and to engage in gross motor activities generally. As in the days of the Colosseum in ancient Rome, we have become a nation overly preoccupied with sports. As a result, we give time and attention to the development of balance and large-muscle coordination in young children. We do not typically give similar attention to fine motor coordination and the development of the hand, wrist, and fingers.

Other nations today do encourage the efforts of infants to develop their hands. In Japan, an example of a society that treasures exquisitely made products of the hand as part of their national heritage, very young babies of fourteen months or so are encouraged to put wooden spindles the width of toothpicks into holes no larger than those found in the tops of salt shakers. Children need time to sit with small objects that help them to develop their fingers for such intricate action. Perhaps in the United States we have become so conscious of safety that we do not allow our young children to explore small items: a pebble, ladybug, piece of grass, shell, or—if inside the house— the fringe on a rug, a button, the lid of a perfume bottle. Of course, we must attend carefully to our children when small

things are available to them. This attention is time-consuming
and diverts us from other occupations. Is this part of the problem? Are we not taking the time to observe our youngest children so that they can safely manipulate the details of their
environment?

Whatever the reason, in America we tend not to give sufficient
attention to the child's development of refined hand movements
in the first three years. We misinterpret children's early fascina-
tion with tiny objects such as buttons and their first efforts at precise coordination, such as putting keys and other items into small
holes. Twelve-to-fifteen-month-olds continue to use their hands
for gaining information, but they are also involved in working
with their hands. We miss this transition from the child's learning
to the child's seeking to work. We see children using their hands
and interpret this activity as more exploration. Yet, what are they
really doing when they are opening cupboards and drawers,
emptying them and putting things back, sliding drawers back and
forth, putting clothes on and off, refilling the water glass over and
over, putting sand in the pail and dumping it out—all very typical
activities of the fifteen-month-old? In fact, this activity represents the child's work, not further exploration.

We need to ask ourselves what the purpose is of this new mile-
stone in the child's development. Why do fifteen-month-olds
begin to tend more toward work than toward mere exploration?
Clearly, they do not work for a finished product as an adult does:
the rearranged shelf, the cleaned cupboard, the full pail. The
sheer repetitiveness of their actions belies this goal. Montessori
surmised that fifteen-month-old children are driven to activities
of "work" in the home because doing all of these activities
requires more and more control of their hands, and results in
further development of the feedback loop from hand to brain to
hand again. Their intelligence is developing even as their hands
expand the knowledge to be passed on to their mind through

engaging with the environment in this entirely new way. They thrive on these experiences and cannot seem to get enough of them.

Sadly, we deprive fifteen-month-olds of such opportunities for work in the home or a homelike setting. Instead we give them a schedule of planned activities, expensive toys, television, and VCRs to keep their mind off their real needs. What they actually need are what Montessori termed practical-life activities (described in detail in Chapter 6). Practical-life activities keep fifteen-month-olds at the leading edge of their skill development, building their intelligence, deepening their concentration, and giving them a new appreciation of their expanding capabilities.

In addition to doing practical-life activities at home, many children by the time they are eighteen months old are ready to spend three hours a morning doing these (and other activities) in a setting outside their own home. For this reason, Montessori designed such a setting for children ages eighteen months to three years in her schools. In our school we refer to this environment as the Young Children's Community. It is important, however, to understand that this Montessori setting outside the home is not the optimal environment for all eighteen-month-olds. For a child to benefit from the Young Children's Community, his will needs to have developed sufficiently for him to fully engage himself in activities while in a community of peers. This means that the child cannot be constantly interfering with other children. Nor can he create a commotion by going continuously from one activity to another, unable to stay for any length of time with one material.

We help the infant to develop his capacity to stay more reliably with an activity by creating possibilities for sustained attention from birth. We have discussed some ideas to aid this development already and will present more in Chapter 9, The Developing Will. However, one point should now be clear: by rushing about with our children without giving thought to their needs for developing focus or, equally damaging, by allowing them to become mesmerized in front of a TV or VCR, we destroy both their conscious attention and the development of the will.

Parents observing the calm and happy demeanor of children in our Young Children's Community sometimes want us to enroll a child who, in our judgment, has not yet developed sufficient ability to stay with a focused task. Fortunately, this does not happen often but, when it does, parents inevitably have difficulty understanding that their child will be worse off (in terms of the development of focus) in a classroom or other group setting than in a home environment. The Young Children's Community has many activities available to each child and is not confined to a choice of one or two, as can be arranged for children at home. Further, the classroom is full of children doing all these activities. As a result, there are double the distractions for the child in the classroom versus the home. These unprepared eighteen-month-olds will not develop their abilities for concentration in the midst of these distractions. The best thing their parents can do is to choose an environment that limits distractions and that offers positive activities for focus under the direction of a knowledgeable and loving adult. Unfortunately, the worst environment of all for a child who is slow to develop the ability to stay with a structured activity is the group-play-oriented settings typically offered for very young children. Not only are such settings usually full of chaotic activity and distractions for the child, but they provide neither activities for focus and development through the work of the hand, nor an adult model of focused work such as that which the child can observe in the home.

When the child is three years old and ready to enter the Children's House (Montessori's name for her primary school classroom for three-to-six-year-old children), he will find there one of Montessori's unique contributions to education: the utilizing and further refining of the child's fine motor control through specially designed materials. These attractive materials have special appeal to the precision of the hand and introduce the child to every aspect of our cultural heritage: oral and written language, mathematics, geography, science, music, and art. In their very first years of schooling, then, three-year-olds trace sandpaper letters in cursive writing, copy them with chalk on a chalkboard, and make phonetically spelled words with letters of a movable alphabet of cursive letters. The appeal of miniature objects for a young child is utilized by matching dollhouse-size items that can be spelled phonetically, such as a tiny cup or box with a prewritten slip. Almost daily from the time they are three until they are six years old, the children voluntarily choose to trace the geometric shape of metal insets and precisely fill them in with controlled lines. Such is their hand control from these and other activities of precision, such as sewing and use of art materials, that they develop careful cursive writing by the age of five.

They learn to read through their own writing, discovering that books contain the ideas of others in written form, just as their own stories give their thoughts to others in a visual representation. By the time they are in the first elementary class for six-to-nine-year-olds, they are writing long stories and reports, sometimes of twenty or more pages. All the human tendencies are at work here: exploration, orientation, order, abstraction, manipulation, repetition, control of error, perfection, and, most of all, communication and sharing of ideas with others. The hand now operates as the instrument of the intelligence by making the ideas of the mind visible through the fluid motion of cursive writing. The unity of intellect and hand is complete.

A similar process takes place even more dramatically in mathematics. The tiny golden beads that Montessori uses to introduce the decimal system to three-year-olds appeal to young children precisely because of their interest in refined work with their hands. The children count each tiny bead in long cubing and squaring chains of ten bars, nine bars, eight bars, and so forth, putting a small ticket with the appropriate numeral by each bead bar. The concept of exchanging for a higher category as each quantity reaches ten is introduced with the beads as well. The mathematical operations of addition, subtraction, multiplication, and division, involving numbers to the thousands and higher, is explored initially with the bead material. Further materials, also involving refined hand control, gradually carry each mathematical operation to a higher and higher level of abstraction. Similarly, geometry and algebra are introduced with concrete materials for the hand to manipulate and discover the abstract processes that they represent. Because every intellectual idea is given to the hand first, the children develop a deeper mathematical understanding. By the time they are twelve years old, they have developed a pattern of problem solving rather than problem doing. How to get the answer is as important to the children as the answer itself.

Geography, too, is given to the hand first. With their hands the children feel a globe of the world with land areas covered with sandpaper and oceans depicted by smooth surfaces, thus experiencing how much of Earth's surface consists of water. Later they are introduced to puzzle maps with each country represented by a cutout piece with a tiny knob for lifting it in and out of the map. They are introduced to the concept of land and water forms such as lakes, islands, bays, capes, straits, isthmuses, and so on, through small trays with models of their shapes. The children pour water into the appropriate indentations, thus creating a specific land or water form. In the elementary classes, maps with tiny flags on pins are used to denote capitals of countries, mountain ranges, deserts, rivers, and seas. Again, it is the uniting of hand and intellect that allows for in-depth understanding and encourages increasing interest in further learning.

You may wonder why we have not mentioned computers in our discussion of the child's hand development. We are concerned that, far from aiding hand development, extensive use of computers by young children may retard it. Moving a mouse involves neither fluid, independent use of the wrist, nor refined finger movement. When the keyboard is used, the child is engaged in a monotonous punching of the keys, each with the same pressure, rhythm, and repetitive movement. Contrast this action with the use of the hand and fingers when drawing or sewing, or in playing the piano where each finger moves differently and many fingers strike the keys in different combinations at one time. Further, in playing the piano there is a difference in how the right and left hands are used; the rhythm constantly changes and the strength of touch varies. We are concerned with the development of the hand as a tool of greatest flexibility, precision, and delicacy of movement—"instruments of the intelligence," as in a surgeon's hands. It is movement guided by thinking, not mechanical actions, that we need to encourage.

Our technology is a result of the precision of the human hand and a developed intellect; it does not produce them. We cannot predict the specific skills needed for the child's adult life. Our role is to help the child develop himself as a complete human being "adapted to his time, place, and culture." To the extent that we meet this responsibility, our children will have the capacities and experiences necessary to find meaning and fulfillment in their lives as adults.

FIVE

Crawling to Coordination

We have traced the development of the child's hand and brain from birth to three years old, as depicted on the lower half of our Time Line (see p. xxii). We now turn to the upper half of the Time Line and the other major area of the infant's self-construction: the large-muscle development of legs, arms, back, and trunk that will give the child an upright position. These two areas of formation comprise the whole of human development from helpless newborn to independently functioning three-year-old. They do not represent a point of arrival, however, but a point of departure. After three years of effort, the child is a wholly unified human being in all her complexity, but her mission is only beginning: she now starts her exploration of the whole world with head, hands, and feet. We will trace the infant's progress from helpless baby in a horizontal posture, to intrepid explorer on her own two feet, and discuss the ways in which we can best assist that journey.

The human infant's achievement of independence in movement in the first year to year and one-half is an astonishing feat. From the first moments of life, the supine child must commence preparing the instruments that lead to the conquering of the environment from an upright position, developing and coordinating the large muscles of torso, back, arms, and legs, which will eventually enable her to move her whole body in space.

The nine months of life within the womb are a period of internal gestation during which the baby is attached to the mother through the placenta and umbilical cord. After birth a period of external gestation begins. Although now in the outside world, the infant continues to be attached to the mother, this time through her arms and breast. The father, too, now becomes essential to the infant by bathing, diapering, and attending to the child's needs of dependency. However, if all goes well, a "second birth" occurs when the baby is eight to nine months old: the child begins to crawl. Thus begins a voluntary separation from both mother and father and a dramatic shifting of attention from them to the external world. Finally, after a period of crawling, then pulling up to stand, the child walks away from her parents and into that external world as an independent being. There are several aspects to consider in contemplating this monumental task of the human infant in achieving equilibrium and independent movement of the whole body. They are the natural pattern of development of the child's large muscles, the aid that we can give to enhance that development, and the gains to the child as a result of her independent movement.

Before the child can move the muscles of the arm, back, and legs at all, the neurons controlling those muscles must be myelinated. This process is accomplished according to the infant's internal timetable and cannot be outwardly influenced. We have to wait upon the child and her individual progress in development. Differences in the rate of myelination are one reason some babies are off and crawling, or sitting alone, or taking those first steps several months (or more) before others. Once the myelin sheath is formed around the necessary neurons, the brain begins to direct those muscles, and information is subsequently sent from the muscles back to the brain, altering the actions taken according to the new knowledge gained. This connection of brain to muscle makes possible the infant's coordinated, purposeful movement as opposed to aimless, random movement. But, unlike myelination of the neurons, the coordination and strength of the large muscles can be encouraged by outer circumstances. Interest in specific objects in the environment initially rouses the baby's brain to action and causes it to send its messages to and from the large muscles. This interest in items of the environment gives us our opportunity to influence the infant's development of coordination.

Strength in the large muscles of the infant is developed through their repeated use, just as muscle strength is only maintained in adulthood through vigorous physical exercise and training. Incentives to scoot and crawl, and opportunities for the infant to lift, pull, climb, and so forth are necessary to achieve optimal muscle strength in the baby. Again, providing these incentives becomes our opportunity for influence.

In discussing the specific aid needed by the infant as she seeks to develop her large muscles, we must first describe what not to do. This seems an odd beginning. Surely, in our modern world, loving parents do not obstruct an infant's positive moves to develop an independent and fully functioning body. Unfortunately, we do so everyday. Our present commercialization of childhood contributes to these obstacles in the infant's path as she works to develop her body for full use and independent movement. We have manufactured every manner of conveyance and confinement for young children: cribs, playpens, high chairs and eating tables, infant seats, jumpy seats, car seats, infant swings, walkers, strollers, bicycle carts, carrying backpacks, front-facing slings, and so forth. When young couples travel today, they sometimes appear to be moving a small furniture store.

Some of these items were developed for safety, others for the convenience of adults, and still others from a false idea of what promotes meaningful skill development in children. In fact, of all of these expensive products, the only one that is necessary for safety is the car seat and, because of the strict confinement it imposes, children under three years old should spend as little time as possible strapped within it. As for other products, parents must choose very carefully from among the items produced for adult convenience. In every generation, adults find it frustrating and inconvenient to readjust their lives to accommodate the demanding needs of the young children in their midst. Self-formation is arduous, and the young child's need for aid in its completion is a twenty-four-hour, seven-day-a-week responsibility. Nature has not changed its plan for human childhood, which requires the constant presence, dedication, and, increasingly, wisdom of loving adults. Amidst so many choices of products that enable us not to be bothered by our children, parents need to think through very carefully which of them to bring into their lives, and why.

Contemporary affluence also contributes to another area of constraint in movement for infants. Adults in previous generations indulged themselves on occasion by dressing their children for admiration and show, rather than for comfort and ease of movement. However, except for the very wealthy, they did not have the means, or the time, to do so on a daily basis. Babies spent much of their time in simple, practical attire that allowed for maximum movement. We will discuss clothing for the child under three in detail in Chapter 7. Here, however, we want to stress a key principle in choosing appropriate clothing for the infant: the child must be dressed so that she can move unhindered. Every choice of clothing should reflect this principle.

Let us compare ourselves to the baby for a moment. What do we choose to wear when we want to be active? Adults have inactive states, but a baby is pretty much active all the time. If not sleeping, she is moving to whatever extent she can, unless she is temporarily immobilized in a conveyance. If, as adults, we put on clothing that does not bind and is made of natural fabric that breathes when we exercise, how much more do we need to give our infant similar clothing. Furthermore, the infant needs to be comfortable when lying in a prone position. This means that her clothes must be free of big buttons, bows, and other ornamentation. Clearly, the baby should not wear dresses, for these prevent her from drawing herself up on her knees and pushing off, first to scoot and eventually to crawl. Remember that dresses were the everyday clothing for both male and female babies in the Middle Ages in part to create difficulty in crawling. Superstition of the time held that crawling indicated the baby might be a "changeling"—that is, part human, part animal. Therefore, crawling was considered an animal, not a human act, and when possible was discouraged.

Appropriate clothing for the infant allows her to get her knees under her, push off, scoot and crawl, just as soon as coordination and muscle strength make these actions possible. On her upper body, the infant wears layered clothing: a soft cotton undershirt and, if needed, a long-sleeve cotton shirt as well as a lightweight wool sweater buttoned up the back. Her cloth cotton diaper should be twisted once over in the middle so that the part between her legs is narrower, thus reducing the diaper's width and allowing the legs to come closer together for freer forward movement. You can add a nylon cover with elastic at waist and leg openings, to cover the cloth diaper when protection from the environment is necessary. (We discuss the many disadvantages of disposable diapers in the section on toileting in Chapter 7. Here we mention only that paper and plastic restrict movement because they do not stretch or yield.) For the rest of her dress, the infant has bare legs with booties or socks with ankles just tight enough to stay on her feet. If she is going to be on a chafing surface such as a rough carpet or stone patio, she may need a pair of cotton leggings for protection. (Sweat pants are an option but parents should realize that they do contain at least a small hindrance to the child; the knee slips within the pant leg's looser space when the infant scoots or crawls.) Thus simply attired in bootie, diaper, cotton shirt, and sweater, the baby is dressed for action.

We are not often conscious of a third obstacle that we place in the way of the children's progress in movement and self-formation. It is not connected to any visible object, as are confinement in devices for safety and transport or the constraint of movement through poor choice of clothing. Yet, this obstacle has the potential of being more damaging to the child because it relates directly to her developing attitude toward struggle and her view of herself. We are referring to the inhibiting of the child's initiative for movement by adults' responses to her. From the first weeks, we constantly prop up the infant. Very soon we are sitting her up, even though her muscles are still very weak and uncoordinated, and it is a very long time before she can sit up on her own power. Next, we pull her up to stand, although her bones are still weak. Eventually we "walk" her by holding onto her tiny hands high above her head and, by this process, turning ourselves into an infant "walking machine." Potentially the most damaging of all to her developing sense of self, we continue to sweep her up according to our own needs and whims and carry her about in our arms long after she is walking stably on her own. When we make such actions habitual, we teach our child to depend upon us. We take from her pleasure in the results of her own efforts and the joy of conquest.

From the first months of life, the infant strives to see things from an upright position. Just as in language acquisition, it seems that something is programmed within her leading her to respond to her environment in a prescribed manner. Hence, as soon as she is able, she holds her head vertically—not sideways or on an angle—and she loves to be carried upright in our arms. However, by constantly propping and sitting the infant up at every opportunity, we take away some of her incentive to get herself upright on her own. Make no mistake; it is incredibly hard work for her. We have only to remember the stroke victims we know who must retrain their large muscles for sitting and walking. It is painful to watch the intensity of their struggles. Yet, we know that we make it far more difficult for them to achieve full recovery if we too readily substitute our actions for theirs. They need incentives and encouragement with just the right amount of challenge, but the effort to develop muscle coordination and strength is theirs alone.

A last area of obstacles to the infant's development of movement relates to a topic past generations had little reason to consider. It concerns the gift of time: time free of a barrage of noise and endless "entertainment." Time to concentrate and focus without distractions is essential for the child's self-formation in every area of development, and muscle coordination and strength is no exception. From the beginning, the child has a strong drive for coordinating and strengthening her large muscles. However, she is diverted from these efforts when her attention is consistently drawn to something else. The television set creates just such a compelling distraction. If it is turned on where the infant can see it, she becomes mesmerized by it—not because she can understand what she sees there, but because the constantly changing images and movement on the screen engage her orienting response.* The baby sits immobile, staring at a television screen as precious moments go by that could have been given to developing her physical coordination and strength.

Later in her life, after school or in the evenings, the child is similarly immobile, parked in front of her computer, surfing the Internet, or playing electronic games. One of the greatest chal-

---

*Robert Kubey and Mihaly Csikszentmihalyi, "Television Addiction Is No Mere Metaphor," *Scientific American* 286, no. 2 (February 2002): 74–81.

lenges facing parents today is determining the proper role of technology in family life. Rightfully, modern technology should be a great boon to our lives, providing both parents and children with more time for study and reflection than any previous generation. The fact that this is not the case is clear evidence that we are missing important opportunities to better our personal lives and increase our happiness and sense of fulfillment through this latest of human achievements.

We turn now to the specific aid needed by the infant as she seeks to develop the large muscles required for moving her body in space. Throughout this discussion of developing coordination for movement and equilibrium, it is important to remind ourselves of our purpose in giving this aid. Our goal as we prepare the infant's environment for movement is not to rush her development so that we can have a baby that develops faster than others. Our purpose has to do with psychological rather than physical reasons and reflects our attitude toward the child. In preparing the infant's environment, particularly the child's own room, we clearly reveal this attitude. It should reflect the view that this infant is an individual who is going to grow and change and separate; this is not someone who will remain a baby forever, to be carried about and cared for by others. Our purpose then is to foster the child's self-formation into an independent being. To accomplish this mission our assistance to the baby has to be well grounded and thorough, hence based on knowledge of infant development and guided by each child's individual timetable.

Parents need to be very careful here. After the initial period of adjustment, we often find ourselves enjoying the fact that this baby needs us. Without realizing what we are doing, we fall into habits that keep her dependent on us. After the beginning weeks are past, we need to watch for our impulses to carry the baby about constantly with no place to put her down that is not a confined space such as a crib or other holding device. We want to foster the baby's self-concept from the beginning: "I am a capable person. I can do things for myself. I can affect my environment." It is the infant's experiences, as she figures out how to use her body, that will give her this view of herself.

The child-bed in the corner of the child's room (described in Chapter 2) already sends a message that this space is for a person who is going to be mobile and thus eventually capable of fulfilling her own desires. Given the freedom of the child-bed, the baby will begin to "slither" almost from birth, often covering a surprising amount of territory. As we have mentioned, a crib not only limits this early mobility of the baby, it makes the infant dependent upon the adult when she wants to sleep or wake. After a few months the baby can get herself in and out of the child-bed. At no age can she climb safely in and out of a crib. Further, when the baby first manages to pull herself up to stand by holding on to the crib's bars, she typically cannot get herself down again. She must stand and cry until an adult comes to rescue her.

By two months of age, the baby has mastered the control of her head. Her mobiles overhead and mirror next to her on the wall have helped this self-formation. In addition, by providing these items for the child, parents have sent a vital message: "We are not the only interesting things in the environment. You are going to belong to the world, not just to us." No detail should be missed in supporting this message. For example, Montessori suggested mobiles that are moved by the wind or the child's own motions, rather than wind-up, mechanical ones that require the mother to make them move. In effect, in things large and small, parents are continually preparing their infant for the day that she will be in the world without them. Such an attitude toward the child reflects the parent's selflessness and establishes that their relationship is for the child's benefit, not their own. As we continue to follow the infant's physical development in these first three years of life, you will note that everything we suggest reflects such an attitude and helps parents assist the infant in her gradual self-formation as a separate and independent human being.

For this outcome to occur at the natural time in each succeeding stage of children's development, it is important that the infant is accustomed from birth to spending a significant amount of her waking time on her stomach. When the necessary neurons are at last myelinated, the muscles of the baby's back, buttocks, arms and legs are ready to begin the lifting of head and upper torso from the child-bed or mat. However, the infant's brain has to direct these muscles in order to coordinate them for this action, and continuing practice is necessary to make them ever stronger. "Push ups" with the arms from the stomach position are key in forming this needed coordination and strength for all of the subsequent large-muscle development of the infant. Pediatricians today recommend for safety reasons that infants fall asleep on their backs. Thus they are not given as much time on their stomachs as babies in the past who typically were put to bed on their fronts or sides. When these babies awakened, they exercised their bodies from the stomach position and developed very good muscle coordination and strength in their backs, buttocks, arms, and legs. Our Time Line is not geared to this recent practice of babies sleeping on their backs and may therefore show development several months ahead of schedule when compared with your own infant's progress. This is all the more reason to accustom your baby to being on her stomach whenever awake. Again our goal is not to push the infant ahead of her individual timetable, but to help her meet it. When the infant develop skills at the natural time for her own self-formation, she is not only happier but her cognitive development is also affected because her brain is ready for the new information that moving about in her environment gives her.

By approximately four months of age, the infant who has spent sufficient time on her stomach can roll from back to front and vice versa. She takes pleasure in this movement for its own sake, but we have also assisted her by giving her more things to see. Her mirror enables her to observe herself moving, and she can follow the movements of others there as well. Most important, from her position on a mat or child-bed, she can see all about her.

As we have mentioned, in order to move our bodies efficiently, we have to develop knowledge of the area around us. Therefore, we want to make it possible for the infant to experience her environment visually before she begins to crawl about in it. To help you understand how best to help your baby in this regard, we are going to suggest an experiment. Lie on your back on the floor and survey the room around you. Next roll to your stomach and compare your experience from that position. Your infant needs first to explore visually the distances about her in this way for many weeks. Now try crawling out into the room and see what it feels like to cover the space to different objects. This is the process that the baby follows in developing self-awareness in space and an understanding of distance as it relates to sight and body awareness. Because she is seeing the room from a position down on the floor, the baby forms a correct impression of the space she will soon move out into. She builds an internal map of the floor—a floor plan, if you will—with "points of reference" in the room to guide her when she begins to scoot and then crawl. In the beginning, her movements are slow. By the time she can crawl, and then walk, rapidly in the room, she is safe in doing so because she has learned gradually how to judge distance and speed.

We have helped in this process of gradually understanding distance and space by allowing the baby sufficient experiences in a familiar environment. It is not helpful to her if we constantly carry her about to other people's houses or to shopping malls. This is another instance where we need to give our child the gift of time. On this occasion, this involves her remaining in a familiar environment, her own home and yard or other customary daytime settings: to study them visually and then very gradually to begin to move about within them.

Movement in space is driven by the child's curiosity and interest in the external world. The mirror on the child's bedroom wall helps fuel this interest. We can provide further opportunities to the baby to move her whole body by offering her specific incentives to movement. We can put a small toy or cloth ball just barely out of reach and allow her to try to get to it on her own. Our instinct, of course, is to anticipate her desires and give her everything even before she indicates an interest. This is a natural response for adults, as we are accustomed to dealing with each other. It is helpful to hand desired objects to another adult, as we already know how to reach things for ourselves. The baby, on the other hand, is in a process of self-formation. Trying to get to something on her own power represents an opportunity for her. Of course, we are not going to allow an infant to get overly frustrated. We will see to it that there is a balance between effort and success. However, a constant attentiveness and hovering over the baby by parents, family members, or other adults is not helpful. Such behavior negates her initiative and cripples her at the threshold of life.

As soon as the baby is scooting (at about four months on our Time Line) we want to give her as much "floor time" as possible. It is helpful to have mats throughout the house for this purpose. (Vinyl-covered foam pads, sold for use in playpens, work well for this purpose. They are stiff and do not bunch up as the infant slithers and scoots.) In this way she can be near us wherever we are, exercising herself, exploring a cloth ball with her hands, pulling her knees up under her, and scooting after the cloth ball that has rolled ever so slightly out of reach in order to explore it again. Thus the infant's drive for self-formation in one area parallels her interest and abilities in another. As we have discussed, the development of the baby's hands proceeds to purposeful prehension at four months of age, and she wants to examine all objects in her adjacent space. Now at four months the development of her body allows her to reach those objects on her own power. The combination of the needs of the hand and body soon results in a baby who is busy scooting about and exploring with her hands all the objects in her immediate space.

This is the time—well in advance of her rapid crawling and complete mobility—to "baby proof" the entire house, just as we have previously done with the infant's own room. Cover electrical outlets; place lamps out of reach; use chests or easy chairs to block access to electrical cords; remove wastepaper baskets; and keep floors clean and free of items small enough to swallow. All open stairs should have gates, and a portable gate is useful for individual rooms. When we know the baby is safe in another room of the house, we can allow her to have several minutes there out of our sight. As we go about our work, we can talk to our baby from the next room and reassure her of our presence if she calls for us. If we do this gradually—at first just a few minutes at a time—the baby learns that she can manage without us for brief periods. We lay a foundation for an understanding, so important in a healthy adjustment to life, that physical presence is not essential to trust and a feeling of oneness with loved ones.

Many parents neglect to consider this key concept until their babies are older, perhaps age fourteen months or more. By this time, the child becomes accustomed to one or the other parent's constant presence and attention whenever she is awake. Such dependence becomes trying when the baby is older and is ready for more interaction with the environment. This is the time when many mothers and fathers wonder, "Where did our perfect baby go?" The baby is no less "perfect" than before, of course. What these parents mean is "Where did our perfect relationship go?"

Because the child is now physically so active, she is demanding in a new way and it is harder to keep up with her needs.

Perhaps earlier, these parents adjusted well to their infant's total dependence on them. Now they are not adapting to their baby's new needs, as development proceeds and she must take the first steps in learning how to depend on herself. Because these new needs are not being met, a reaction sets in—either passive or violent according to the baby's personality. Sometimes parents, in seeking to return to an earlier symbiotic relationship, begin to micromanage their child's every waking moment. Thus they set the stage for even more difficult problems later. Parenthood involves a series of adjustments to each new stage of the child's self-formation and plane of development. This is why it is essential that parents familiarize themselves with the natural development of childhood and early adulthood, thus preparing themselves for each new stage before it arrives. It is also why being a parent is so interesting and challenging; it helps us to understand human nature generally, and the self in particular, as few life experiences can.

At approximately seven months a baby who has had a good deal of floor time on her stomach develops arm muscles that can push her up to a sitting position. The muscles of her back are not yet strong enough to maintain this position for long, however, without a support behind her. We can supply this support for brief periods with a pillow or other means. Montessori designed a special chair and table out of heavy oak for this purpose, useful at the infant's mealtimes and occasionally for other activities if not prolonged. This oak table is proportioned for children from the time they are sitting up until they are approximately eighteen months old. (Montessori built another table of lighter wood and with a different design for children from eighteen months to three years old.)

During this time when the infant is trying to push up on her arms into a sitting position, it is important not to continually sit her up as if she were a rag doll. Sitting up should come to the child as a discovery of her own power. Further, the act of sitting up through the infant's own efforts strengthens her back muscles and develops her balance. If others constantly prop her up, she has little incentive to put forth the strenuous effort on her own that such development requires.

By approximately eight months of age, the baby can not only sit up, she can maintain this position comfortably without support. As we can see on the Time Line, her hands have progressed from intentional work to hand-to-hand transfer and the first stages of control of the fingers. Again we have the perfect balance of development proceeding apace in hands and body. The body is now upright in a sitting position thus freeing the hands from helping the body to scoot and crawl. At the same time, the hands have developed the capacity for more intricate study and manipulation of objects.

In the next period of development, beginning at age eight months, your baby will reveal herself as a "sitter" or a "crawler." "Sitters" are those babies who at eight months, in spite of every incentive that we have previously provided, prefer visual exploration of their world to crawling about within it. Although they appear to us not to be very active, in fact a great deal of activity is occurring within. "Sitters" very often acquire language early, for example, and tend to be very verbal throughout childhood. It is as if the brain cannot excel in every area of development at once and, for the moment at least, has opted for language over locomotion.

We have to be certain that waiting to crawl is the child's choice and not ours, however. We continue to avoid constraining the baby in infant seats, swings, jumpy seats, and strollers. From age six to eight months on, we add new incentives for crawling to the infant's activities. Balls of rubber and wood, and other objects that roll more easily and thus further, such as a cylinder with a bell inside, are substituted for the cloth and knitted balls of the earlier period. It is important, though, not to use these new items as a "gym lesson" for the infant. Nature meant such exercising to happen naturally all day long, directed by the baby's internal timetable, not determined by adults.

Given sufficient opportunity, the majority of infants do turn into "crawlers," not "sitters." They begin crawling everywhere with great enthusiasm and energy at approximately eight months. Crawling not only requires great strength in the infant's back, arm, and leg muscles, it also necessitates a bilateral coordination of right arm with left leg, left arm with right leg, in an alternating pattern of movement. This bilateral movement becomes the foundation for walking upright in a balanced position in the future.

Some infants develop very unorthodox patterns of crawling. Since there is no evidence that these methods have any effect on their later development, we doubt that it makes any sense to try to change them. The possible exception would be crawling backwards. When starting to scoot at four months some infants develop a pattern of pushing back with their arms, thus propelling their bodies in the opposite and undesired direction. This tendency can eventually lead to crawling backwards. When your baby tries to scoot and propel herself forward to a desired object, you can help by allowing her to press her feet against your hands or the wall, thus blocking her backward motion and, at the same time, helping her to develop strength in her legs for going forward.

At about nine months, the infant tries to pull herself to a standing position. Just as for her sitting up, it is best not to substitute our actions for the child's efforts. The joy of achievement in getting to a standing position rightfully belongs to the child. We can, however, help the child by making certain that there are items in her environment that she can use to pull up on: an ottoman, a couch or coffee table, and in her room a low toy shelf. You can also secure a bar or handrail on the wall. (As depicted on the Time Line, this is similar to an exercise bar or ballet bar for adults. The infant bar is approximately one and a half to two inches in diameter and fourteen inches from the floor.)

After several months of pulling herself up, the child will find a Walker Wagon useful. The Walker Wagon consists of a wooden rectangular box or tray attached to four small wheels. It has a stationary vertical hand bar that the child uses to pull herself up to her feet and thence to push the "wagon" in front of her as she walks forward.* Use this aid on a carpet or grass until your child is ready for the faster movement of a wooden floor or hard surface. However, it is essential to avoid all other commercial items advertised to "help infants walk." These products put the infant on her legs, thus causing her to bear her full body weight before her bones are sufficiently developed. They also constrain the child in an unnatural position—one she is not ready for—to enable her to walk forward. As a result, the child receives the wrong messages about maintaining balance.

When the infant first pulls herself up on a low piece of furniture or the wall bar in her room, she does so with two hands. In the beginning she moves along on tiptoes, continuing to hold on with both hands. Her hand development now includes the thumb-finger opposition that makes the pincer grip possible. This new ability facilitates her firm handhold, particularly on the wall bar. The baby can also now hold objects tightly to her body with both arms, again demonstrating that development in one

---

*Child-size items described in this chapter can be purchased from The Michael Olaf Company, 65 Ericson Court #1, Arcata, CA 95521 (http://www.michaelolaf.net). We suggest that you ask for their catalogue "The Joyful Child," which contains helpful text as well as items for purchase.

part of the body (the arms and hands) is supporting that of the rest (the legs and feet.)

When you first discover that your baby can pull herself up, it is wise to check the house and yard again for safety. You may have a walking child sooner than you expect and there are new aspects of the baby's environment to consider. You can cover sharp edges on tables and counters with tape, for example. Be prepared for bumps and bruises. Babies have no judgment when beginning to crawl up furniture and onto counters and stairs. Such judgment must develop very gradually over a very long period of time through continuous activity. Parental vigilance, patience, and ingenuity are therefore required during this phase. For example, the parents of an unusually lithe and active ten-month-old who had begun to walk, put a thick knitted ski hat on their baby whenever she was awake. The well-padded hat afforded at least some protection from her continual mishaps.

After pulling up successfully, the next task for the baby is adding balance to her upright position. First, she lets go of one hand and walks along while holding onto her supporting structure: a piece of furniture or a wall bar. Finally, she lets go entirely and in a triumphant moment stands on her own two feet without assistance. The struggle to develop this first experience with balance into true stability and then add to it the alternating use of one side of the body, then the other, in normal walking is arguably the most dramatic challenge in human childhood. For most babies it will require endless energy, courage, and persistence over a several-month period.

At the same time, we see that the baby's two hands are beginning to work together now, too, so that she can thoroughly explore whatever her two legs can get her to. The human child, usually over a twelve-month or longer time frame of continual effort, has now arrived at a point of development corresponding to that of the newborn foal.

Although the struggle for the baby is a prolonged one, we

need to be very careful that we do not rush her through the early stages in learning to walk. Solid development is predicated on fully completing the demands of each phase before moving on to the next. Just as "dropped stitches" in a knitted sweater result in an incomplete product, so children hurried through any stage of development are not as strong as they could have been.

On the other hand, allowing the separation from the parents, as represented by the child's walking, for example, to occur at the right time with the right help paves the way for an acceptance of life's inevitable attachments and separations as natural processes. Such an acceptance helps children to understand that relationships with others will evolve and change throughout their lives. This ability is especially crucial in the first years of the child's life. We want to help children realize that when they leave someone or something, the gain can more than offset the loss. In this way, we transform the child's experience of attachment and separation into a process that enhances trust and security in life. For such a result, the parents have to perceive the value in separation and be ready for it in each stage of the child's development. Most often, it is harder for the adult to separate from the child than for the child to separate from the adult. We tend to cling to the child, not quite trusting her abilities.

We have mentioned one physical aid that we give babies as they begin to walk: the Walker Wagon. For the child who is somewhat older and walking more stably, Montessori also designed a small wooden stairway with handrails and steps at a specific distance and height. This is an expensive item because it is custom built, and it is certainly not necessary for the home. However, it is not as costly as many pieces of apparatus such as backyard or basement jungle gyms, and it provides endless practice and repetitive use to help the infant learn to go up and down stairs safely.

More important than these few physical means, however, are

the habits that we develop in relating to the child who can walk with stability. If we give in to the temptation to carry her with us everywhere, we are not giving her the right help at the right time in her development. She needs now to be up and out of our arms at all opportunities. Similarly, she must be freed from being pushed and pulled about in various conveyances: strollers, wagons, and so forth. She needs to develop an impression of herself as a capable person: "I can walk like other people do."

This is the time to begin the habit of a daily walk with your child. This walk should be a meandering one, one that follows the child's mission, not the adult's. The child stops to inspect everything. The purpose of the child's walk, then, is not to get more exercise. The baby gets plenty of exercise by being in perpetual motion for most of the waking day. However, there is a benefit to the adult in the "child's walk." In our accomplishment-oriented lives, we lose sight of the joy and beauty of living in the moment and of savoring the details of life. Forced to slow ourselves to the child's slow pace and walk without an outward goal, we recapture something of our own childhood and therein find a means of reflection, peace, and relaxation. Furthermore, the adult is soon surprised by the developing abilities of the young child who walks daily. Children as young as two years old, given the opportunity to go at their own pace, are capable of quite long walks, sometimes covering as much as a mile in different types of terrain and in all kinds of weather. By the time these children are four or five years of age they may well have developed into good little hikers.

During all this period of pulling up, standing, holding on, and developing balance for walking, the muscles of the arms, torso, legs, and feet are strengthening through use in the new manner. Just as the legs have remained bare to facilitate movement and sensorial awareness, so should the feet be bare whenever feasible from the time that the infant pulls herself up to stand.

Because of concern about temperature, the parent needs to feel the child's feet occasionally to check for their warmth. However, if the house is at room temperature, an active baby tends to maintain good overall body temperature and there are numerous benefits to the infant in having her feet uncovered. Bare feet enable the baby to take in many new tactile experiences: how squishy the soft ground feels underfoot, the coolness of earth and grass, the texture of the carpet, the smoothness of the wood floor, the impact of weight as the infant increases in weight over time. This information of the world stimulates mental development for the child, just as do sensations of temperature, texture, and weight acquired through the hands. When we cover the child consistently from head to foot with clothing and shoes we take away these opportunities.

In addition, freer use of the foot develops stronger muscles. This is particularly true once the infant pulls herself to an upright position. She balances herself differently when she can use muscles all over the foot. Further, bare feet do not slip and the child learns that she can count on her own feet. When socks or shoes slip, they send the opposite message and the child decides, "I can't trust my body." Try taking your own shoes and socks off and compare your experiences in walking and balancing. When shoes are necessary for the child's protection, such as in public places or going out for walks, choose those with flexible soles to minimize constriction and those that have reasonable traction. If it is important to cover the child's feet while in the house, choose nonskid socks (socks with rubber on the bottom which retards slipping).

There is one other topic that is important to consider when children begin to walk stably. If we want them to be on their feet and walking on their own as much as possible, we need to consider how to manage this when we are in public spaces both indoors and outdoors. Outdoors it is a matter of safety. When we are getting out of cars, crossing public parking lots and streets, or walking on busy sidewalks, it is tempting to pick young children up and carry them to our destination. We recommend a different solution. Take your child firmly by one hand so that she must walk by your side, holding your hand. A fourteen-month-old child, having just found freedom to move on her own, typically resists this constraint at first. However, she is much less likely still to be resisting at age two or three years than the child who has not been asked to walk quietly by your side earlier and to hold your hand from the beginning.

This is a habit of discipline that should be established as early as possible for several reasons. Paramount is safety. Children are at least four or five years old before they have sufficient self-control to stay reliably by our sides in public places without holding our hands. A second reason has to do with the child's developing will. Asking the child to hold our hand for short periods in public places is an opportunity to help her accept necessary limits in her life. When indoors, compliance is more a matter of learning manners than safety, but it is no less important. The habit of "indoor manners," consisting of quiet voices and no running about, helps young children to develop awareness of their environment and respect for other people. Such controlled behavior in public places can only be introduced to very young children if they are on their own two feet, yet within our reach. (We discuss this topic again, as well as other ways to aid the child's developing will, in Chapter 9.)

What has a twelve-to-fifteen-months-old child gained through her great achievement of independent, coordinated movement of both hand and body? Movement is essential to understanding life and having an effect on life. The result of the conquering of movement for the infant is a deepening knowledge of the world, as well as an exhilarated attitude toward life and a positive view of herself. She realizes that she is a capable person: "I can move from here to there. I can do what I set out to do. I can affect my environment and I can affect others." Because she was not restricted in movement in the early months, as so many babies are, she is less frustrated. She has gotten to the experiences that her brain was ready for and on her own power. There is no way that we could continually have guessed for her what, of all the stimuli in their environment, she wanted to master at each given moment. She had to have the ability and the freedom to move within her own space at will.

A moving baby learns continuously about her world, filling in information of distance, speed, and time on her visual maps, as she goes from one object to another, one place to another, all day long. She discovers what the objects she sees feel like once she gets to them: what do rounded or sharp edges feel like? Does that shiny wood table feel hard or soft? She discovers visual perspective: an object that looked smaller from a little distance is actually larger when she gets to it. She develops body awareness as she inadvertently bumps into obstacles and objects, and she gains in agility as she eventually learns how to avoid them.

Finally, in addition to giving all this knowledge of the world and of the self, movement is the "playing field" for the development of the child's will. When the baby wants to get to something, she must direct her body through distractions—inhibiting some actions and carrying out others. She even must learn to inhibit an impulse to pull herself up on a table when she is told, "Don't go there." Or perhaps experience teaches her that this table not only falls over, it falls over with her every attempt to pull up, and thus she develops both memory and concentration.

At fifteen months the child has reached what Montessori called "the stage of maximum effort." She walks carrying a heavy object and holds on to it while climbing rapidly in and out of a chair. She climbs the stairs over and over. Balanced walking not only frees her hands to carry objects, it also enables her to use her hands for work in structured activities. Thus she is ready to be part of the culture around her. She moves into high gear, propelled to action. She realizes that she is capable of her own learning, and works and works for mastery. She is frustrated often, as she tries to develop each new skill. She is excited about life, and it is hard to sleep.

What are we going to do for this child who is always on the move, who wants to explore her whole world and is filled with such incredible energy? Montessori had an unusual answer for this age-old dilemma of parents. It involves a new approach to the child's activities, one that requires a different adult role and a renewed dedication on the parents' part. At the same time, this new approach, because it so successfully meets the needs of the child in her self-formation, results in solid collaboration between parent and child, and therefore a more fulfilling life for each of them.

SIX | Practical Life

Children who walk steadily at age fifteen months are at long last independent beings, ready for a new kind of work in their self-formation. For many months before they began to use their feet, they used and exercised their hands; now that they can walk, Montessori said, the hands are ready to become "educated if only they are given the opportunities."[*] This is a great moment for the parent. Yet it is one of great difficulty, too. Before, the child had to stay put wherever he was. Now he is everywhere, investigating all over the house, taking and moving objects, climbing and carrying at will.

Montessori described these newly independent fifteen-month-olds as "very different from the children who a short time before needed help in taking their first unsteady steps. Theirs was not independence because they relied on others for help. At the time, they were fighters but now they are victors; now they are really independent." And how do we respond to this great conquest of independent action? "Today we make a square box, a playpen, and put the child inside. . . . This is the reward for the independence that the child has conquered, this is the amount of freedom that we allow him."

Caging the child in the playpen when inside and in the pram

[*]Quotations in this chapter are from Maria Montessori, "Lecture on Movement by Dr. Montessori, London, 1946," in *Communications* 1 (2001): 30–33.

when he is out, means that we cannot learn about the child's needs in development: "We cannot study their psychology." Montessori advised one mother who was seeking to learn about her daughter: "Leave the child alone and watch what she does. Do not abandon her but watch from a distance; you can go to her if she needs help." This little girl proceeded to leave her many toys and began carrying a very heavy footstool all about the house. Montessori described other children of this age doing equally surprising things: carrying a heavy jug of water across the rug and making every effort not to spill a drop, carrying a loaf of bread almost as large as the child himself to the table, emptying a large wastepaper basket, then picking up all the bits of paper and putting them back in the basket again, dusting all over the house with a duster, putting a stopper in and taking it out of a perfume bottle over and over, taking freshly ironed napkins and laying them out in a nearly perfect straight line across the room from one corner to the opposite one, then just as carefully re-piling them all over again. To Montessori all such freely chosen behavior offers clues in understanding the child's needs in self-formation.

Montessori expected that adults would find her suggestion of simultaneously giving more freedom of action and carefully monitoring the movements of fifteen-month-olds, unsettling—even difficult—at first. Certainly it would require sacrifice on the parents' part. In particular, giving up the playpen meant giving up freedom from having to watch the child. Yet Montessori insisted: "To give children freedom and be watchful and ready to help is not easy, but we must be prepared to do all this."

Through observing newly independent children in their free-dom, Montessori reached a startling conclusion, one that is not properly understood even today: "At this age just toys, especially light toys, do not satisfy the child. He can do nothing with them." What the child wants at this age is to do things that require his maximum efforts. In the preceding phase, the child's goal was to exercise his hands and master his body. Now in this new period of independent movement, it is "to conquer the environment." For this purpose, children want to "do what they can as soon as they can." More than merely conquering their own bodies as before, now they must master the world. It is no wonder that their energy and determination are so boundless.

The child's first step in meeting this expanded goal is to become newly conscious of the parents' actions in everyday living. Before, the child watched what his parents were doing; now, he tries to imitate what they are doing. At this point, parents need to understand that the child tends to learn what the parents do. On the other hand, the child must understand that he cannot imitate immediately. There has to be a period of training and preparation first. The newly independent child is not going to be free, then, to do whatever he likes, whenever he likes. To do the things that adults do, he must willingly accept our help in preparing himself. Montessori used the example of someone learning to play the piano. A person "cannot play music on the piano merely by imitation; he has to learn to play it. We cannot do anything only by imitation; training is also necessary." Training for playing the piano involves a series of exercises for independent practice. The purpose of the exercises is not a direct one but an indirect one—not the playing of music but a preparation to do so. To imitate the adult successfully, then, the child must first learn and repeat certain exercises in preparation.

At the same time, the child is intrigued by the preliminary exercises themselves because they represent a full "cycle of activity." Montessori noted, "Children naturally like to have exercises which are complete in themselves, even if they serve no direct outer purpose . . . but are a preparation for the activity which is to come. These are what we call 'cycles of activity.' Children do these things that seem useless, with great care and interest. They seem useless to us but the child is preparing himself and learning to coordinate his movements." Montessori used an example of the child making the most strenuous efforts to climb into an armchair and then climb immediately out of it. "We may wonder why he should make such a great effort if he does not want to enjoy the armchair once he has got up and into it. But no, he climbs out of the chair, across the arms, and down to the floor again. It is a 'cycle of activity,' an effort that brings a special co-ordination of movement."

These cycles of activity not only aid the child by preparing him indirectly for later actions, they deepen his concentration and perfect his personality, developing in him "constancy and patience." It is this positive effect on the child's concentration and personality, and therefore ultimately on his ability to learn, that most impressed Montessori and led her to make exercises that involve cycles of activity the foundation of her approach to the child's later education.

Montessori recognized that meaningful learning requires a willingness to follow each successive step in the process of acquiring new information. It is essential to repeat each one of those steps as many times as necessary to know and to understand the specific learning involved on the deepest level. To complete such a cycle of activity requires a "depth of engagement" on the child's part. It is just this engagement of the whole personality that is necessary to all meaningful learning throughout life.

Montessori suggests that the appropriate time to address the challenge of engagement is when the child first achieves independent action at approximately fifteen to eighteen months old. What the child now needs is "work with structured materials" that follows his natural interest in completing cycles of activity and in imitating the adults in his environment. For "this new kind of play," as Montessori called it, toys will not do. The child needs items that are real and relate directly to the adult's everyday activities. Montessori called these items the practical-life materials.

Because the practical-life materials are to reflect the country and historical period of the individual child, Montessori could not designate specific items and activities. She could only establish principles for parents and Montessori teachers to follow in selecting them for an individual situation. Similarly, the way in which the adult presents the materials to the child, and helps him to follow through in using them, follows general guidelines but differs in detail according to the specific culture. In this chapter we discuss these principles and guidelines as they apply to children living in Western cultures today. However, they are easily translated to other cultures and societies. As we have said, human children are the same everywhere and their needs in self-formation are the same. Their developmental pattern and their mission to become "a complete human being adapted to time, place, and culture" do not alter whatever the historical period or specific circumstances.

The exercises of practical life should involve manual activities that the child sees adults engaged in on a regular basis in daily life. Therefore, parents select from among their occupations the ones that "they have to do anyway in their everyday life," and by doing so, parents avoid the feeling of pressure to do even more for their child than they have hitherto been doing. They are simply including their child, according to his interest and capability, and as time allows, in setting and clearing the table, unloading groceries, preparing food, baking, pouring water and juice, wiping the table, washing dishes, sorting and folding laundry, putting away clothes, dusting, sweeping and mopping, washing a mirror or window, polishing a vase or shoe, picking up a room, emptying wastepaper baskets, watering plants inside or outside, and arranging flowers. When the child is somewhat older, this may even include ironing, sewing, weeding the garden, and raking leaves.

Obviously, by including the child in their own work, parents are slowing down their own efficiency and the time of accomplishment. Why would Montessori, in other ways such a practical woman and one of great personal achievement, recommend such a seemingly impractical approach to children once they become fifteen months old? She suggested making the child the adult's daily companion in these simple activities of home and family for one reason only: out of respect for the possibilities of human life as found in the small child.

The reason for following Montessori ideas and practices, then, is not to be a better mother or father or to have a better child, or even because as a parent you love your child so much. It is because you respect your child and what he represents in the continuum of human life. With tasks undertaken in this spirit, and, in following Montessori's attention to detail in setting up and introducing each new activity, parents all over the world have found their children capable of doing far more than they ever imagined. As a parent, you may also discover that you feel a new "lightness" as you go about necessary household duties and that the time spent is far more interesting and rewarding than before. You are no longer a servant; you are an educator. Our goal for the remainder of this chapter is to help you understand and respond to Montessori's ideas for the practical-life exercises and their materials in a realistic way—a way that truly helps you to help your child in his self-formation. Otherwise, you may consider these beautiful ideas but of little use.

The following anecdote from one of our parent child lectures illustrates the dilemma that many parents experience when they begin to include their children in the work of their daily life, and serves as an introduction to the practical application of Montessori's ideas. One of our mothers in the parent child course prepared her kitchen with a Montessori table and chair, her child's own dishes and silverware, a little glass pitcher and glasses for pouring his own water, and a little sponge for wiping up the table after his meals—all as we had suggested in our lectures and home visit. After some weeks had gone by, she asked us, "What do I do if he doesn't use the little sponge on the table for wiping up a spill? Do I ignore it, insist that he does, suggest he does? I don't know how much I am supposed to teach him."

In answer to this mother's question we emphasized that the parent, in becoming a teacher instead of a servant, still remains a parent. She might best be described as a "mother-teacher" with an emphasis on mother, rather than a "teacher-mother" with the teacher role dominating the relationship. There are two reasons why this distinction is important. First, the intensity of the parent-child relationship tends to lead both parent and child to overreact in their responses to each other, particularly when demands upon behavior are involved. Second, home is a harbor for both parent and child and it is important that there is a softening of expectations there—not an abandonment of expectations but a softening.

For these reasons a definitive answer cannot be given to a specific situation involving a practical-life activity with parent and child. However, when parents are uncertain about how to respond to their child involved in a practical-life activity, they need to remember that collaboration is the basis of all healthy human relationships. We are the collaborating species; our ability to collaborate is the basis of civilization. The trouble for human beings begins when the skills for collaboration are not developed and used. Nowhere is this reality more apparent than between parent and child. The practical-life exercises are the predominant means for developing the skills of collaboration in both parent and child; in other words, they provide the best opportunities to become a "mother-teacher" or a "father-teacher" to a fifteen-month-old child. We will discuss possible answers to the mother's questions, later in this chapter. However, it is in observing and working with your own child that you gradually find the answers to your questions as specific situations arise.

Let us begin then to describe how to set up practical-life exercises. First, we must give the child materials that he can use successfully to carry out these exercises and the cycles of activity they make possible. To achieve this, we must select materials that are structured for the child's independent and repeated practice after the adult has demonstrated their use. They must be real, child-size, and arranged in a simple, straightforward, and orderly way.

To prepare any activity for the child, it is necessary for the parent to think through every detail ahead of time. For example, is the cracker stiff enough to spread the peanut butter on or does it crumble with the pressure of spreading? For a fifteen-month-old child to slice apple wedges into smaller bite-size pieces, the wedges have to be laid on their sides so that the skin is easier to split, and so forth. All of these difficulties become apparent in the preliminary practice period by the adult prior to a presentation to the child. Such practice gives us an appreciation of just how complicated our simplest everyday actions are. Practicing also makes us aware that, as adults, we automatically think through all our actions before we perform them. "First, I have to get the tray with materials and set them up. Next I must get a carrot for peeling. Now I have to pick up the peeler and stroke from left to right, put each peel in the bowl on the right," and so forth. It is this practical experience with organized activity in the practical-life exercises that helps the child eventually to begin thinking logically and in an organized way, and to become aware of the results of his actions.

Because the materials selected for a specific purpose such as food preparation are set on a tray in order and sequence for use, from left to right and top to bottom, the child mentally incorporates this precise order and it becomes part of his functional intelligence. We recognize this specific mental order as that required for efficient reading and writing, for example. Thus in these cycles of activity with practical-life materials, children indirectly prepare themselves for written language in the future.

The needed materials for each specific activity are gathered together on a tray for the child. This preselection by the adult is necessary because, as we have noted, the child has an absorbent mind rather than a reasoning mind. Before the age of six, the child cannot reason through what materials he will need and know where to find them. (After age six, the child has developed the necessary reasoning mind, and can think through and plan for what is needed. This is why in an elementary Montessori classroom, items for different exercises, such as science experiments or art projects, are deliberately left for the child to gather from different places in the room, much as you would gather needed utensils and supplies in your kitchen if you were going to bake or prepare food. Having to gather needed materials from around the room provides an opportunity for elementary school children to exercise their newly formed reasoning minds and is part of the stimulus to action.)

After you have planned each detail of an activity, organized a tray of materials, and practiced with them, you can model a cycle of activity with them for your child. Do so very slowly and methodically, pausing briefly after each step. Your child wants to imitate you but his thinking skills are limited. He relies on habit, pattern, and repetition. You need to show him what to do exactly in the same manner and in the same order (left to right, top to bottom). In the beginning, using the same system each time makes it easier for him to remember. Later when he is older, he will develop his own system, but for now repetition and exactness are essential for success.

Children imitate whatever adults do. They cannot understand exceptions. When you are setting the table with your child, for example, you need to carry a plate with two hands and with your thumbs on top of each of its sides. If you are in a hurry, use a tray for multiple items, rather than carrying an item in each hand. This is important because you cannot expect your child to understand that you can carry a glass in each hand while he must carry only one glass with his two hands. Children will proceed to do as you do, not as you say, and mistakes and failure will follow. Eventually, your child will learn that using a tray is the efficient way to carry more than one object at a time.

After the adult has demonstrated the use of a practical-life exercise, it is the child's turn. Observe what he does and help as needed. It is important to remember that your child is interested in the process that you are both engaged in, not the product. He enjoys wiping the table but his goal is not a dry table. The mother in the parent child lecture with the question about responding to her son's spilled water, needed first to consider how to draw his interest to the activity of wiping the table. She could have tried several options: looking at the spilled water with exaggerated attention and concentration, using language—"Oh, I see a spill here"—or by picking up the sponge herself and demonstrating how to wipe the spill very carefully and methodically using left to right, top to bottom strokes.

Montessori referred to such specific responses of the adult as "points of interest." It is points of interest that draw children deeper into an activity once engaged, or back to it after they have lost their concentration: the last drop of water from the pitcher while pouring, the tiny piece of cheese left on the chopper, the spot of flour on the rolling pin, or the flower stem that just reaches the water in the vase. Points of interest, then, help the child to clarify the challenge in an activity. Seeing the challenge in an activity is the motivator to carrying it through to completion and repeating it.

If, however, points of interest fail to revive his interest, it is still important that the child see the activity completed. In our anecdotal situation, the adult simply takes the sponge and very precisely completes the task for him. Because language is so powerful for the young child, it often helps to focus his attention if you verbalize your actions. You might say, "I'm going to wipe the table. Watch." Then proceed to wipe the table. We will discuss the motivating role of language in the child's self-formation in further depth in Chapter 9.

After you have demonstrated a practical-life exercise, and once your child has begun to use it with concentration, you must take care not to interrupt him. This is sometimes difficult for adults, even trained Montessori teachers. As one Montessori teacher of a Young Children's Community said, "It is a great temptation for me to help too much. I feel I should be doing something. I come from a 'world' where I am programmed to be constantly active." Yet, the essence of collaboration is give-and-take. Once the link is successfully made between the child and the materials, the adult needs to back away and allow the child to work in peace. The child's will and concentration are still very fragile in the first three years. If you interrupt the child unnecessarily, he finds it very difficult to go back to an activity. If he is fully engaged and there is something more that you would like to show him, try to wait for another opportunity.

Adults are often surprised to learn that even praise represents an interruption to the young child engaged in work. Yet, as mentioned in Chapter 2, commenting or clapping for children's accomplishments can break their absorption with the experience and draw their attention to you. Further, parental cheerleading, if overdone, can interfere with the child's independence and create the expectation of an audience for even normal accomplishment. If your twelve-month-old child pours his tablespoon of water very carefully from a little glass pitcher into a tiny glass without spilling, you can share his pleasure in that achievement with a warm smile. Such a low-key response indicates that you are happy for your child because you know that he is happy. You are happy not because your child is a "super baby." At any age, developing an inflated idea of self leads eventually to isolation and loneliness. Our goal is to help children appreciate that they are unique human beings and special to us. However, we want them to realize that all other human beings are unique, too.

In the process of using a practical-life exercise each day with sufficient concentration and effort, children gradually become more and more proficient. Because of the feedback loop from hand to brain and back again, practical-life exercises are self-corrective. Children see their own errors and strive to correct them. A little water spills from the watering can as he takes care of the plants, some of the water remains after his first attempt to mop it up, and so forth. The adult's modeling of the exercise, and re-presenting of it as needed, helps the child to understand the goal to be reached. However, adults must be very patient as they work with children in their long process to perfection. Children have all the time in the world for their self-formation; they cannot be rushed. When we fall into the trap of trying to be the perfect parent of the perfect child, we inevitably become overly controlling, trying to push him for accomplishment. The eventual result is a tense child and a "put upon" parent. We can learn instead to give children the aid they need and then allow them to work for perfection on their own timetable.

The first environment to prepare for practical-life exercises is the kitchen. Inevitably, this is where the adult spends the most time in activities that the newly independent child can imitate. Each kitchen is different but there are a few items that are necessary in all cases. The most important one is the child-size table and chair designed by Montessori for children just over fifteen months old. The dimensions and material of this table and chair make it possible for the child to sit safely and comfortably for long periods and be independent in his coming and going. Climbing up on a stool to work at a high counter is neither safe nor comfortable for children. We have only to imagine how we would feel about working in comparable conditions for our height and level of competency. The one item that might be kept at counter height is a small sponge (approximately one and one-half by two inches) in a little dish by the kitchen sink. This sponge is for wiping the child's table. If we provide the child with a safe stool,* he is able to get the sponge on his own and eventually to wet it independently as well.

At the end of a counter or on the wall, we hang other materials for daily clean up: a small broom, dustpan and dust broom, wet mop (with bucket below), and towel for drying the floor. A wash cloth is a good size for a child to use as a towel.† The parent introduces these items—broom, dustpan, mop, and towel—one at a time to the child over a period of several weeks. Each presentation is given in a careful and precise manner and repeated for the child periodically as necessary.

Parents need to remember to practice alone first. You will soon see that it matters exactly where you place your hands on each item, what direction you sweep or wipe or dust, and what type of motion you use: circular or straight, fast or slow, hard or soft, haphazard or methodical. The child cannot see the order in our minds. Adults can sweep casually and it will work. For the child, we need to demonstrate every activity systematically. He needs to see that in sweeping, for example, we are getting all the dirt from every area to one spot before using the dustpan. Thus by acting deliberately we make our decisions and thoughts prior to our actions visible, and thereby accessible, to the child as well.

Because your child sees you sweeping, he wants to sweep with

---

*See Cosco, Rubbermaid, and L. L. Bean.
†See the Michael Olaf catalogue cited in the footnote on p. 84.

his broom, too. No matter how clumsily the child does something at first, allow him to keep practicing and repeating on his own. You can re-present how to use the broom from time to time when he is not already using it—if that seems required. If in the midst of sweeping, however, your child decides the broom is a stick to swing or wants to use it for any other purpose, put it away and distract him with another activity. Very young children cannot tell us directly that they are tired or bored or can no longer concentrate. They do so by getting silly or disintegrating into fantasy or becoming destructive. We need to be alert to these messages and help the child by responding promptly and firmly.

A child-size carpet sweeper is a nice addition to the housekeeping materials when the child is a little older (approximately twenty months old). We do not recommend a vacuum cleaner or Dustbuster, because the child cannot see the mechanism by which they work. A digital clock presents the same problem when the older child is learning to tell time. Always choose the simplest materials possible for your child's use. One of our goals is to help children understand the world and how it works. Children need to see what is happening with the objects they are using. Another goal is for children to develop respect for the items in their environment. This respect follows from their understanding of an item's function. Thus a broom or carpet sweeper becomes a tool with a purpose, not for use as a hobbyhorse or a gun.

The preparation of food and the setting of his own table (as opposed to the actual process of eating, which belongs to the category of personal care and is dealt with in Chapter 7) are among the first practical-life activities in which the child can participate successfully. To store the necessary items, you can purchase a wire or wooden three-shelf cart from a household supply store. An even better solution is to make space in your existing kitchen cupboards for the child's dishes by storing rarely used items elsewhere. In this way, the child's dishes and items for food preparation are behind cupboard doors and thus not visible or accessible to younger siblings. By giving the child an empty cupboard of his own, we help him understand that his work is also part of the family's work and that his contribution is valued as such. It is very important that items for setting his table are precisely arranged on the shelves in order of use. On the top shelf from left to right, put a rolled-up cloth place mat, folded napkins, and a small basket of flatware consisting of six to eight identical spoons and forks. It is important not to mix and match different types of spoons and forks. It is hard for the young child to quickly and easily recognize the difference between a spoon and a fork if the spoons already differ from each other. Further, we want the child to focus primarily on the sensations of taste and the temperature of the food he is eating, not the shape and feel of the utensils in his mouth.

On the second shelf, put four to six bowls and next to them four to six small plates. Dessert or salad plates are a good size. Again all the bowls and all the plates should be the same shape and type. The child needs to see at a glance, "These are my bowls. These are my plates." In this way, we aid the child's developing ability to categorize and classify.

On the bottom shelf, we can put two or three tiny glass pitchers and eight to ten small glasses. Cylinder-shaped votive candleholders make good glasses for young children. Again we want all the glasses and pitchers to match each other. They must also be transparent so that the child can see how much liquid is in them. This means they should be glass, not porcelain or metal. Glass also has the advantage of being breakable. Of course, whenever the child is using breakable objects, adults must pay close attention. If we want to help the child to develop controlled movements and care in handling his environment, we have to give him items that he cannot handle roughly, or throw about, without realistic consequences. If an accident occurs—a glass is broken and water spills—we demonstrate how to clean it up. By our matter-of-fact attitude, we indicate our acceptance of mistakes as part of the learning process. Because some accidents are to be expected, we should always choose inexpensive and replaceable items for the child's use.

When all the child's dishes and utensils are stored in the orderly and clear manner we have described, the child is able to take them from the dishwasher and replace them on the proper shelf on his own. At least part of the time, you may choose to set up a practical-life exercise to allow your child to wash his own dishes rather than using the dishwasher. For this exercise, purchase two Tupperware tubs (one for washing and one for rinsing), a brush, drying towels, and a dish rack. In the beginning, you can use a pitcher to fill the tubs with a small amount of water. Later, the child will enjoy filling them with your supervision. Again, the child can replace the dishes in their storage place on his own when finished.

When you show the child how to set his table, begin with the place mat, then proceed to the napkin, bowl or plate, and finally the fork, spoon, and glass. At first you can fill his glass from a larger pitcher within your reach. Later, you can fill his small pitcher with just a half-inch of water (at first, and later somewhat more) and then he can pour it into his own glass. You can refill his small pitcher from your larger one as needed. A three-inch-high glass pitcher is ideal for the child's first pitcher. You can purchase one, as well as all other items for the child's use described in this chapter, from Montessori Services, 11 West Barham Avenue, Santa Rosa, CA 95407 (http://www.montessoriservices.com).

Once the child is pouring well (usually at about twenty to twenty-four months old), you can begin letting him pour his own milk and juice. You can also progress to amounts of liquid that exceed the size of his tiny glass, as he learns to stop pouring before reaching the top of the glass. A five-to-six-inch-high glass pitcher works well for this purpose. It is helpful to use water initially as your child works on mastering this new level of challenge.

Remember, this is the age of maximum effort and joy for the child in carrying items while moving. The newly independent child loves the ritual and repetition of setting his table. Be certain that he carries only one item at a time and sets it down very carefully in its proper place. He should use both hands around each glass and plate, with his thumbs carefully placed on top of the plate to grasp it. As he gradually becomes proficient, he can help set the table for family dinner as well. He can even learn to count out the items needed: "One fork for daddy, one fork for mommy, one fork for my sister—one, two, three, three forks." Clearing his table after eating is part of the cycle of activity for the child and should be given just as much attention. Eventually he can scrape his own plate with a food scraper and put them in an opened dishwasher, or wash his dishes with the materials we have described.

For your child to prepare food alongside you, or independently later on, you need to prepare materials for him. For food preparation, the child needs two small bowls that differ in appearance (one for refuse and one for the prepared fruit or vegetable), a cutting board, and a small cleaver. You may want to file the tip of the cleaver slightly. If he is going to wash vegetables or fruit, he also needs a small colander. A small basket can be used to hold a spreader (for spreading cream cheese or peanut butter), a peeler, and any other small utensils needed in simple food preparation.

Keep these materials on a low shelf so your child can get them and return them on his own. Again, try to clear out one of the kitchen cupboards for this purpose so that your child will understand how important his work is to the family. A child-size apron that he can put on and take off independently is also essential to the child's work in the kitchen. The act of putting on and taking off the apron helps to define the beginning and end of the activity for the child. It also helps to remind him during the activity that he is involved in a process, which thereby helps to limit distractions. It is helpful if you wear an apron, too, when you prepare food or bake with your child present. To the child, an apron is a costume. When you both put them on, he knows, "Now we are cooks."

As in all practical-life exercises, the adult demonstrates the activity first. Usually children under two and a half years of age will dive in and not be able to wait for you to complete the activity entirely. When this happens, you can guide their hands here and there, but they tend to walk off if you do not allow them to participate. They want to be constantly involved. When the child approaches three years old, he has a more developed will and can wait for longer periods while you show him what to do. Sometimes language such as "My turn first, then your turn" helps a two-and-one-half-to-three-year-old develop his control of self as he waits and watches you during a presentation. After washing your hands and putting on your apron, carry the materials one at a time with two hands on each item to the child's table. The child always sits to your left during a presentation and anytime that you need to sit with him to help. Unless you are left-handed this is the least awkward positioning for you both.

Cutting a banana is a good first exercise for food preparation. In the beginning you need to cut the end of the banana ahead of time so it is easy to begin peeling in strips. Carefully pull each peel down and put it directly into the bowl on the left of the cutting board. Take the cleaver and with your right hand on the handle and your left hand on top of the cleaver, press down to cut a slice of the peeled banana. Put this cut piece immediately into the bowl on the right. It is very important to always put the finished fruit or vegetable directly into the food bowl and any piece of garbage immediately into the garbage bowl. In their enthusiasm, children are likely to cut several pieces at a time and will therefore need an occasional gentle reminder to follow the process of "cut, then place." Of course, as adults we would not work in so methodical a manner. However, it is important for the child to work this way to incorporate the orderly and sequential manner of the entire process. Although a boring approach for us because we are focused on the finished act and product, this step-by-step method and complete cycle of activity are fascinating to the child.

As soon as the last piece of banana is cut, remove the food bowl to a place out of sight until the tray is wiped clean, dirtied utensils are washed and replaced, the tray is put back on its shelf, and aprons are removed. If the food remains in sight during the cleaning-up process, the child most often wants to eat it right away and does not concentrate on the task at hand. If during preparation the child puts food or a utensil in his mouth, remove it right away, saying, "Now I have to wash this." It is very important not to let the child develop the habit of eating during the process of food preparation. It becomes a distraction and he misses an opportunity for developing his will. Children as young as eighteen months old learn to wait patiently, food already placed in front of them, before a meal or snack begins. Children with good impulse control can even do so at fifteen months, particularly if you do not present this activity when they are hungry. (By the time they are three years old, children can refrain from nibbling when preparing food even before mealtimes.) If you have a child who cannot keep from eating during food preparation whether at fifteen or eighteen months of age, it is better if you save this activity for a later age. On the other hand, you may decide to use preparing food as an opportunity to work on impulse control. Realize, however, that you might need to stop early on in the process if your child becomes frustrated. Again, gentle firmness is key.

Washing, peeling, and cutting most fruits and vegetables make good practical-life activities for young children. Potatoes can be scrubbed in a shallow bowl of water with a small brush (mushroom brushes are a good size) and baked for dinner, vegetables cut for stir-fry, lettuce washed for salad, and fruit cut up for dessert. All of the food for dinner can be prepared right after lunch so it is ready for cooking and requires only last-minute attention at the end of the day. On a beautiful day, it is a pleasant experience to take the child's small table and chair and do all of these activities in the back yard.

Baking is another good practical-life exercise. You need another shelf set up with baking materials: a small mixing bowl, spoon, spatula, wooden board, and child-size rolling pin. You can put a few simple cookie cutters in a basket, a small muffin tin, cookie sheet, timer, and child-size mitten-style potholders on the shelf next to a folded child-size apron. When you bake with your child, you need to pre-measure all the ingredients. Your child can then put them in the bowl and mix them together. Young children are capable of following all the other procedures of baking: rolling biscuit dough, putting cookie dough on a cookie sheet, putting muffin batter into the muffin tin cups, and so forth.

The child of eighteen months and older can also prepare his own snacks. Again the adult needs to think through the preparation process very carefully. You cannot, for example, just choose a small jar of peanut butter, jam, or cream cheese for your child to use in spreading crackers. You need to measure out carefully just the right amount for your child to use for this particular snack, and put it in a small dish or coaster. Other good snacks for the child to prepare are raw vegetables and cut-up fruit.

If possible, empty the bottom shelf of the refrigerator door for your child's prepared snacks: a small pitcher of water, cut carrot or celery sticks, a piece of fruit, sliced cheese, and yogurt. However, only let your child get these foods out at designated times. Children need to develop the discipline of eating only on an appropriate schedule and only when sitting down at a table. In this way they are helped to develop both self-control and good eating habits. When proper guidelines are set, young children love the independence of choosing and preparing their own snacks. They learn that this special part of the refrigerator is for them alone and that other shelves are not. Such habits when established early can be a boon to parents in the child's elementary school years. (In addition, we would suggest from the beginning keeping only healthy foods in the family refrigerator, and storing beer and any other alcoholic beverages in a different place where it is seen by, and accessible to, adults only.)

Food preparation and baking are the major activities of daily living for the kitchen, but you may choose to do other practical-life activities there as well. Flower arranging, polishing, folding small pieces of laundry, and watering plants all lend themselves to working on, or from, the child's table in the kitchen. Organize each activity with its own basket or tray of materials. For flower arranging, precut the flowers and use tiny glass vases and doilies to put each finished vase on. A funnel may help for pouring just the smallest amount of water from a small glass pitcher, but be certain not to use the same pitcher that your child uses to pour his water, milk, and juice. Using identical pitchers for different activities confuses children and makes it more difficult for them to establish their sense of order and of what materials go with what actions. Remember that children cannot reason yet and, unlike adults, must rely strictly on memory and order to aid them in their activities. When watering plants, use a six-to-eight-ounce watering can with a long spout and show your child how to hold the spout in one hand and the handle in the other while walking. Doing so helps keep the spout upright and therefore from spilling en route. You can add a one-to-one-and-one-half-inch sponge (cut from an adult-size sponge) to wipe the leaves of houseplants. Show your child how to hold one hand underneath a leaf and support it while wiping the top. For window or large-mirror polishing arrange a small basket with a child-size sprayer containing water with a teaspoon of vinegar, scraper, and cloth or folded paper towel. Demonstrate a methodical top to bottom, left to right, spraying and scraping motion. Remember the child's attraction to order focuses attention and effort. Haphazard movements tend to disintegrate into play and silliness.

When your child folds small items of laundry such as napkins, show him how to match each corner. The exactness and order of careful folding have a special appeal for very young children. When you are folding the child's shirts show him how to match one sleeve to the other. Pants, too, can be matched pant leg to pant leg. Fold again the whole item of clothing from the top to the bottom if a smaller size is desired. When preparing laundry, show your child how to separate light, dark, and medium colors into separate piles before loading clothes into the washing machine.

When you are finished with any of the activities completed at the child's table, show him how to squeeze out excess water from his sponge at the sink, then very methodically cover his table with left-to-right and top-to-bottom strokes. It is important to show him a way of wiping that will cover the entire table. At first, he will have difficulty in covering the whole surface and will need gentle encouragement from you as he develops this skill. Also in the beginning, the child does not necessarily see any connection between crumbs or spilled polish and wiping the table. Be patient and model the appropriate actions from time to time. It also helps you to understand how much coordination and concentration the child must develop to carry out the simplest actions (such as wiping a table, pouring water, or putting a flower in a vase), if you try doing them sometimes with your nondominant hand.

Other activities that we have mentioned as practical-life exercises, such as dusting, emptying wastepaper baskets, and "picking up" rooms, are done throughout the house. You will have to discern the best method of doing them in your own setting. Order and method and the child's size and strength are the most important factors to consider. It also helps to categorize and classify whenever possible. For example, when you pick up a room, pick up the towels first, next the clothes, then the toys or other objects, verbalizing for your child what you are doing—"I'm picking up the towels"—and so forth. In effect, you are breaking down the activity into more manageable steps and making the process logical for your child. If he experiences sequence and order, routine and ritual, organization and logical thinking through the practical-life activities with you at home (or, if you are working full-time outside the home, in another appropriate setting with a loving adult), it will become natural for him to look for order elsewhere in the world.

Again the spirit with which you do the practical-life exercises with your child is the key to their success. Do not let the idea of these activities overwhelm you, or try to do them all at once. It is best to introduce one activity to your child and stay with it for several weeks until it is smoothly incorporated into the rhythm and routine of the day. Present the exercises gradually, one at a time, as your child grows and you grow along with him, observing what he is ready for. The adults' tendency is to get the child "busy" so that we can be free for our own occupations. Instead, we must accept that these practical life activities are for the child to do alongside us as a collaborative effort. We are not freed to do other things, but because we are meeting our child's needs in self-formation, the days begin to go more smoothly and happily for us both.

It is our collaborative approach to the practical-life exercises that enables children to let their human tendencies and desire to imitate us guide their energies. We are to be leaders rather than "pushers." We might say, "Oh, look, crumbs, I'm going to clean them up." Or "There is water on the floor here, let's get a mop." Or to the fifteen-month-old who is bothering an older sibling: "This is Kristin's work. You can push in your chair." Help your child to develop the habit of pushing in his chair whenever he completes his work at a table, and before returning materials to the shelf or cupboard. For a child under age two and one-half, try to catch him before he has slipped away from the table. If your child is close to three years, you can actually bring him back to the table and give the reminder: "Chair first." For children of any age, your faithfully pushing in your own chair each time you get up is a key teaching technique. Again in your role as leader, not pusher, say, "It's time to wash your hands," "We walk inside," "You may feed the gerbil another day," "I see a tissue to put in the wastepaper basket," and so forth. When the child says, "I don't want to," you can respond, "Let's do it together." If need be, you can clean up the room while he watches. However, as the child approaches three years old, you can require his participation. Always remember that a fifteen-month-old tends to want to do what he sees adults doing. Use a "Tom Sawyer approach": make learning to "pick up" a room look as interesting and fun for you as it inevitably becomes for the newly independent child, once he is fully engaged in the activity.

If we are following the Time Line, we see that, through the practical-life exercises beginning at age fifteen months and continuing until the child is three years old, we have met the child's needs for "activities directed toward work with structured material." We have done so by providing opportunities to "educate" the hands and use "maximum effort" in developing coordinated, purposeful movement. The feedback loop from hand to brain to hand has continued to build the child's intelligence, as it has been doing since the child's birth. Most importantly, by making the child's life meaningful to him as a member of his family in this challenging period from fifteen months to three years old, we have helped him to integrate his personality and develop a positive attitude toward himself.

We would like to close this chapter with a portion of a letter from Silvana Montanaro, M.D., AMI Assistant-to-Infancy trainer and examiner. It was written to Lynn just before she started attending the Assistant-to-Infancy Course in 1984, when her first daughter, Margaret, was not quite two years old. The letter addresses the purpose and joy of collaboration with young children in practical activities of the home:

> I can assure you that your daughter will, very soon, not only prepare your breakfast but become your best collaborator: please ask her to do things for you and ask her with the kindness and seriousness with which you would ask anyone else. Children are the most generous, loving and interested human beings you could work with. Through the work with you, she will learn: she is able to do things, she is needed in her family, and she can give something to others. Ask her to set the table, to bring things from one place to another, to wash cups and other little things. You will be surprised how much and how well a small child can work. At the same time you must never forget to set the limits of her activity. Children need to know where they can go and what they can do in order to feel secure.

> To educate is a great task but it is to put our personal effort at the service of the next generation for the benefit of all humanity. Our effort in education is what will be left of ourselves in life.

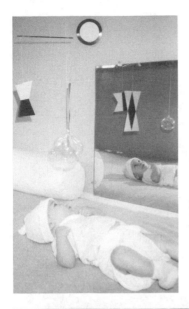

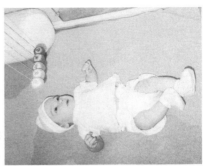

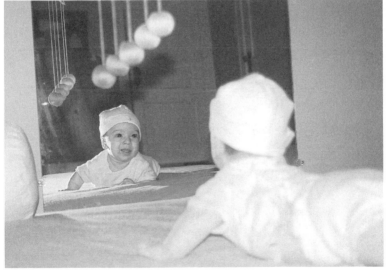

Two-month-old baby on his Montessori child-bed. The Munari shape mobile is for newborns; the Gobbi gradations of color mobile is for newborns to eight weeks. The baby has the opportunity to raise up on his hands, thereby strengthening his arms, torso, and head control, and has a view of himself and his room in the mirror. *(All photos in this section copyright © Karin Olsen Campia)*

The baby sleeping on his Montessori child-bed. Note the rug to protect him if he rolls onto the floor, and the simplicity of the furnishings—the low toy shelf, the nursing chair.

Nine-month-old baby, sitting at the weaning table and chair, drinking from a cup.

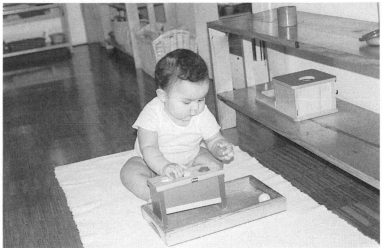

Nine-month-old baby with her mother, who is showing her how to use the toy.

Now the baby can use it by herself. Again, note the uncluttered room and toy shelf.

Lynn with eighteen-month-old. Lynn is helping him core and slice an apple. Now he cuts the apple slices, which Lynn has laid out next to the cutting board, into smaller pieces. Note the placement of the bowl for discarded apple scraps and the bowl to put the finished pieces in.

This eighteen-month-old
is putting on his own sneaker.

This eighteen-month-old is practicing on the Montessori stair and enjoying the walker wagon, a favorite among babies from ten months to two and a half years.

This twenty-month-old has set up his own lunch, using the placemat, cup, bowl, and fork. Now he can pour his own water and eat his lunch with his fork.

SEVEN

Personal Care

We habitually serve children; and this is not only an act of servility toward them, but it is dangerous, since it tends to suffocate their useful, spontaneous activity. We are inclined to believe that children are like puppets, and we wash them and feed them as if they were dolls. We do not stop to think that the child who does not "do" does not know how to do. He must, nevertheless, do these things, and nature has furnished him with the physical means for carrying on these various activities, and with the intellectual means for learning how to do them. And our duty towards him is, in every case, that of helping him to make a conquest of such useful acts as nature intended he should perform for himself. The mother who feeds her child without making the least effort to teach him how to hold a spoon for himself and to try to find his mouth with it, and who does not at least eat herself, inviting the child to look and see how she does it, is not a good mother. She offends the fundamental human dignity of her child; she treats the child as if he or she were a doll, when instead, this is a human being confided by nature to her care.

Who does not know that to teach a child to feed himself, to wash and dress himself, is a much more tedious and difficult work, calling for infinitely greater patience, than feeding, washing and dressing the child oneself? But, the former is the work of an educator; the latter is the easy and inferior work of a servant.

—MARIA MONTESSORI,
The Montessori Method, 1912

In the beginning weeks, the infant is totally dependent upon adults for all her needs: sleeping, eating, clothing, washing, and grooming. The first time that we must assume complete responsibility for another human life is an overwhelming experience for most of us. As new parents, we struggle with our feelings of inadequacy and conflict over our new role. Yet, if we are fortunate enough to have support from those around us, within a few months we become used to the new demands upon us, and reorder the priorities of our lives accordingly. In fact, we learn to enjoy having this helpless being completely dependent upon us. We are in control, not in the sense that now all goes smoothly—because it does not—but rather because the decisions and actions are ours alone to make. We become accustomed to being in charge of all that relates to our child, and gradually we become adept in doing so. In the area of personal care, parents readily perform all actions for their babies—feeding and dressing them, putting them to sleep, bathing them, and so forth—and, in addition, discover easier and better ways to do so as time goes on. We discover something else as well: performing these actions for our children is clearly faster and less complicated than helping them to take part in their own personal care. This remains true until they are at least three years old, and often even older.

Yet, we have said that our mission as parents and educators is to aid the development of "a complete human being . . . adapted to his time, place, and culture." Only through their own self-formation can children fulfill this destiny and become contributing members of society. The infant therefore cannot remain as a lump of clay with everyone doing to her and for her. If a mother and father insist on treating their baby this way, there is a great risk that she will grow up to believe, "I need my parents." We want children to become instead people who have confidence in their ability to take care of themselves. Confidence is necessary in every case for a fulfilling life. Without confidence we do not assume the risks involved in living creatively, nor do we accept the responsibilities that make life meaningful. For children to develop confidence in their own abilities, they have to be helped to care for themselves independently just as soon as they are able. The parents' role is to begin working for this goal within the first few weeks of their child's life.

Thus the stage is set for conflict between the needs of the child and the real, if unspoken, desires of the adult. The adult wants to dispatch all the areas of the child's personal care with efficiency and in a timely manner. The child is thrust forward into her self-formation with all the power and energy of the human tendencies. Her goal is to accomplish complete independence in all her actions just as soon as possible, but her timetable for developing each separate skill is not her own. It is dictated for her by the Sensitive Periods established in human development. She is not interested in efficiency or speed; her focus is on process and on the repetition and practice that are required to work toward perfection in all processes. The child is patient as she works for her self-formation because she is a child; she has all the time in the world.

How are we to help? We need to become aware of all the ways in which we hold the child back from becoming a fully functioning human being: the sink and counter that she cannot reach, the mirror that is too high for her to see herself, the chair that is too big for her to sit comfortably in, the table that is too high in relation to her chair, the pants that are too tight for her to pull up and down, the brush and comb that are too big for her little hands, the crib and high chair that imprison her high—and unsafe—off the ground, the drink of water and the piece of fruit that she cannot get to without our help.

We also need to follow nature's plan, as represented by the Sensitive Periods, for the child's self-formation. We cannot determine arbitrarily at what age a particular challenge is best dealt with—such as toilet awareness, for example. There are optimal moments for each human skill in personal care. If we familiarize ourselves with the developmental stages of childhood, we can find those moments, and thus cooperate with the special energies of childhood—instead of finding ourselves pitted against them. We discover that the child's interest in mastering skills for personal care peaks somewhere between twelve months and two years. This period is sometimes referred to as the "time of self-affirmation" for the child; more often it is called "the terrible twos."

Because we readily become accustomed to doing everything for the infant, we tend to miss the optimal periods in the child's self-formation for personal care. Hence, it is common to see three-year-olds who stand like mannequins, waiting for an adult to put on their coat and button or zip it up; two-and-a-half-year-olds who cannot soothe themselves to sleep; two-year-olds who cannot, or will not, use the toilet; one-and-a-half-year-olds who cannot pour themselves a small drink of water; and one-year-olds who cannot feed themselves or drink from a normal cup.

Each child is different in response to our attentiveness to her inner drive for independence in personal care. There are children for whom it is imperative to give optimal help. Mike, for example, is a good natured and very large ten-month-old. He is crawling but he is clumsy in his movements. He does not appear to be thinking his actions through. He has a somewhat vague or vacant look about him. Paul, on the other hand, appears thoughtful in his responses to independence and self-care despite little direct help from the adults around him. At just one month older than Mike, Paul is already walking. He has a look of intense involvement with the surrounding environment and really fixes his attention on the things around him. His mind appears to be constantly active and thinking about what he is doing. Conceivably, Paul could be raised in a "vacuum" of parental guidance in self-care and still develop into an intelligent, confident child—although perhaps one who was hard to live with as a two-year-old. The latter outcome would be the expected result for a capable, energetic child who had to struggle for individual competence without good parental support in the first years of life. Conversely, Mike must have the guidance of knowledgeable and wise adults in whatever he undertakes if he is to develop the confidence that comes from success in these early years.

A note of caution before we explore the approximate ages for optimal response from the child in specific areas of self-care: we need to watch our expectations very carefully. Personal care is one area where parents tend to jump from expecting too little of the child to expecting too much. We are impatient with the learning period the child requires for gaining any new knowledge or skill. We tend to skip the critical stage of the child's prolonged practice and collaboration with us. We go directly from presenting the way to do something, to expecting that the child can do it. When she cannot readily follow our directions or imitate our actions, we are inclined to take the easy way out. We decide that we were premature in asking her to try a new task—to feed herself or dress herself—and we go back to doing everything for her.

We forget that the child under three years old is very, very little. We are helping her to achieve a far-off, not an immediate, goal. Our aim is not for the child to become a little adult who can dress herself so that she is out of our way and we can do something else. Our goal is a three-year-old child who feels capable in the complex act of eating or dressing for her own sake. If the child is helped at the appropriate time and in the appropriate manner, she can achieve competence in dressing and undressing herself at three years old—including putting her coat on a hanger and placing it in the closet, her hat and mittens in a basket by the door, her dirty clothes in a laundry hamper, her shoes in their specified place. The exception in this independence would be tying her own shoelaces, but even there she should be part of, and engaged in carrying out, some part of this process, not necessarily at every opportunity (because sometimes we must hurry), but a sufficient number of times to maintain her interest. The key point to remember is that we do not want to miss the child's independent streak just because she still needs our help. It is at precisely this time, when all acts of self-care are still difficult for the child, that she is so interested in participating in them.

To help the child under three years old to become successfully involved in her self-care, we have to recognize the complexity of each task and break it into steps—much as we did in the practical-life exercises. Tying shoes, approached in this manner, becomes a process in which it is feasible for a two-and-a-half-to-three-year-old to participate. At first the child is shown simply to cross the laces over each other and drop them, making a cross. In time, when this task is automatic, she can learn how to put the top lace under the bottom one and pull it through making a simple tie. For a long time, the adult needs to make the loop for each lace, but very soon the child can grasp each loop with a pincer grip and pull the bows tight, completing the tie action. Of course, the child is very pleased at this stage for she believes she has produced the tie herself. It is breaking the process into simple steps, then doing them in the same way each time, slowly and methodically, step by step, for a very long time that leads to this success for the child.

We always have to wait for the child's response in any procedure of personal care. We tend to rush the child because again, as in the practical-life activities, *our* goal is to get the action done: to get her shoes on her feet, for example. We automatically put the shoe on the child's foot without even considering the child. Instead, we need to think ahead to the child's goal. Turn the shoe around so it is facing the right direction for the child to put it on, open the shoe wide while pulling its tongue out so that the shoe can be slipped on, and wait for the child to respond. In every act of personal care, keep thinking, "Is there a step that I am taking away from my child that she could do for herself?" We need to pay close attention to the child's development in all four areas of self-formation and be consistently in tune with her efforts. We know that "struggle is good" and that she is in a period when exerting maximum effort appeals to her. On the other hand, when healthy struggle is about to turn into frustration, we know that we need to step in.

As in the practical-life exercises, it is important to be matter-of-fact about the child's accomplishments in self-care. After all, everyone in the world eventually dresses herself, goes to the toilet, feeds herself, and so forth. Certainly we are pleased with our child's accomplishments because they mean that she is growing up. It does not help children, however, to draw attention back to ourselves through applause or excessive comment. As we have discussed, self-confidence for all of us is a result of our genuine achievements, not someone else's assessment of them. Adults cannot give children self-esteem. They must earn it for themselves through their own efforts. No arena is more opportune for the success of these personal efforts than that of the child's independent care of self.

SLEEP

We begin with sleep. Sleep is a paradox; it is a passive state that is highly productive. It is as key to health as exercise and nutrition. We know that sleep deprivation leads to inadequate functioning—including emotional instability, irritability, and poor motor control—but research studies indicate that approximately two-thirds of the adult population in the United States still do not get the necessary average of eight hours of sleep per night during the workweek.

Sleep is not one continuous state; it occurs in cycles, each of which has its own function in restoring energy and maintaining health. Throughout the night we experience a number of ninety-minute cycles of sleep, each one followed by a briefer period of what is called rapid eye movement (REM) sleep. Each complete ninety-minute sleep cycle consists of four stages.

The third and fourth of these stages are referred to as "delta sleep," or deep sleep. They are important for two significant areas related especially to young children. In delta sleep, the body receives almost half its daily dose of human growth hormone (HGH). The latter promotes growth, maintenance, and repair of the muscles. By repairing body tissues and storing energy, we can recover from the previous day's stress. Conversely, loss of delta sleep results in weakened muscle tissue. This is important because the more muscle we have, the more fat we burn. Muscle, then, is key to keeping our metabolism energized. This is why, if we are sleep deprived, it is better not to get up early and go to the gym for a workout. Delta sleep is also important for children because of its relationship to the immune system. Loss of delta sleep results in the body's production of fewer natural killer cells (NKCs) for combating infections and major diseases. It also decreases the activity of existing T cells and interleukin in signaling the immune system to respond to infection.

Most of our dreaming occurs in REM sleep and appears to have a very different function from any of the four stages of the complete ninety-minute sleep cycle. During REM sleep the brain is very active. In fact, this brain-wave activity mirrors wakefulness. If delta sleep is the period of repair and restoration,

REM sleep is the time for increased blood flow to areas of the brain involved in memory and emotion. Problem solving and sorting out of experiences appear to take place at this time. This may be why limiting REM sleep results in a feeling of mental dullness. The periods of REM sleep lengthen during the night, with the longest one occurring in the last hour. Thus sleeping only six to seven hours a night deprives us of the last, and possibly most productive, period of REM sleep.

We have gone into some detail to describe the role of sleep in contributing to healthy living, because sleep is so central to the child's well-being. It is clearly essential that she learn to be independent in sleep as a part of her care for herself. From the beginning, the parents' goal is to teach their child how to put herself to sleep and to sleep by herself as a preparation for sleeping well for life. A corollary to this goal is to help her, as she grows older, to accept her part in the collaboration of family life. Just as she needs to sleep well for her own sake, she eventually must also learn not to disturb other family members from their sleep.

How much sleep is required for good health? Although it varies with individuals, newborns typically need sixteen to eighteen hours of sleep a day. At approximately age three and a half months, the number drops to fourteen or fifteen hours, with more of those hours reliably occurring at night by age two to two and a half months. By six months, the baby sleeps through the night with two daytime naps. The morning nap is more active in REM sleep. The afternoon nap represents a quieter period. By the time the child is two years old, REM sleep occupies twenty to twenty-five percent of her total sleep. This amount stays relatively constant throughout the remainder of her life. Between the ages of two and five years, the child needs twelve hours of sleep a night with one afternoon nap or rest period.

It is almost certain that at some time between ages one and two years your child will make a fuss about going to bed. We discuss how to respond to this situation later in this section. We want to mention now, however, that it is important to know that cutting back on the children's naps does not help them to sleep better at night. Instead, this practice leads to over-tiredness and irritability, and they have an even harder time relaxing for a good night's sleep. Children over three years old should not typically sleep more than one hour in their afternoon nap. Doing so can interfere with their day-night sleep pattern. Five-year-olds usually do not need to nap, but it is important that they have an hour of quiet time at some point during the afternoon.

Six-to-nine-year-olds should have ten hours of sleep at night. Ten-to-twelve-year-olds are in a period of optimum energy and health and usually require only eight to ten hours of sleep. Twelve-to-fifteen-year-olds are again in a very vulnerable and fragile period similar to the child's first three years of life. They again require as much as ten to twelve hours of sleep. They also benefit from periodic ten-to-twenty-minute rest periods, or even naps, during the day. Adults, as we have noted, routinely need eight hours of sleep, although some adults may require as many as nine hours and others may need somewhat less than eight.

Our first responsibility to newborns in regard to sleep is to help them sleep through the night as soon as they are capable of doing so. For most babies this is possible when they are two to three months old. By sleeping through the night, we mean from approximately a ten o'clock evening feeding to a six o'clock morning feeding. It is essential to work toward this nightly sleep pattern from the beginning. Otherwise a "wake up" nighttime habit becomes firmly established. Such a habit results in loss of sleep for the child and is disruptive to the whole family.

After the first days when the mother and baby are occupied with adjusting to each other and their new relationship, start to keep a chart of the baby's sleeping, nursing, and diapering times. You are looking for patterns—in particular, one longer sleep cycle. To establish this longer cycle of sleep in the nighttime, we need to listen for the type of crying we are hearing. After the first two weeks, we do not need to rush to the baby at the first whimper. Monitors are almost too efficient at this point. Often a newborn fusses a bit and then goes back to sleep, or will entertain herself for a little while before crying in earnest. In the days before monitors, this kind of "fussy crying" often went unheard, and the baby had a little time to be awake by herself, exploring her new world, before going back to sleep on her own.

It is very helpful, particularly for a new mother, if there is another person in the house to participate in establishing the baby's schedule in the early weeks. It takes work to help the baby to a nighttime pattern of sleep. Sometimes the father wants to take this role, or other family members can help, particularly if they are experienced with newborns. Through experience we learn many ways to space night feedings further apart. One of Lynn's baby helpers put a fifteen-watt bulb in the nursery lamp. She turned this dim light on and took up her knitting while waiting to see if the baby was going to fully rouse himself or instead go back to sleep in fifteen minutes or so. If he was definitely going to remain awake and had not been fed for several hours, she would make certain that he had waited as long as he could manage without hard crying before eventually taking him to his mother to be fed.

Experience teaches us not to overhandle the newborn at any time, but particularly at night. Constant handling, jiggling, walking, and rocking result in an overstimulated and excited infant that has difficulty relaxing into sleep. At the same time, it may be necessary to put your hand gently on the baby's stomach or back for reassurance or place her on your chest where she can hear your heartbeat and breathing. Each baby is different and it takes time to learn what does, and does not, help her to relax.

There are good reasons why it is difficult for the mother initially to manage establishing the infant's schedule unaided by another adult. In the first weeks, she is exhausted. Her body is making an enormous hormonal adjustment and at the same time she is experiencing sleep deprivation. It is hard for her to think straight in the middle of the night when her baby cries out. Rather than work to help the baby get to a suitable schedule, she tends automatically to nurse the baby, hoping that they can both then go back to sleep. Unfortunately, continual feeding during the night does not help the baby establish a nighttime sleep pattern and can lead to indigestion and discomfort. Both mother and baby remain overly tired and unable to sleep well during the night. The baby soon becomes dependent on constant attention, handling, and feeding both day and night. For these reasons every effort should be made to have another adult in the house to help the mother in the beginning weeks. The sooner that you can get the baby into a nighttime sleep pattern, the sooner you can be a better parent. If by three to three and a half months, your baby is not on a stable schedule, it is time to get seriously to work on it.°

During the day, naps are important for both mother and infant. The mother should sleep whenever the baby sleeps in order to compensate for the mother's sleep loss during nighttime feedings. Babies must have naps in order to get a sufficient amount of sleep in each twenty-four-hour period. Babies who are not encouraged to nap become overstimulated and keep themselves on autopilot, often staying awake for hours. We know one six-week-old, hitherto very placid, baby who stayed awake for thirteen hours straight after enduring constant handling and attention during a family reunion weekend. It took days for her to return to her normal eating and sleeping patterns.

°Marc Weissbluth, *Healthy Sleep Habits, Happy Child.*

As babies get older, routine and ritual become increasingly important. As a general rule, the more routine and ritual in the first three years of children's lives, the more comfortable and relaxed they become and the more in tune with their daily schedule. This is because the child under three years of age is in the Sensitive Period for order. We will discuss the role of order as the basis for the development of language and intelligence in the following chapter. For the moment, it is the relationship of order to routine that is important. By helping the child to know what will happen next, routine and ritual help her to build trust in the world and to feel secure in her life.

Routines give information to children about their world that they are not ready to receive through words. Hence they learn what will reliably happen next, by experiencing it, rather than by being told. Bedtime is always at seven o'clock because that is when it occurs every day, not because a parent has told them that it is at seven o'clock. The child cannot even think what seven o'clock means. Of course to the adult it means that the child needs a certain amount of sleep and going to bed at seven o'clock is the way to get it. The child will not get these needed hours if she goes to bed at eight o'clock. We take all this information for granted. Unfortunately, we see the child's refusal to go to bed as willfulness, not as her inability to think as we think. We compound the problem by routinely varying children's bedtimes for the convenience of our schedule or by capitulating to their whims and demands for one more story, drink of water, or trip to the bathroom. The more faithful parents are to setting a firm hour for going to bed, the better are the chances that their children will be able to get to sleep on their own and sleep well through the night.

The ritual and manner of preparing for bed also have a great effect on the child's ability to put herself to sleep. From the time she is an infant, the period before bedtime should be a quiet, relaxing one. When a parent or sibling engages the baby in roughhousing or teasing play just before bed, it most often over-arouses and excites her. Since the baby needs to slow herself down in preparation for putting herself to sleep, this is unfair to her. Bath time can also be a stimulating experience for a child. For this reason it is often best for children even as old as four or five years to take a bath and get into their pajamas before dinner. This schedule allows ample time after dinner for cleaning up the dishes together in a relaxed manner, brushing teeth, going to the bathroom, and getting in bed for a cozy story time before the child's light is turned out and the door closed for the night's sleep.

The child-bed on the floor, instead of the traditional crib, is a big boon to the baby's sleeping habits. Even as early as six weeks old, the infant who has a dim night-light watches shadows and reflections in her mirror and in effect plays herself to sleep. At eight weeks, she discovers her hands and explores around her a bit more for what she can feel and touch in this comfortable and familiar place. When the baby begins to move more, she may manage to get out of her bed and onto the floor. When this happens you can put a small rug, or other buffer, by her bed. Because the baby is dressed warmly, it does not matter if she sleeps out of her bed. After a short period, the baby can scoot to get back to her bed, just as she was able to get out of it, and she learns to go back to it on her own.

Meanwhile the baby in a crib at this age is beginning to encounter difficulties. Not only is the small space very confining for her; typically, she can now pull herself up by the bars. Because at first she cannot get down again, she stands and howls until a parent comes to get her. Often this is the beginning of another disturbed sleep cycle for both parent and child. Worst of all, the time comes when the baby might try to climb over the bars. As we have discussed, severe injuries to the head, neck, and spinal cord have all occurred to young children in the process of trying to climb out of their cribs.

From the time children are infants, it is important to keep their bedroom doors closed while they sleep. We close the door for safety whenever the child is sleeping but also to establish the habit of sleeping with a closed door. Such a habit is important for the child throughout life when security against disturbance and a guarantee of privacy and quiet are essential to a good night's sleep. Children who are accustomed to sleeping with a closed door from infancy will still go through a period of protest at some time in early childhood. When they do, parents must close the door deliberately and tell them, "You cannot come out. I will see you in the morning." Speak with finality in your voice. You are doing them a favor, after all. They need to sleep.

Again, a predictable schedule and order of events develops your child's trust and ability to unwind, relax, and be ready for sleep. Do not vary it. This is a great challenge for parents today. As adults, we are constantly on the move; we thrive on change. It is stimulating for us, and because our sense of order and trust in the world is already established, it can even be an antidote for mild depression and loneliness. We have experienced the cycles of night and day and the seasons of the year that follow each other inexorably throughout our lives. We understand the designations our civilization has assigned to the hours, days, weeks, and months, that define for us these cycles of light and dark and different displays of weather. Our children, on the other hand, will not fully understand these things until they reach the age of the reasoning mind at about age six years. In the meantime, it is our responsibility to give them sufficient routine and dependability in their daily schedules, especially in regard to sleep.

A word of warning: if we always rock and hold a baby to get her to sleep, she learns to need this action as part of her daily routine. Similarly, if we put her to bed with a bottle or pacifier, those also become a necessity for her. If the baby awakens and cries during the night, it is the adults' role to check her and soothe her, but the ultimate goal is for the infant to learn to soothe herself. This happens most readily if you simply reassure the child with a pat on the back and then see to it that both parents and child go back to sleep in their own beds. If you want to add a "transitional object" for your child's sense of security give her a soft stuffed animal or small blanket. If you use a transitional object, buy several replicas of the same item. If one gets lost or is in the wash, you can substitute a new one.

Most importantly, parents need to set a good sleeping schedule for themselves and to maintain a healthy attitude toward sleep. As we have discussed, sleep is not a luxury but a need—not an inconvenience but an "opportunity for the mind to create." Throughout history, scientists, mathematicians, and other creative people have awakened in the morning with the answers to problems that were troubling them the night before. It is not necessary to remain sound asleep all night. Just drifting in a kind of twilight state or "resting sleep" is often enough. The main point is to be still in body and mind and to use discipline to keep negative thoughts of the world from intruding.

FOOD

Just as in helping infants to sleep well, our goal in teaching babies to feed themselves involves helping them to develop the right attitudes as well as competence. From the beginning, children are developing their understanding of food and what it means in their lives. For the human species, eating is not limited to a biological experience; it has the possibility of expanding the joys of life in many ways. It involves preparing food that we have shopped for or grown in the garden, selecting food that is balanced and nutritious, and exploring the varieties of foods and their preparation. It also involves a recognition that we eat for spiritual as well as physical health. All over the world and throughout history, human beings have eaten in collaboration with others as a social and celebratory experience. In our own time, we put candles on the table and decorate it with flowers and beautiful place settings. We value the companionship of family mealtimes and dinners alone with our spouse, in extended family gatherings, at backyard barbecues and dinner parties with adult friends, because they are opportunities to deepen the intimacy of our relationships. It is not only how, when, and what to eat that we want our children to learn; it is to understand that *why* we eat involves more than filling our stomachs with food.

Nature provides for the infant's initial nutrition, a collaborative and intimate experience: the act of nursing from her mother. Except for the birth itself, breast-feeding is the baby's first experience with human collaboration. The infant's sucking stimulus aids the uterine contractions that help restore the mother's body to its prepregnant state. The mother in return gives of herself by nurturing the baby from her own body. We do not know in what way the experience of nursing arouses the infant's potential for a spiritual and social response to life. However, women who have nursed their babies know that the experience of breast-feeding goes beyond the instinct of a purely animal act to encompass an intimacy that fulfills the human spirit.

The depth of this experience is certainly not reached in the beginning weeks of nursing a first baby, however. It takes time— a long time of mutual effort by both infant and mother. In the beginning, biological feelings dominate. There is discomfort; the uterus hurts when it contracts during nursing. For some mothers there is a momentary feeling of gloom from the hormonal rush preceding the release of milk from the breast. Further, the milk supply is not yet established. Sometimes there is too much and the breast becomes engorged. Sometimes there is too little and the nipples become aggravated and sore from the baby's vigorous sucking. Sometimes the infant needs help in learning to suck successfully or has a physical malformation that makes sucking difficult for her. A new mother may feel like a cow, useful primarily for the milk that she can supply. New mothers sometimes are concerned about the adequacy of their breasts for the new experience of breast-feeding. Women with small breasts worry that they cannot produce enough milk. Women with large breasts worry that they will produce too much. In fact, breast size is not the determining factor. Breast size has to do with the amount of fatty tissue within the breast, whereas the level of milk production is based on the efficiency of the glands in producing milk. The factors involved in producing adequate milk for your baby are sufficient rest, good nutrition, plenty of liquids, and nursing regularly every three to four hours.

If you are a first-time mother, expect it to take eight to ten weeks before the full transition is made from experiencing nursing as primarily a biological event. It is at this time that the milk supply becomes adjusted to the individual baby, and there is less discomfort from too much milk in the breast or too much sucking from a hungry baby. Unfortunately, this is just the moment when many first-time mothers give up breast-feeding, believing that they have failed in their efforts to develop the feelings of intimacy and closeness with their babies that are described by experienced nursing mothers.

How do we avoid this unnecessary outcome? Most important is the mother's attitude and the attitudes of those around her. Although fashions come and go, it is now incontrovertibly established that breast-feeding for six to eight or nine months is best for both the mother's and the baby's health. In support of this goal, the nursing mother deserves unqualified support and encouragement from everyone around her. For her own part, she needs to believe in nature's plan and have confidence in her ability to serve her own baby. She can remind herself that if they were marooned together on an island, one way or another she would certainly manage to keep her baby alive all on her own. This is one of those times in life when belief in yourself, and a little stubbornness, can go a long way in producing the best outcome.

The mother's knowledge of the fundamentals in breastfeeding is key. The essential fact to understand is that complete emptying of the breast at each feeding is the signal to the body to produce more milk. Allow the baby twenty minutes at one breast. The baby may well empty the breast in ten minutes but the additional sucking ensures that this occurs while also giving the breast sufficient stimulation to increase milk supply as needed. If the baby is still hungry after twenty minutes on one breast, offer the other breast but be certain that you initiate the next feeding on this breast. In doing so, you are assured that it too is completely emptied before offering the other breast. (If your baby is an unusually strong and vigorous sucker, in order to protect your nipples from soreness, limit her to ten to fifteen minutes of nursing on each side in the earlier weeks.)

Even small babies usually can go two to three hours between feedings. Larger babies may thrive on feedings spaced at four-hour intervals. In the beginning weeks, it is important to remember that the more often the baby is fed, the more milk your breasts will produce. However, if a baby is fed within less than two hours, she may develop indigestion and regurgitate, or get a stomachache. In addition, frequent feedings mean that you have to take care that your nipples do not become sore. It helps if you have prepared them before the baby's birth by rubbing them gently with a washcloth to toughen them. There are good commercial mammary ointments to use between feedings that help the nipples to heal if they do become chapped from the baby's sucking. If this is your first experience with breast-feeding, it is a good preventive measure to use a lubricating mammary ointment routinely after each nursing and not wait until soreness has developed.

It is also necessary to understand the importance of intimacy in the relationship between nursing mother and baby. Before birth the infant stores knowledge of her mother: the motion of her body, the rhythm of her breathing, and the sound of her voice. When babies begin to nurse, these known points of reference help them to keep their bearings and give them a sense of security in an otherwise foreign environment. If the mother nurses the baby in private or, on occasion, in the presence of the father only, her knowledge of her baby and his or her comfort in her presence is extended and deepened. If the mother is distracted with company, phone calls, or other activity during a nursing session, she cannot devote her full attention to her baby. The significance of what she is accomplishing for her baby may elude her, and she is more likely to feel that she is merely the baby's "milk factory." On the other hand, if she takes the baby, along with a nourishing drink of her own, to a private place in the house so that she has only the baby and herself to consider, the nursing session becomes a peaceful, relaxing time for them both. The mother soon looks forward to these sessions as breaks in an otherwise stressful day.

Make no mistake; despite the sentimental picture of happy, healthy mother and baby created by advertisers and the media, life for both mother and newborn can be exceedingly stressful. Both mother and baby are facing new and unanticipated challenges. This is why an involved father is so important to both mother and child. In the beginning the father's role is primarily a protective one. His chief responsibility in the first eight weeks is to act as a buffer for the mother and child from the outside environment. That outside environment may include friends—and even family members, including the baby's siblings, if they do not sufficiently respect the mother and infant's need for rest. Because the mother is sleep-deprived and in a generally fragile state, she may not make the best judgments about her need for privacy with her baby. Most often, new mothers try to overextend themselves, either to please others or to bolster their feelings of adequacy in this vulnerable time. Fathers need to help them keep reality and expectation in balance.

The father soon finds that his role as protector of his wife and baby's privacy is not an easy one either. If this is the first baby in the family, he must establish well-defined parameters for the visits of friends, neighbors, and extended family—a role most often involving diplomacy, tact, and firmness. If there are older children in the family, he may find that helping siblings to understand the mother and infant's need for privacy and intimacy is one of his greatest challenges. It helps if mother and father have accustomed siblings to less exclusive attention by the mother before the baby is born. No matter what parents do to prepare them ahead of time, however, siblings will be jealous. In fact, one of the benefits of having a new baby in the house is just so that the older children can learn to accept and deal with their jealousy in productive ways.

For the parents' part, they need to remember that they have given more than a new challenge to their older children. They have given them a new friend for life. Eventually, siblings accept and appreciate this happy reality. In the beginning, however, it helps to take a matter-of-fact and accepting attitude toward their very natural jealousy. Expect that siblings will alternately express dislike and hide it by being oversolicitous of the new infant. Never leave the baby alone in their presence if siblings are six years old or younger. Ask them to get a diaper for you or some other task to show your respect and appreciation for their capabilities. If they are older (over ten years), show them how to hold the baby upright against their shoulder to burp her and let them settle the baby back into her child-bed when a nursing session is completed. If the father manages to protect the privacy of his wife and infant from older siblings during nursing and resting sessions in the beginning weeks, he is amply rewarded by the much quicker recovery of the mother and adjustment of the whole family to its new member, and thus a return to normal family life.

After the two-month period for establishing nursing has passed, mother and child have approximately six months remaining before the process of weaning from the breast is completed. It is in these intervening months that the new mother begins to discover the true meaning of motherhood. Through experience, rather than abstract information, she learns that motherhood consists of more than fulfilling physical needs and is more than just loving a baby. Becoming a mother involves developing intimate knowledge and respect for another human being and her path to self-formation. For her part, the baby in this period is learning that this new world into which she was born is a predictable place in which she can have trust and confidence. By now she has progressed to an established schedule of five to six feedings a day with a longer sleep cycle at night and several daytime naps. She can handle small discomforts and occasional fussing and crying because her deepest needs are consistently attended to wisely and in a timely fashion.

If all has gone well in this beginning period of approximately nine months, mother and child have moved successfully from internal attachment through the uterus and umbilical cord, to the external attachment of the mother's arms and breast. Now at nine months, mother and infant are challenged with a new mission—that of separation. Just as birth represented the child's freedom from the limitations of the womb, weaning from the breast is a move toward independence from the mother and represents the child's further embrace of the world.

The timing of weaning from the breast varies in individual situations but ideally it should never be abrupt. Weaning involves a process of at least four weeks to several months and begins with dropping one feeding at a time with intervals of several days to weeks in between. By the time of weaning at approximately six to nine months, the baby is most often on a schedule of five meals a day, usually at six and ten o'clock in the morning and two, six, and ten o'clock in the evening. The last feeding at night is a sensible one to drop first. The mother's milk is the least abundant at the end of the day and her supply adjusts more easily to the omitted feeding at that time. The two o'clock nursing, as a middle-of-the-day feeding, is often a convenient one to leave out next. As nursing periods are dropped, the milk supply slows down in response. It is not a perfect adjustment, however, and mothers need patience. Your breasts are typically uncomfortable for a day or so each time a feeding is missed. You also need to protect your clothing with nursing pads as your breasts may tend to leak excess milk. As you spread out nursing sessions, you can relieve the pressure in your breasts by expressing by hand a small amount of milk with a warm washcloth.

Giving up nursing is felt as a loss to the mother and invariably the absence of the intimacy and loving companionship of the experience must be acknowledged and mourned. On the other hand, the mother is free now of an immense responsibility. Her energy level returns to normal and, after so long a period, it is a relief to become more fully engaged again in the wider world. Similarly, the baby may show an indication that she too is ready for new and wider experiences of the world. In the first few months of life, she gives the impression "My whole world is my mother." She is excited about her mother and very focused on her, spending much of her time staring at her mother's chest and face during nursing sessions, stopping her sucking only now and then to smile up at her. Gradually, as she grows older, she tends to pull away from the breast during nursing sessions, to gaze out toward the world, to look at the interesting things out there. Eventually, some babies even get somewhat restless in their mother's arms. However, many infants give no overt indication that the moment for weaning has come. It is the mother who understands the baby's biological processes and needs, and who must finally choose the appropriate moment for each new learning experience, including weaning, to begin.

So far we have only discussed weaning as it relates to breast-feeding. However, there is a corollary to the process of weaning the baby from the breast; other types of nourishment are introduced to take the place of the mother's milk. These new sources of food are given very gradually and well in advance of the cessation of breast-feeding. At about age six months, the baby begins to produce enzymes that are capable of digesting foods other than breast milk. At the same time, the infant begins to require new supplies of iron to meet her needs for healthy growth and muscle development. Therefore, breast milk alone is no longer sufficient to meet all her nutritional demands. This is why we begin the introduction of solid foods when the baby is are approximately six months old, and other types of fluid such as water and small amounts of fresh juice on a spoon or in a glass even earlier.

Just as we previously prepared the infant's bedroom for independence in sleeping, so we need to carefully prepare the environment for the infant's participation in the new mealtimes of solid food and liquids. The adult's first consideration is the baby's position. The infant is not in her mother's arms as in breast-feeding. Just as the child-bed met the baby's needs for the sleeping position, we need to find a suitable piece of furniture for the baby's new experience of sitting to eat solid food and to drink fluids from a glass. Montessori designed the weaning table and chair mentioned in Chapter 6 for this purpose. Both table and chair are sturdy and heavy with the seat of the chair low and wide, with legs spaced far apart for stabilization. The chair has arms so that the child is held securely within it.

Seated in her chair opposite her mother or father, the child both receives a new message of separation and independence from her parent and can see what her parent is doing. Thus she is given an indirect lesson in feeding herself in the future. She observes the distance from bowl and spoon as the spoon comes toward her mouth and back again to scoop more food from the bowl, and so forth. Her absorbent mind is busy at work, incorporating the totality of the experience and indirectly preparing her to imitate the adult's actions as soon as her eye-hand coordination and muscle development permit.

In our discussion in Chapter 6 of setting the table as a practical-life exercise, we described the types of utensils, bowls, and plates for the child to use at mealtimes. For personal care, the baby also needs a bib. Try altering the closing device of a standard tie or snap bib by substituting a Velcro fastener in front or sewing on an elastic piece that allows you to slide the bib comfortably over your baby's head. Babies often want to see what the adults are doing with their hands and do not want to cooperate while you tie or snap a bib's fastener behind their necks. A pullover bib also has the advantage of independent use because eventually the baby can pull this type of bib over her own head by herself. You also need to place a sponge approximately two inches wide by three inches long on the child's table. If there is a spill, sponge it very carefully in front of your child so that even the simple act of wiping the table becomes an opportunity for her developing concentration. Remember that throughout the baby's first months you are continuing to encourage focus and engagement whenever your child is present. No activity of personal care or practical-life is merely for the purpose of accomplishing a task.

Prepare everything for the child's meal ahead of time so that once your child is seated in her weaning chair, you are not distracted. For this reason, it is best not to eat at the same time as your child until she is self-sufficient in eating. You can eat either before or after your child. Because it is always important to be a good model for your child, especially do not give in to the temptation to stand and eat in the kitchen during the child's mealtime.

To develop good eating habits and avoid the danger of choking, young children must always remain seated while they are eating or drinking. Because from ten months or so onward, the baby can crawl in and out of the weaning chair, you need to place the chair against a wall and pull the table up to the arms of the chair. This position holds the chair firmly in place while the baby is learning to sit and eat on her own. Hold the table in place with your feet if she pushes away, so that she cannot leave the table until the mealtime is over. At fifteen months, however, the baby is ready to learn that she must remain at the table. This is the time to say, "You are getting up. You must be finished, then. I'll put your food away." Remove the dish and end the meal. When the child sees that her mother means business, very often she will sit back down again to finish eating. If your child does not do this, however, do not be concerned. She is not going to starve. Just be certain that she waits until the next scheduled snack or mealtime to eat again. Children will soon learn that standing up and leaving the table signals the end of a meal.

Pediatricians alter their advice on what kind of solid food to give infants and at what age to serve it, depending upon the latest research into the nutritional needs and digestive capacities of babies. Within reason, parents should follow their doctor's advice. However, Paula remembers when pediatricians told mothers to feed their infants commercially produced baby cereal as early as three weeks after birth. After initially trying to follow this advice, she soon realized that it was very impractical. She was nursing her baby for thirty to forty minutes at each breast-feeding session. Adding an equivalent period of time to force-feed baby cereal into her baby's reluctant mouth made no sense.

When a digression from accepted historical practice is introduced in child care, parents need to think it through carefully, based on their experience with their own children, to see if it follows common sense.

Initially, when you offer food to your baby, it needs to be almost liquid in consistency. The temptation is to put too much of this nearly fluid food on the spoon. Just the tiniest taste on the edge of the spoon is sufficient at the beginning. Although for some time, the baby needs the adult to feed her, allow her to grasp her own spoon as soon as she is able. She needs to experiment with the feel of a spoon and to develop her grip on it. Given this opportunity to explore her spoon, she soon manages to get it to her mouth on her own.

By eight to ten months, the baby has progressed to picking up finger food. Cheerios cereal pieces or small pieces of bread or toast are a good size and texture for the the baby's first experimentation with eating with her fingers. However, be very careful what type and size of finger food you offer your baby. Choking is a real danger at this early age. Be certain to seek your pediatrician's advice in this matter.

From the time that the baby is six months old, it is important to offer water at mealtimes. At first put a few drops of water on a spoon. Soon you can proceed to using a glass. A petite glass such as a shot glass is the right size for the baby's tiny hand to hold. In the beginning you must hold the glass and pour a few drops into the baby's mouth. Keep a small pitcher on the counter next to you for refilling the glass. Fill it with just a little water (less than an ounce). At first, the water will go right down the baby's chin. Gradually she will become more and more competent in swallowing it, and less and less liquid will dribble down her chin.

When the baby drinks water or juice competently from her shot-size glass, you can also serve her milk to her in a glass. It is important not to substitute bottles or sippy cups of milk at this time. Baby bottles and sippy cups are unnecessary for babies who have nursed for nine months and who therefore have had sufficient opportunity for sucking. If the infant is introduced to drinking from a glass in a gradual manner from six months onward, her ability to do so by nine to ten months develops naturally. If the parents are concerned that their child at nine to ten months is not consuming enough calcium through drinking milk from a glass, they can supplement her meals with other calcium sources such as yogurt, custard, cottage cheese, and grated cheese.

Introduce a fork when the baby is twelve to fourteen months old. Try cutting soft bread or French toast into a small piece and guiding the child's hand to stab it onto the fork. Babies vary in all their competencies but many are successful in using both fork and spoon, as well as drinking from their own glass independently, by the time they are fifteen months old. Such accomplishments send a message to the child: "You are a capable person who can take care of many things for yourself, not just someone who is waited on."

Although the fifteen-month-old still needs to experience the independence of using the weaning table and chair for most meals, she can join the family for dinner at a larger table in the evening if it is a beneficial and enjoyable experience for all. This means that the mealtime is an appropriate length for a baby and takes place at an early hour. Otherwise, it is better for the baby to eat her own dinner at five o'clock and come to the family table at six o'clock just for fruit and milk. When she comes to the larger table, the baby should use a junior chair rather than a high chair. Junior chairs are usually available for purchase from unfinished-furniture and antique stores. Junior chairs differ from high chairs in that they have a step both to climb up on and to rest the child's feet when seated. Junior chairs also pull directly up to the table, eliminating the attached feeding tray of the high chair. Thus the child is not imprisoned in the junior chair but can climb in and out of it independently. Again the message is sent to the child: "You are not a rag doll that gets picked up and placed where it is supposed to go. You can get to your place all by yourself."

In closing this section on guiding the baby to independence in eating, we want to share the following anecdote describing how one mother was able to help her child. Note that the first thing the mother does is to be certain that her child is really hungry before inviting her to sit down and eat. One day we went to visit eleven-month-old Maria and her mother. When we arrived, Maria had recently gotten up from her morning nap. She was now investigating a very large box that had arrived from Federal Express while she was asleep. She was pulling herself up to the box and standing, holding on with two hands. Her mother said to her, "We got a package. It is a box. Box." After investigating the box for several minutes, Maria then looked over to the table next to her and said, "Da." She was looking very intently at a metal horse from Thailand on the table. Her mother said, "You want to see the horse. Sit down and you can see it." She then gave her the horse. "You are seated. You can look at that—a horse from Thailand." Her mother sat on the floor next to her. Maria explored the horse with amazing finger and hand dexterity, going all over its legs and body. Next she started to crawl with the horse in her hand. "Let's not crawl with that," her mother said. She repeated, "Horse, horse." Maria stopped to look at the horse again before continuing with her crawling. This time her mother took the horse away and put it back on the table. She did this firmly, if gently, and we got the distinct impression that this was a ritual that had been repeated before. Maria went back to investigating the box.

"Are you getting hungry?" her mother asked. "Box, feel the box." And again after a few minutes, "Are you getting hungry?" After Maria investigated the box for a few more minutes, "Shall we start lunch? Come on in the kitchen with me." Maria finally crawled into the kitchen after her mother. "Let's put on your bib—I'll get the rest of your food together."

Her mother told us that she had gotten Maria's lunch ready after breakfast. Now she took only a minute heating up her meat and vegetables in the microwave. She explained that she always fixed extra food from her own dinner the night before so that Maria could have it for her lunch each day. She had also prepared a tiny dish of yogurt and had a small pitcher of juice on the counter next to her. She sat on a very low stool next to Maria's weaning table. "Are you ready to eat? You need to sit in the chair first." After another minute, she said, "We will begin when you are seated." Maria now crawled rapidly to the weaning table, pulled herself up into the chair that was pressed against the wall, and sat down. She then pushed herself back in the chair. Her mother pushed the table against the chair so that Maria could not get out easily. Her mother explained that she was finding the weaning table much more practical than the high chair she had used initially. "Now the food doesn't go on the floor," she explained. "She just drops it on the table. I can keep putting it back on the plate. I think she was just interested in seeing the food hit the floor from that great height [of the high chair]."

Maria began to put food in her mouth, using her fingers. "That's a lot of food in your mouth." "Do you want to practice with your spoon?" Her mother put a little yogurt on a second spoon and handed it to Maria. "You feed yourself." Maria very carefully put her spoon to her own mouth. "That's enough yogurt on your spoon," her mother said. Maria had scooped into her bowl for more yogurt. Her mother took some of the yogurt onto the spoon that she was feeding Maria with, at the same time mentioning to us that Maria had just started in the last three days to use her own spoon to feed herself. "Before this she just banged it or hit her food with it." Now she said to Maria, "This is the spoon I'm going to use." Maria was trying to imitate her mother by taking yogurt from her mother's spoon and putting it on her own spoon, as she had seen her mother do a minute earlier. She did this repeatedly, although she had only seen her mother do this once before.

Maria stood up in her chair for a moment, as if she were finished, then she sat down again. "Yes, we need to be seated," her mother said. "You would like some juice?" Her mother then poured what seemed a large amount of juice for an eleven-month-old to handle into what looked like a glass votive candle-holder. Surprisingly, Maria took this "glass" in both hands and drank to its bottom all in one sitting and without spilling a drop. Her mother explained that she had started giving Maria a tiny shot glass with a teaspoon of water in the spring when she was seven months old. During the summer for some reason she started spilling it. "She still spills from the shot glass but not from the votive glass." Her mother speculated that she might be experimenting with the shot glass since it was clearly easy for her to manage it without spilling at this point. Her mother continued speaking to Maria: "Would you like more? We'll have one more glass—We put the other end in our mouth." (Maria had put the handle end of her spoon in her mouth.) "We need to wipe your hand then you can get up." "I'm going to take these things to the counter." Her mother made several trips to the counter, holding each item with two hands as a good model to Maria. Then she said, "I'm going to wipe the table." She wiped the table very carefully from top to bottom, left to right, sitting to the right side of Maria so that she could see all of her arm motions. Her mother mentioned that one night at dinner after she and her husband had finished, she inadvertently left a cloth on the table. Maria picked it up and started to wipe the table following the exact pattern of her mother's movements when wiping Maria's small table each day. Her mother said they were both amazed.

As we left, we remarked how surprising it was to see Maria

crawling rapidly to her chair and seating herself so competently at the beginning of her meal. Her mother replied, "It's not something I worked on. I had said to her each day before her meal, 'You need to sit in your chair.' But I was really just talking out loud to her. One day I noticed that she started to move toward the table when I said this. I was startled. They always surprise us. They know more than we think they do!"

DRESS

Let us consider now the child's dress. As in every area of personal care, independence for the child is our ultimate goal. Independence in dress has many facets. We do not want this independence for the child in order to free adults from dressing her. Our primary aim is not even to get clothes on the child. Our purpose in teaching the child to dress herself involves her self-formation. It is how the child feels about herself after she is dressed that is of ultimate importance. A corollary to this purpose is the appropriateness of the child's dress to the occasion.

Just as understanding health is key to eventual independence in sleeping and eating, so understanding the appropriateness of dress to the occasion is a major part of independence in dress. Parents not only need to focus on how to help their children learn to dress themselves and be responsible for their own clothes, but must also help them become aware of the appropriateness of their clothes to a specific situation.

In first considering the topic of their child's clothing, parents need to ask themselves, who am I thinking of when I dress my child? As a parent, are you seeing your child as a living human being with specific needs or as an object for your pleasure and self-enhancement—even as a symbol of your success in life? Human beings, of course, dress themselves for many different reasons. Every civilization throughout history has regarded clothing and personal adornment as an important part of its culture.

Adults use dress as a means of impressing others by indicating wealth and status, of inspiring fear as in dressing for battle, and of expressing themselves in creating beauty and joy for themselves and others. It is this last purpose that is pertinent to children. How we dress always says something about ourselves. "Is this what I want to say?" is the question we want to teach our children to ask about their clothing as they grow into adulthood.

As a consequence of their needs in self-formation, children under six years old are already focused on themselves. We have learned that this is not an unhealthy focus at this early age. On the other hand, it is not a view that needs to be fostered or exaggerated either. Unfortunately, giving in to the temptation to dress the child under six years old in excessive ways heightens the child's already existent emphasis on self. It is particularly unfortunate when the child is dressed with so much adornment that we see not so much the child as her outward decoration. The message that we inadvertently send to the child is "What is important about you is not what is inside of you but what is outside of you."

When we dress young children we want to choose clothing that allows them to move comfortably, that is appropriate to the occasion, and that allows them to dress themselves just as soon as they are able. In addition, we give them limited choice as soon as they are capable of choosing for themselves, and we show them how to care for their clothes. If parents follow these guidelines, the chances are good that their child will become an adult who is appropriately confident and expressive of self in her dress.

We discussed the appropriate outfit for a newborn in Chapter 5. Freedom of movement, sensorial awareness of the environment, and comfort were the main considerations behind our selection. After choice of clothing, the next step for adults is to elicit the infant's cooperation as you dress her. From the time she is a tiny baby, talk to her and tell her what you are doing: "Now, let's put your arm in this sleeve," and so forth. Dress the baby in the same order and in the same way each time. Try to do so in distinct steps, and slowly enough so she can track what you are doing. As in all activities with young children, allow for cooperation. Ask for it and wait for it with patience. You need to do this before you think your baby can respond. It is very likely that the baby's ability to copy your actions and her understanding of your language while dressing her, will occur before you expect it. Again, being orderly and repetitive in your movements and words is important.

As the baby grows up, the adults should extend the choices for her clothing. The principles remain the same, however: freedom of movement, comfort, ease of dressing, and appropriate dress for the occasion. Buy shirts that open at the top or are a few sizes too large so that they fit easily over the baby's head. Turtlenecks are a poor selection for a child under five because they are difficult for her to put on by herself. Pants should have elastic all the way around the waist. Avoid sweat pants with tight cuffs at the ankles; they also are difficult for the child to get on and off. Sweaters need to have buttons that fit easily into their buttonholes. If the buttonholes are tight, try enlarging them or replace the buttons with smaller ones. Because children can handle buttons on coats before they are capable of using zippers, try to avoid the latter in the beginning. Children's felt coats, originally designed in Europe, have buttons large enough for children to fasten independently at an early age. Make certain that mittens and hats are loose enough for the child to pull on and off with ease, and are comfortable. Look for hats and scarves with a soft inside lining of acrylic. After the child is too old to wear shoes with flexible soles (as advocated in Chapter 5), the best all-around shoe is a simple, low-cut tennis shoe. Not only are boots, high-top shoes, sandals, and party shoes difficult for children to put on and take off, but loose buckles and leather soles are a safety hazard.

When showing a child of two years or older how to practice buttoning a coat, put the coat on a table opposite her. Demonstrate how to grasp the edge of the button with finger and thumb of one hand and poke it through the buttonhole, grasping it with the pincer grip of the other hand to pull it through. Practicing over and over again with her own coat in this way, makes it much easier for the child eventually to button her coat when she has it on. The same procedure of practicing on a table is helpful with zipping a coat, buttoning a shirt or sweater, and so forth.

When teaching the child to put on her socks, use the fingers and thumbs of both your hands to scrunch the fabric of the sock into a small bunch at the toe. Put this much of the sock over the end of her foot. She can try to pull the sock up partway onto her foot but for a long time you will have to get it over her heel for her. After it is over her heel, she can finish pulling her sock the rest of the way up her ankle.

If you take the time and effort to select your child's clothes carefully, show her how to dress herself, and allow her to practice, she is likely to get her clothes on and off by herself as early as fourteen months. She is well on her way to developing full independence in dress. However, there are two further aspects involved in making this newfound independence complete. She needs to make her own choice of what to wear and to take part in the care and storing of her clothes.

The idea of giving choice to children in many areas of their lives has become widely accepted in recent years. Unfortunately, the necessity of limiting choices to a manageable level for young children is not so well understood. Young children can handle two options; three is too many. They cannot think through the appropriateness of their dress for a particular occasion or the current weather. Parents have to make selections for them that meet such criteria. A good way to allow for some choice but to keep it within the child's capabilities is for the parent to put out two outfits for the child and let her choose one of them. If the child does not choose readily, the adult must then choose. Do not let dressing become an opportunity for negotiation or manipulation. If this happens, it is a sign that clothes are taking too important a place in the young child's life. It is best then to forget about choice with regard to clothes and concentrate on allowing limited choice in other areas of the child's life, such as a choice of the vegetable to prepare together for the evening meal. Choice is an important element in the child's developing will, as we discuss in Chapter 9. However, too much choice in too many areas is overwhelming and confusing for the young child. Thus, instead of building self-confidence, choice can destroy it.

Give children the opportunity to help in the storage and care of their clothing so that they can learn independence in dress. Put a clothes hamper or large basket in the child's room or bathroom where she can put each item of clothing as she removes it. Young children are in the Sensitive Period for order. If they are accustomed to seeing clothing on the floor, they develop the idea that it belongs there. It is wise, therefore, to develop the habit that all dirty clothing goes directly from child to laundry basket or hamper. Similarly, plan for a customary place in the closet where shoes are placed side by side, as soon as they are removed.

Store clean clothes either in drawers, bins, or on an open shelf. Arrange them in order: on the top shelf or in the top drawer, place the first items to be put on and progress down to the last ones. Socks and underwear, then, are on the top, shirts in the middle, and pants on the bottom. Sew large rings in the young child's first coats and sweaters so that she can hang them on hooks in her closet. When the child is three, she can learn to hang coats and dresses on child-size plastic hangers and place them on a rod in her closet lowered for this purpose. Keep mittens, hats, and scarves in a basket by the front or back door so that they are handy when the child arrives or leaves home.

In clothing, as in so many things for young children, less is more. If you stay with the basic amount needed, you not only make your child's goal of independence more attainable for her, but you also make your own life simpler. For even an eight-year-old, four to six pairs of pants, four to six shirts, one pair of sneakers for school with the almost outgrown pair saved for outside in the yard, one good dress or good pair of trousers, and one pair of dress shoes are enough. With this manageable and practical wardrobe, the elementary school child is always ready to run, play, and climb—activities that should fill her early school years. If this limited wardrobe is sufficient for even an eight-year-old, it is certainly not necessary to burden the two-to-three-year-old with more clothing.

TOILET TRAINING

If our purpose in dress is independence in the child's personal care, toilet awareness is an integral part of the help that we must give to the infant from birth. In addition, there are at least two other reasons why toilet awareness deserves the serious attention of the adult from the beginning. First, learning to control her bowels and bladder is the first accommodation that is asked of the child by her society. As such, it involves an understanding and acceptance of the expectations of the civilization into which she is born. Second, this is an accommodation to her society that requires knowledge, as well as conscious effort and willing cooperation on the child's part. It is not a feat that the child is able to accomplish on her own. She must have the focused attention of the adults around her. As a result, it is the child's first major experience in collaboration with an adult for an educational purpose. It is clear, then, that toilet awareness is more than a matter of "dry pants" for the child.

The myelination of neurons necessary to ready the body for

control of bowels and bladder is completed by the time children are approximately twelve months old. She is now able to feel the impulse to control her bodily functions. The child needs, however, to learn to execute this control. Everything that you have worked toward to date in the child's personal care is an aid to her in achieving this goal. Eating and sleeping are now on a routine schedule. The child is independent in dressing to a significant degree due to the loose clothing selected and your attention in helping her learn to dress herself from the beginning. Most importantly, you have helped your child from birth to develop an awareness of the sensations of wetness and dryness, by changing diapers as soon as they are wet. This means that you may have changed as many as twelve or more diapers a day in the first months.

For the baby to develop the necessary awareness of wetness and dryness it is also essential that she wear diapers made of a natural fabric such as cotton. Unfortunately, adults consistently choose disposable diapers rather than cotton ones, because the former are quick and convenient. Often they do not realize that there are diaper services in most areas that make the use of cloth diapers both handy and economical. In addition, parents may not be aware that disposable diapers present obstacles to the child's work in self-formation in two ways. First, they draw the moisture away from the child's body, thereby eliminating the uncomfortable sensation of wetness. In fact, they even become comfortable for the child after urination because a chemical reaction within the diaper creates a "sauna effect" or feeling of warmth next to the child's body. Second, because it is difficult to tell when the child has urinated, the adult does not change the child in disposable diapers as often as a baby in cloth ones. In fact, studies show that babies in disposable diapers are changed as infrequently as four to six times a day. This is an unfortunate outcome because diapering is a time when parents are fully attentive to their babies. They talk with them, play simple games, and smile and sing to them. Babies in disposable diapers, as compared with infants in cloth diapers, are therefore missing many additional opportunities for social interactions with an adult during the course of each day.

If, from the baby's birth, cloth diapers are used and changed as soon as they are wet, the infant gradually becomes aware of the opposite conditions of wet and dry. The next step is for the baby to connect her bodily sensations of elimination with the accepted place to excrete those wastes. As in other areas of development, the child has a Sensitive Period for interest in this process. You can help your child respond to this interest if you begin to diaper her in a standing position as soon as she can stand readily by herself, in other words from approximately twelve months old. From a standing position, she can more easily observe her body and the actions involved in cleaning her, disposing of her waste, and putting on her clean cloth diaper. To help your child realize that the bathroom is the natural place for human waste, always clean and change her in the bathroom after the early months. It also helps if she is aware that other members of the family go to the toilet in the bathroom.

The child's Sensitive Period of interest in toileting occurs between twelve and eighteen months of age. Your child may indicate this interest in obvious or in more subtle ways. It is important to keep in mind that like all Sensitive Periods this interest is a temporary phenomenon. If it is missed, learning to use the toilet becomes a remedial endeavor. Unfortunately, as in other areas of the child's developing capacities, the child is often ready for the adult's help in toileting before the adult is prepared to give it. How then do we prepare the environment to facilitate the child's use of the toilet beginning at no later than twelve to fifteen months?

First, place potty chairs in all bathrooms after the first months, thus ensuring that the baby becomes accustomed to seeing them there. (See the Michael Olaf catalogue for the most appropriate potty chair we have found for young children.) Prepare each bathroom in the house further, with a diaper pail with water for soiled pants, a basket of clean underpants, a small mop, wash cloths, and—for the parents' access only—a bottle of Nature's Miracle (available at pet shops) or other carpet stain remover.

Parents need to choose a time for toileting within their child's Sensitive Period of interest and when they can devote sufficient attention to the process. Most often, it takes three to six weeks of intensive care to help a child learn to use the toilet. During this time it is important that your child is in the environment that is most comfortable to her. For many children this means remaining at home during these weeks as much as possible. Therefore, you will need to curtail unnecessary activities and trips outside the house for this time frame. It is also helpful to choose a time when the weather is mild enough for lighter clothing and outdoor living. If the baby can go naked, or nearly naked, during these weeks, she will more quickly associate urine trickling down her legs with the muscular tension and urge that preceded it. Wearing only cotton underpants during the learning process also facilitates changing and re-dressing, thus helping everyone to remain patient with the procedures involved.

The next step is to help the baby urinate while sitting on the potty. For this connection to occur the child needs to sit on the potty at various times throughout the day. The most likely times for success are after the child's first waking up in the morning or from naps, and after meals and walks. It is helpful if you keep a record of your child's urination and excretion so that you can more easily predict her need for elimination. Scheduled promptings by you throughout the day can thus help your child anticipate her need to use the potty. You can keep a basket by the potty with a book for the child to look through. Sit with your child during "potty time" but this should not become a time when you are providing entertainment. Children will quickly get more interested in the attention they are receiving from you than in the work at hand. Keep your attitude matter-of-fact, encouraging, and confident, as in any learning situation with your child. When she is successful, empty the potty in the toilet, and then let her flush it. Establish the habit of her washing her own hands immediately afterward. Acknowledge her use of the toilet with appropriate matter-of-fact comments: "That is urine. You have put your urine in the potty."

Successes on the potty are few and far between at first. For many children, even under the optimal conditions described so far, these are not accomplished easily. During the long process to full control, cleaning up when the child does not make it to the potty is ongoing. From the beginning it is essential that the child participate in each clean-up session. Again, the goal is not dry pants but a child who feels appropriately in control of herself and her life. Let her be as independent as possible in getting her wet pants off and putting them in the pail of water in the bathroom. If they are soiled, have them hand them to you for a preliminary cleaning by rinsing them in the toilet. The child can soak up her urine from the floor with the small mop and cloth, and she can wipe herself with her wash cloth and towel. She can put her other soiled clothes and the items she has used in cleaning up into her laundry hamper. She can then wash her hands and dress herself in fresh clothes. At this early age, children find the process of dressing and undressing themselves independently to be of great interest. Capitalize on this interest in dressing and undressing to keep them focused on the toileting process.

The adult needs to keep in mind at all times the comprehensiveness of the toileting task for children. As we have said, this is their first experience in compliance with societal expectations. Respect them in this serious task by using adult terms for their genitals and bodily wastes. Acceptance of bodily functions in this early period as natural and part of physical health can contribute to the children's development of responsibility and a respectful attitude toward sexual maturing in later childhood and early teenage years.

Parents tell us that positive toileting comes faster if the child is in underpants both during the day and at night. Thus the child is not confused by a concept she cannot understand: sometimes it is all right to have diapers on and other times it is not. Some parents, however, prefer to concentrate first on the child's use of the toilet during the daytime. If you make this choice, continue using cloth diapers until the child remains dry through the night or has established good control in the daytime. When this point is reached, you can remove diapers from the house or relegate them to the closet until a new baby arrives. Removal of the diapers from the young child's environment sends a message to her that she is growing up and is capable of taking responsibility for use of the toilet. If necessary, several pairs of heavily padded training pants with a waterproof vinyl covering can take the place of diapers at night for a transition period.

When your child begins to sleep without protection at night, keep a change of pajamas, clean sheets, a blanket, and other items for the child's care close to her bed. To make middle-of-the-night changing easier while the child is learning to stay dry, use a piece of two-by-five-foot rubberized flannel tucked in the sides of the bed where they sleep. As in the daytime, let her help to clean up after herself. For your own part, limit your child's fluids from late afternoon onward and concentrate on establishing as calm and stress-free an atmosphere in the home before bedtime as possible.

Just as most children succeed in early learning situations if they are given sufficient adult support, so most young children can become independent in personal care including toilet awareness before, or soon after, their second birthday. In fact, studies indicate that in the 1950s when Paula was raising four of her five children, ninety-two percent of babies were using the toilet successfully during the daytime by eighteen months of age. Certain historical changes have occurred in the meantime that account for a much lower percentage currently. However, children themselves have not changed. Given sufficient support and attention by their parents, most young children today respond well to the process of toilet awareness that we have outlined. There are exceptions, of course. Just as some children have difficulty following three sequential directions, learning to read or memorizing math facts, so some children are slow in the learning processes involved in control of their bodily functions. Obviously, such children need more adult attention, patience, and consistent effort to achieve success in their toilet learning than others. Unfortunately, when difficulties in toileting arise, parents today are too quick to abandon their child's mission of self-formation. They put her back into diapers, usually disposable ones, and miss the opportunity that appropriate timing with their child's Sensitive Period provides.

Our society as a whole shares the blame for this failure, just as fifty years ago our culture was responsible for the substitution of bottle feeding for breast-feeding by the majority of parents who could afford to do so, as well as the total anesthetizing of mothers during labor—both practices with negative consequences for mothers and infants. The appropriate response of parents whose child is having difficulty with toilet awareness is not to give up on her but to redouble their efforts to help. Just like parents of a child having trouble with reading or mathematics, parents of a child having difficulty with toilet learning need patience and must use their resources and ingenuity if their child is to succeed. However, as in any hard-won accomplishment, the victory in the end is sweeter. If parents remember that their mission is not a child in "dry pants" but a child successful in her formation of independence, coordinated movement, language, and will, they will know that their hard work on their child's behalf is worth the effort.

GROOMING

Just as with independence in sleeping, eating, and dressing (including toileting), areas of personal care involving grooming are best addressed before the child reaches the age of opposition at approximately age two years. Ritual and order are again the child's major resources in learning. You must analyze each procedure of personal grooming: brushing and combing hair, brushing teeth, wiping the nose, taking a bath, shampooing hair, washing hands and face, brushing fingernails, and so forth. Prepare your child's environment, giving great attention to each detail, and establish the necessary routines and timing for each activity.

For brushing hair, your child needs a child-size brush and comb in a small basket. A stand-up mirror on the same table, or a wall mirror at the appropriate height for her viewing, should be placed next to it. With most personal grooming activities you need to alternate turns with your child. After your child makes her attempt, say, "Now it is my turn," without mentioning that her turn did not quite do the job. At times you will need to put your hand on your child's hand to guide the action to be taken. As in everything we do with children, you need to be gentle and move at their slower pace, inviting their participation. You are offering your child a learning opportunity. Keep in mind that the journey to successful independence in personal grooming is a long one. However, the child's participation on some level is necessary from the outset.

For brushing teeth, the child needs a small tube of toothpaste and a toothbrush in a small cup. This is a good use for a baby cup if your child has received one as a gift. The child holds the brush and the parent holds the paste, squeezing a very small amount onto the child's brush. After your child has a turn, you can gently place your hand over hers on the brush and continue brushing. Fortunately, the young child's teeth are baby teeth and thoroughness in brushing is not vital. In later years when complete brushing is necessary, the child is old enough to brush her teeth competently on her own. What is important during this early period is to establish the habit of brushing teeth when your child's interest is greatest.

To help your child become independent in wiping her nose, keep a small basket with a few tissues folded into quarters by her mirror. Take a tissue and demonstrate how you wipe your own nose. Fold the tissue from a square to a rectangle and place it over your nostrils with two hands. Blow gently but do not close off either nostril. Doing so can force mucus up into the nasal passages and increase the risk of infection. Slide your fingers along your nostrils until they come together. The tissue is now in a square again. Pat your nostrils on each side with the used tissue. Keep a small wastepaper basket for discarded tissues by the low shelf or table where you have the basket of folded tissues. Folding the tissues each day is a good practical-life activity for mother and child, or an older sibling, to do together.

You will find that young children are fascinated with the process of blowing their noses. As classroom teachers, we are always amazed by the rapt attention of children, even as old as five and six years, as we give a lesson in nose blowing. We think that this occurs because parents often neglect to show children how to carry out this necessary procedure for themselves. Eventually, older children do figure out how to blow their noses on their own but usually very inefficiently, grabbing tissue after tissue and smearing mucus across their faces. Nose blowing is of course a simple process for adults, yet it is a complex one for children. It is a good example of how we unconsciously undermine the child by constantly doing for her under age five or six years. Suddenly as she enters kindergarten or first grade, we expect her to do for herself ever after with competency and ease as if by magic and without any previous preparation.

For independence in bathing, provide a hook low enough for your child to reach, a towel, and wash cloth small enough for her easy handling. A hand towel or bath towel cut in half and then hemmed makes a good towel size. You may want to use a small facial sponge instead of sewing a small wash cloth. The soap must be small enough for the child to use readily. Hotel-size is ideal. If necessary, cut a large bar in half. Again the goal in bathing is the child's participation. Let her do some part of each step in the process with you.

Washing hair is often traumatic for young children because the adult tries to control the whole process. Instead, squeeze a small amount of shampoo onto your hand and help the child rub it onto her hair. Eventually, you can try putting just enough shampoo for one soaping in a small bottle. Let your child squeeze it onto her own hand. The child will rub, of course, in only one spot, but you can take a turn next saying, "Now it's my turn." Your child can participate in rinsing her hair if you allow her to dump cups of water over her head. Again, alternating turns helps achieve the desired result.

Washing hands is one of the most important grooming habits to establish early. As such you need to give this process a good deal of thought. You must supply a sturdy step stool to the bathroom sink, a tiny bar of soap in a soap dish, a small towel (a wash cloth is a good size) for hand drying, and, if desired, a small fingernail brush. If you take time to demonstrate hand washing to your child in a methodical manner, as in all personal care and practical-life exercises, you will find that she not only becomes competent in washing her hands at a surprisingly early age but truly enjoys doing so. The child can also wash her face when necessary. As when wiping her nose, she needs a small mirror available for this process.

Success in children's mission of independence in their personal care depends upon the extent of collaboration that parents establish with them. Enjoying collaboration with children involves taking an interest in them as human beings in the process of development. The adult must be intrigued with this process, willing to give time to understand it, study it, observe it in action, and support it. Indeed, everyone who works with children must have such an attitude. Within the home, our goal is to treat the child as a respected member of the family. She is not the family pet to carry about, feed, clean up after, and groom as we do the family dog, but a human being, capable of starting on the road to independence from the first days of her life. This independence is built not only from making a contribution to the family through the activities of practical life described in the previous chapter, but involves every issue of the child's personal care, from sleeping, eating, dressing (including toileting) to each process of individual grooming—brushing and combing hair, brushing teeth, wiping her nose, taking a bath, shampooing hair, and washing hands and face. When these processes are introduced in the Sensitive Period of interest, each of these achievements along the lengthy road of independent self-care brings great joy, pride, and confidence to the child under three years old.

EIGHT

Language and Intelligence

Infants develop their capacity for abstract thought and its expression not only through the coordinated movements of hand and brain interacting with the environment, but through their early experiences with language. The intelligence of children is therefore intimately connected with the quality and extent of their exposure to language. We can define intelligence as consisting of two key interrelated components. First, intelligence involves the creation of ideas and intentions, together with the capacity to study and understand such thoughts by reflecting on them and subsequently forming them into systematic relationships and logically organized patterns. Second, intelligence requires the ability to take these creations of analytic and synthetic thought and use them to better understand and transform the world. To accomplish the latter, we must have a well-developed skill for expressing ourselves symbolically. In other words, we must be able not only to act productively and independently from our creative, disciplined thinking but to explain what we have done and wish to do next, to others. Our story of developing language and intelligence in the child, then, involves both the capacity for symbolic thought and the skills of communication.

The ability to communicate effectively evolves gradually from the first days of life. Parent and baby engage in a dialogue with each other whereby, through gesture and expression, the infant seeks to make his needs known and the parent tries to interpret and meet these demands. From the beginning, then, body language is a key component of human communication. But sound is also an essential aspect of this preverbal dialogue between parent and infant. All babies cry, and most cry a great deal in the early months. An infant cries in different ways to express different needs: "I am hungry," "I am cold" (or hot or wet), "I need to sleep," or "I need activity." If the parents combine listening for these different cries with carefully observing their baby's behavior, they gradually learn to respond appropriately.

It is in this first communication with another that the infant begins the long journey toward discovery of self as an entity separate from the rest of existence. Through communication of body and sound the child both initiates and receives the actions of his parents throughout his preverbal life. Thus he experiences influence over another. To the degree that this influence in the first years of life is not absolute, he ultimately reaches a healthy understanding of his place in the world as one human being among many. If, on the other hand, the parents are overly anxious and therefore anticipate the child too much, they inadvertently give him a false sense of omnipotence that bodes ill for his future relationships and his acceptance of the limitations of human life. Thus it is that long before sound and symbol are united in oral language, the necessary foundation for thoughts about reality—of who, what, and where we are—as well as for our ability to communicate effectively with others about this reality, is already established.* We will now begin to trace the connecting of sound and symbol in the human infant's language: a process that develops the human intelligence and, together with the hand's pincer grasp of forefinger and thumb, is unique to the human species.

---

*See Stanley I. Greenspan, M.D., *The Growth of the Mind.*

THE DEVELOPMENT OF ORAL LANGUAGE

We have stated that babies are programmed for symbolic language from the beginning. They recognize human speech at birth having previously heard muffled human voices for many months from within the womb. This prenatal experience results in a preference for their mother's voice from among all others. However, at birth their brains are capable of distinguishing the phonemes represented in all human languages. Thus, adaptability to any human language is possible in the first weeks of life. By six months, however, infants have already activated the neural structures for identifying the phonemes of the language surrounding them, and those for other languages are weakening.

Human language requires that the infant take meaningless sounds and combine them in specific, intricate ways in order to produce meaning. Animals cannot carry this process to the same level of sophistication as human beings. For animals, sound and meaning are essentially one and the same. Human babies, on the other hand, can practice the sound of *c* and *a*, eventually combining them to produce "ca"—still a meaningless phoneme. One day, however, they add "*t*" and the miracle of meaning occurs.

By two months, the motor nerves for the infant's throat, tongue, and mouth are myelinated and the infant becomes capable of babbling. At first, the sounds he makes represent only the vowels. Vowel phonemes are common to almost all languages and are physically easier to produce in the early months. Thus babies at approximately the same age in most parts of the world begin their speech with "ooh" and "aah" sounds.

Once babbling begins in the early months, the infant not only learns through hearing the sounds of others, he also learn from hearing and producing his own sounds. He practices with his sounds as if trying them out for effect and accuracy, thus strengthening his vocal tract and muscles through repetitive use. From two months of age, the importance of producing and hearing his own babbling for the infant's language skills is another significant reason for avoiding pacifiers. Sucking on a pacifier effectively mutes the child as if he were in fact unable to produce sound. By five months old, babies can combine vowels and consonants in producing what is termed "canonical babbling." Through sucking at the breast, they have developed the lip and tongue muscles needed to make the sounds of *b, d, m, n, w,* and *j.* The baby now endlessly creates strings of repetitive sounds: "ma, ma, ma" and "ba, ba, ba," exercising the vocal muscles and listening to his own vocal production.

Interestingly, the amount and quality of the infant's babbling correlates with the amount of attention that parents give to him. If parents respond by listening and imitating, the baby babbles more. Equally, a lack of parental response leads to less babbling. Dialogue then is clearly essential from the beginning. As parents, we need to talk and wait for our babies to respond, whether we are bathing, nursing, or dressing them. Name the objects you are using and describe the actions involved. Do so in simple words but with respect for the seriousness of the child's task in self-formation. Speak slowly, remembering that the neural speed of the child's brain remains at half that of the adult brain until the child is approximately twelve years old. Speak as if on some level the child might understand you. Remember you are laying a foundation for intelligent communication. We never know the exact moment when understanding will come, and it most often surprises us.

Usually, however, by the ninth or tenth month the baby accomplishes this great feat. He discovers that meaning can be conveyed by sound, perhaps beginning to use social responses such as "hi" and "bye bye," and to name family members. Gradually, the baby makes connections between every kind of sound and object and action. He understands more than he can convey, and so he becomes frustrated often—pointing and trying out his sounds, hoping his efforts will result in the desired parental response. We see his frustration as a negative experience, and so we hasten to give him what he wishes as soon as we can guess at his meaning. Yet, frustration is what drives him to go beyond the making of sound for its own sake. It is hard work to make connections between sound and meaning. We have only to think of Helen Keller, and the way the world was ultimately revealed to her through the connection of her senses to symbolic language, to imagine both the effort required and the resulting thrill that children experience in their gradual conquering of language.

At twelve months old, the child has often learned as many as six words. He continues to add a few nouns and expressions each month. However, once a vocabulary of fifty words is reached, a breakthrough occurs and the child begins to learn new words every day. This vocabulary explosion, occurring in most children between the ages of twelve and twenty-four months, dovetails with the rapid formation of the brain at this time. The metabolic activity and synapse formation of the cerebral cortex (specifically, the left parietal lobe, the area of word storage and retrieval in adults) are at the highest level they will ever achieve.

For the next four to five years, the child may learn a new word every two hours he is awake. This incredible facility for vocabulary and word meaning continues throughout the child's elementary school years. It is for this reason that Montessori went to such lengths to introduce the child to extensive facts and nomenclature of the world in the first twelve years of life: first through "keys to the world," as she called her materials in the Children's House for three-to-six-year-olds, and later through "keys to the universe," the term for materials in the elementary levels for six-to-twelve-year-olds.

One of the most intriguing aspects of the child's language

development is the brain's innate response to words as references to the whole and not to the parts of an object or its individual properties—as in the word "leaf," for example. The child also recognizes that there are words that refer to classes of items rather than to an individual member of that class. The word "leaves" refers to all manner of leaves: maple, willow, aspen, and so forth. A third innate assumption enables the child to recognize that a new label given to something with a name already known refers to either a new property of that object or only a part of it. Hence, "green" refers to one aspect of the leaf and "petiole" to one part of it.

Sounds combine with meaning to give us vocabulary and the ability to name everything about us. It is grammar, however, that enables us to convey to others whatever we are thinking. The expansion into grammar begins very soon after children's explosion into words. By the time they are four years old, children have incorporated all the rules of syntax. Grammar establishes that meaning is determined either by the order of words or by changing their beginnings and endings or their inflection. Hence, two-year-olds say, "I run" or "see ball," not "run I" or "ball see" (if they mean that they see their ball). Children begin to string more and more words together in the correct order but at first there is little use of inflection and they omit words such as "to" and "am" and the articles "the" and "a." They might say, "Dog run fast," for "The dog is running fast." Gradually, they begin to use word endings such as "ing," then they begin using prepositions such as "on" and "in," plurals (dogs, balls), and possessives (his, hers). At last they add articles, past and present tense verbs, and third person pronouns: "He jumps on the bed" and "He jumped on his bed."

Logic indicates that children's eventual development of grammar does not come from mimicking the sentences of adults. If the latter were the case, they would not use sentences like "She gots" for "She gets." Nor do children experiment with grammar by trial and error. Rather, they appear to grasp intuitively the rules for how words combine and their various endings, as well as the different functions of words in sentences such as nouns (what something is), verbs (what it is doing), and adjectives (what kind it is). At a certain point, for example, children figure out a rule for verbs, such as add "ed" for the past tense. They then proceed to say "He runned" for "He ran." Interestingly, when they were younger and had not yet determined the past tense rule, they did not make this mistake. There are approximately 180 irregular verbs in English for which children must memorize the correct endings for past and other tenses. They also must learn the plurals of nouns and pronouns, and comparatives and superlatives of adjectives. Typical examples of children's mistakes from overgeneralizing grammar rules when they first grasp them are "foots" instead of "feet" and "goodest" instead of "best."

Because language development influences the baby's understanding of what is happening around him and his ability to tell others of his needs—thus initiating their responses—it has a major effect on his intellect, as well as his social being. Indeed the quality of the language to which an infant is exposed permanently alters both his brain structure and its function. By the age of three, each child's approach to language, and therefore level of achievement in many areas of self-formation, is already largely determined. It is essential, then, to give specific linguistic aid to the baby from birth and, equally important, to remove all obstacles. Ear infections, for example, must receive prompt attention, and tubes must be inserted to drain fluid and facilitate hearing immediately if indicated by the child's medical doctors.

It is true that genes play a part in the baby's ability to acquire language just as they influence his height and eye color. However, researchers have determined that the capacity for reading is only fifty percent inheritable and for spelling, only twenty percent. Such statistics indicate that there is enormous opportunity for environmental influence in these areas. Nor does this influence require that parents be highly educated or financially well off. Rather, research also indicates that the most important variable is the parents' style of interacting with their baby. This finding is consistent throughout the child's elementary school years in all areas of language: reading, spelling, speaking, hearing, and listening.

It is reassuring that parents do not need a college education (or even the ability to read) to help their baby establish a solid base for language development. However, parents do need knowledge about what is helpful to their infant and what is not. First of all, good grammar and clear pronunciation are important and the quantity of words to which the baby is exposed correlates directly to his language development. Most importantly, only those words spoken directly to him count. Overhearing telephone conversations or electronic devices such as televisions and VCRs is of no help to the child. In fact, it is a negative because it places a barrier between parent and infant. The baby can make sense of language only when he can relate directly to the persons and things referenced. He needs to be interacting with you as you speak, and focusing on the real world around him at that moment.

Therefore, it is imperative to talk to your baby often throughout his day, naming objects, discussing actions, relating events, and describing people and their apparent feelings. Keep your speech simple and clear. It seems that raising our voices to the higher pitch and more deliberate delivery preferred by babies is natural to adults, so this will happen even without your awareness. Your baby needs lots of repetition because he must reinforce specific neural pathways in the brain. "Drilling" of information, however, leads consistently to boredom at any age, and certainly has no place in the life of a young child, whatever the area of self-formation involved.

Note that no suggestion we have made for the infant's language requires that parent and baby leave the house for shopping center, play group, or exercise class. The home environment contains all the opportunity necessary. Again, it is face-to-face contact with parents that is critical. Your baby must see you speaking so he can see, as well as hear, how words are pronounced. As for anyone in true conversation, the baby needs to know that he is both being spoken to and heard by you. Pay close attention to his responses. If you miss his first attempts to use sound as meaning—"ba" for ball, for example—he may not try this feat again for some time.

Ask your child questions; use repetition and elaboration to encourage him. Imitate his words and phrases so he realizes that he is a participant in a dialogue. You do not need to be concerned with correction. Children strive to copy the language they hear about them. Restating their phrases or repronouncing their words without additional comment is sufficient help for them. Above all, enjoy the special dimension that language brings to your relationship with your child. Responsive games such as "Peekaboo" and "This Little Piggy" are a delight to baby and adult alike.*

THE DEVELOPMENT OF WRITTEN LANGUAGE

Thus far we have discussed the child's acquisition of oral language. We now consider the development of written language. To do so, we must return to the child's unconscious absorption of the world through his senses as the foundation for his developing language. With all his senses open to the maximum from the first days of life, the child creates a general sense of the world around him, and this global understanding of his surroundings is what enables him eventually to adapt to his "time, place, and culture,"

---

*See Lise Eliot, *What's Going On In There,* pp. 351–90.

including his language. He begins to think about his world, and to describe his experiences of it, in words.

The richness of sensorial experience required in the development of language and intelligence helps to explain why the method of teaching foreign languages that is typical to elementary schools does not work. The child must connect with a word for water, for example, in different ways: how it looks, feels, pours, its temperature, texture, weight, what he thinks about its uses, and what mood or emotion it stirs in him—whether calm and placid, as in a pond of water; ageless and timeless, as in the rolling surf; or violent and uncertain, as in an ocean storm. Only through such experiences can he fully grasp the richness contained in the word "water" and use it in the meaningful, creative, and unique ways that represent good language. He cannot achieve this level of fluency if he is merely presented with an abstract list of foreign words, with definitions and rules of grammar to memorize.

We have introduced the infant to oral language from the beginning of life. We also want to lay the foundation for written language as soon as possible. At first the sensorial basis of language requires that the infant experience real objects: his mother's face and breast, and the baby's own hands and feet. Within weeks, we help him to begin the journey to symbolic representation by introducing small replicas of real objects—a stuffed animal or doll that portrays realistic facial features and balanced bodily proportions, or a mobile of butterflies or birds that reflects the child's experience with them in the real world.

When the child is approximately eighteen months old and his hands and fingers are sufficiently developed through discovering the real items of his environment (see Chapter 4), we can give him miniature objects to explore: pots and pans, kitchen utensils, tools, domestic animals, birds, fruits, vegetables, and so forth. A small basket of three or more of these items belonging to one category can be placed on the child's toy shelf. Introduce a small basket by naming each one of its objects and lining them up left to right on the child's table or on a rug. From time to time, play a naming game with your child, naming an object for him a number of times, and eventually asking him for the object by name. After he has a good deal of experience, and when you are reasonably certain your child knows the answers, you can ask for the identification of an object by saying, "What is this?" This latter question represents a test of the child's knowledge. Therefore, it is introduced only after repeating the first two steps many, many times—both of which involve your naming of the object for him.

Children vary enormously in their capacity for linguistic memory. Repetition over many days or weeks, even months, is the key to helping them develop in this area. The important point to remember is that you are engaged in playing a game with your child, not in giving him a "lesson." If it is fun for you both, it is a productive activity. If it is boring or frustrating for either of you, something is amiss. Instead of a short and sweet five minutes of play with your child, perhaps you are reverting to the much longer "teaching episodes" common in your own elementary school days, thus boring your child. Or, if you are overanxious or overcontrolling in "teaching" your child, then *you* are not fascinated with the process of learning for its own sake. Hence you are the one who becomes frustrated.

After your child is familiar with a basket of objects—different kinds of dogs, for example—you can match them to a set of cards depicting the breeds they represent. In the beginning try to find cards that duplicate the entire animal—the collie rather than just the collie's head, for example. Later, you can use cards that are similar but not exact, thus showing only a portion or a different size of the animal. Cards that are similar (as opposed to exact) require the recalling of more information by the child, and in essence represent the more advanced ability of generalizing.

Finally, you can play a game with your child using the cards only. He must now remember even more information, demonstrating that he is capable of the symbolic act of pictorial representation in isolation.

We want to introduce the child to the importance of books from the very beginning. Have books for the child under six years old that are based on reality, rather than fantasy. The young child needs to explore the real world before he can appreciate a fantasy world created by adults—a world where rabbits talk and wear clothes and go to school, or where lost children fly through the sky at night or pirates look for lost treasure. The child's first books should be of durable quality with pages made of cardboard strength. Keep only a few at a time in a small basket by his bedroom chair. He can also have little baskets of two or three books in other designated places in the house—by a child-size rocking chair in the living room, for example. Never mix books with toys, however. Books are not to manipulate or experiment with in the way that toys are. We teach children from the beginning to handle books with care, turning the pages from the top. Again the number of books available should be limited: four is the maximum for a child two years old. The child's favorite book of the moment can remain out, but rotate other books from a supply in the closet.

In addition to the books freely accessible to your child, keep a supply of books of good literature and beautiful illustrations in a closed cupboard or closet shelf. These are books for you to read out loud to your child each evening before bed or at a special time during the day. As with the books freely available to the child, these quality-produced books also reflect reality and introduce him to a further knowledge of his world. It does not matter if the child understands all that you read to him. In fact, no child comprehends on our adult level, even when he is familiar with the words used and the people, objects, and actions described.

What is important at this stage is the child's absorption of good language and expressive thought.

If your child is able to make an appropriate choice, you can let him select the nightly book for reading from among two or three in your closet supply. However, if your child is one of those children who always want to control, we would suggest that, from the start, you be the one who makes the selection. The emotional interaction between your child and you is the most memorable aspect of your reading time together. It is important that you make this experience enjoyable for you as well as your child. Choose books that you find interesting. Your child is not likely to grow up loving reading if he associates it with parental boredom or an obligatory parental duty. Determine ahead of time how long you are going to read, and stay with that schedule. Do not fall into the "one more page" or "one more story" syndrome that typically represents the child's attempts to forestall the bedtime hour and leads to tired parents much in need of their own evening of relaxation.

Just as essential as reading to your child, he must see you reading for your own pleasure. Children tend to value whatever their parents value. If they never see you reading, they will know that books are not really important in your life, no matter what you may say to them. It is not difficult to read in front of your child in the first months because he stays in one place, and is easily self-occupied with a mobile or rattle. Before long the child becomes mobile, however, and can move rapidly about the house. When this time comes, it is a good idea to set aside a designated time for your own daytime reading. During this time it is necessary to make a conscious decision not to respond to the child, unless, of course, he is getting himself into a dangerous situation. One mother we know chose the first fifteen minutes shortly after her eighteen-month-old child was up from his nap for her reading time. She would sit quietly and read to herself for this period, deflecting his requests for attention. She would simply explain, "I am reading now. I can help you when I am finished." She said that at first this was not always easy for her to do. However, she persisted because she knew how important it was for her son to understand the value of reading. In addition, this was a time when he was well rested and could handle a few minutes without her attention. Indeed by the time her son was two years old he had figured out, all on his own, that he too could look at a book by himself during this "reading time."

As you seek to aid your child's development in oral and written language, it is helpful to remember that children vary tremendously in their path to developing good language and the joy of using language well. One child may have precocious language skills from his beginning months. Another does not. Yet, both may develop into thoughtful, expressive children who write and read well by their early elementary school years. For example, compare the following anecdotes about Tommy and David. One day when Tommy was twenty-three months old, he was playing in his room during naptime instead of staying in his bed to rest or sleep. His mother opened his door and said, "Tommy, where should you be?" He answered with a twinkle in his eye, "In the kitchen baking?" This same child at twenty-one months admonished his mother for letting him cry in his room for ten minutes after an altercation: "When Tommy crying you need come Mama!" Again, at the breakfast table one Sunday morning, Tommy's father picked up the paper to read. When his mother told Tommy that he needed to finish his cereal, he responded, "No Mama, I'm very busy with my reading" and, mimicking his father, he looked intently at the paper, too. He was then twenty-seven months old.

David, on the other hand, was a quiet, apparently thoughtful child who was not inclined to answer his mother often with words. She could see, however, that he put order into his actions.

For example, while playing with two scoopers in his sandbox, he would use both hands, pouring from one scooper to the other with great care and trying hard not to spill any sand. Because of such demonstrations of order in his actions, his mother expected that there must be order in his thoughts. In addition, this was not a child who customarily would tear randomly about the house or, when his mother bent down to talk to him, avert his face and eyes with no sign of response or recognition, and go running off. Therefore, she was not worried about him. True to form, David was not inclined to talk to his teacher, Mrs. Eggerding, either, when he entered the Young Children's Community at age eighteen months. Finally, one day when he was two years old, he was sitting next to her during circle time. He said very quietly, "I like your shoes, Eg." Then he looked quickly away with a shy expression, as if to say, "Oh dear, I let her know that I can talk!"

Both Tommy and David have parents who read to them faithfully and who enjoy reading themselves. There is order in their homes and structure in their daily lives. They have appropriate toys and there is time and space for imaginative play. The television is never on when they are awake, and their parents communicate directly and often with them, speaking slowly and listening carefully. With such wise support from loving and dedicated parents, both of these boys, despite their differences in verbal output in their first years, are well on their way to good language development.

MUSIC AND ART

There are other areas of symbolic language and self-expression besides the written word that are important to introduce to the infant. Music, too, is a form of human communication of mood and message. Music has been part of human tradition since the drumbeats of early humans signaled the beginning of a hunt, a time of celebration, or a danger that was near. The oral traditions of ballad, song, hymn, and poetry represent one of the richest areas of our cultural heritage. Babies love to hear their parents sing to them. The mother's humming or singing of a lullaby is especially soothing to her infant because, as we have learned, he knows her voice from before birth. A nightly song at bedtime is a comforting way to put a child to sleep at any age. How well you sing is not the essential factor. Your presence and involvement in the making of music is what counts. Children can see how vocal sounds are formed, and the repetition and alliteration in song and ballad enables them to develop their capacity for memorization.

You can also play quality musical tapes for your baby. We know that a baby's absorbent mind takes in whatever he hears, indiscriminately. Therefore, as in literature, it is important to introduce him to only the best of our cultural heritage. The classical music of Bach and Mozart with their formal structure and recurring musical themes and patterns, are especially helpful to young children who are in the process of forming order within their own minds. However, it is best not to turn any kind of music into background noise in your home. Set aside a special time for listening to music during the day when you and your child are both ready for a quiet time or involved in an activity that does not require concentrated effort.

If you play a musical instrument, play it for your child. Modeling a love of music is as important for your child as letting him witness your love of books. Children will pick up more knowledge than you imagine. One mother told us that she announced the musical pieces and their composers that she was going to play as she completed her piano practice after lunchtime each day. Her daughter had rested on a blanket under the piano during this period since she was two and a half years old. One day when her daughter was four years old, she forgot her customary announcement of musical selection and began to play Sonata

Number Eight by Prokofiev with no mention of piece or composer. Her daughter drew near to her under the piano and looking up to her said, "More Prokofiev, Mommy?"

When you choose your child's books, be certain to look for ones about composers and the history of music and musical instruments as well. There are many quality books for children on these topics that you both can enjoy in your bedtime reading together. Musical instruments are also a good topic for the language objects and cards described earlier.

Rattles are usually the first thing babies use to experiment with producing sound and rhythm by their own efforts. Even a newborn of seven or eight weeks can grasp and shake the tiny silver rattles made for this age. Of course, a newborn is not at a stage of development when he can initiate sound on purpose. Instead, his little eyes pop open every time his arm and hand movements produce sound with the rattle, as if to say, "What was that? What was that?" By age eight months, the baby enjoys shaking a small gourd and, by twelve months, making sounds by clapping his hands. At approximately eighteen months, he likes to tap a simple native hand drum, wind his own music box, and even use a xylophone. Do not use these as toys, however, but only as musical instruments. Bring them out at special times when you are able to participate with your child. Choose instruments that make real musical notes and not the tinny sounds made by so many toy items manufactured for children's use. For example, the quality in music boxes for children varies widely. And, above all, you do not need to add pressure to your daily schedule by joining the "baby rhythm" or "music" classes so popular today. Everything helpful to the babies' development in music and rhythm, as in other areas of their self-formation, is readily accomplished in the more relaxed and natural setting of a home or homelike environment.

Montessori classrooms follow the same pattern in introducing children to the language of music, as in presenting them with spoken language. First, the sound is identified. Next, a symbol is given for it. Finally, sound and symbol are combined. Thus two sets of musical bells of pure tonal quality are played separately, matching bell to bell, and then by scale. In this way a three-year-old develops his ear for pitch. Eventually, he is introduced to the name "middle C," and so forth, for each bell in the entire musical scale. Finally, he is introduced to the representations of these sounds by musical notes and their placement on a musical staff. These last materials are in concrete form so that children can manipulate them.

The Montessori musical materials are integrated into the classroom environments, both primary and elementary, and available to the children at all times. Therefore, the child is able to discover reading and writing of music independently, just as he did the reading of books. Indeed, Montessori said that the reading of music could occur as naturally for children as their discovery of the connection of oral to written language in literature. Just as the primary school children enjoy writing their own stories before they can read books, so do many elementary school children compose their own songs before they can readily read the music written by others. The elementary school classroom is also where the children most enjoy discovering the music of other cultures and historical time periods.

Art represents another important area of symbolic language and self-expression to introduce to the baby. Art, as well as music, has been part of human tradition from our earliest days. Cave drawings by early humans depicting the hunting of animals represent the first human communication through symbolic drawings. The first written languages portrayed ideas through pictorial symbols, as in Egyptian hieroglyphics. Eventually, the Phoenicians discovered that by making a small sign for each sound in a word, they could eliminate the confusion of using pictures of things and actions, thereby giving us our alphabet in twenty-six characters. However, we still illustrate these words produced with the alphabet, for our books and literature, with drawings and paintings. Furthermore, throughout human culture, painting and drawing unaccompanied by text have remained a very special language through which to express ourselves and communicate with others.

Recognizing the possibility for the child to convey ideas through drawing before he is capable of writing, Montessori aided the development of this skill. By giving opportunities for the coordination of the thumb and forefinger, she enabled children to hold a pencil or paintbrush properly, often by the age of eighteen to twenty months. These first pictures by children are often circular "scribbles," yet by three years old, children will explain that they have made "a tree" or "a house."

Because in the Montessori classroom, art materials are available to the children at all times, it is natural for them to add illustrations to their writing from their first days. Thus children of four years old, who make a story with the Moveable Alphabet* because they cannot yet write, draw a picture to illustrate their story. Through this picture they are able to communicate far more content and detail than they are yet capable of through their "writing" with the letters of the Moveable Alphabet. Their artwork then, by helping them to develop their ability to communicate abstract thought, aids the development of their intelligence. Expressing their thoughts through artwork becomes natural to them, and they continue to illustrate their stories spontaneously after they are capable of writing them in a fluid cursive hand. Indeed the creativity of the children in the Montessori elementary school classrooms as they illustrate their research reports, using not only graphic art but three-dimensional repre-

---

*The Moveable Alphabet is a set of cut-out cardboard letters in cursive form that the children use to make into words by analyzing their sounds and then spelling them phonetically. Thus they can compose their own stories, although they cannot read or write.

sentations of dioramas, sculpture, or models of wood or metal, helps to explain the energy and active engagement readily apparent to visitors to a Montessori environment.

Although artistic expression, just as musical expression, is natural to human beings, environment matters. Parents have a key role to play in their child's production skills and appreciation of art. Just as in music, we want to introduce the infant to the best of our cultural heritage, so in helping the child develop this appreciation, it is important not to bombard the baby with too many artistic images, even as we limit the number of books available to him and do not keep music constantly playing in the background. It is helpful, however, to choose one or two prints of good paintings, or even an original watercolor or photograph, to hang at a low height on the wall of the baby's bedroom. Hang the picture low enough for the baby to see readily but not so low that he can reach to pull it down. Hopefully, there are other works of art on the walls of other rooms in the house for the child to discover. Our own appreciation of art is central, both as a model and in providing opportunities for museum outings appropriate to the child's age and interest level. In addition, parents can include biographies of artists and illustrated books of their works, in the selections for bedtime reading with their child. When your child is two and one-half to three years old, you can have a basket of language cards just with paintings, and teach him their names: Renoir's *Two Girls at the Piano* or *Child in White*, and so forth.

In helping children to produce their own art, parents need to make materials available that match the development of the child's hand and ability to organize a simple activity. We recommend that when your child is approximately two and one-half years old and has developed sufficient thumb and forefinger dexterity, you provide a tray with one colored pencil and a small piece of white paper for drawing. You can cut ten-by-twelve-inch paper in half, or even quarters, and keep a supply for drawing and later for painting as well. Colored pencils have several advantages over other art materials: unlike markers, they can result in light or dark color, depending on the pressure used, and thereby help the child become aware of hand control. Unlike crayons, they maintain a finer point and are easily sharpened if the point does become too blunt and ineffective. Colored pencils are also thin enough for the child's small hand, while many crayons are not. You can gradually add other art activities: painting (at first with one primary color—red, blue, or yellow only), drawing with white chalk on a small chalkboard, modeling potter's clay, cutting and pasting (use scissors of good quality that really cut), stringing beads, sewing yarn on pieces of cardboard, and so forth.

Just as with the practical-life activities, all art activities are organized on trays or in baskets and are supervised by the parents. A presentation in the use of materials is always given first, and they are used with care at all times. This means that if a pencil or piece of clay ends up in the child's mouth, you need to take it away and stop the activity until another day. Because the parents' attention is required, many mothers find that the child's small table and chair in the corner of the kitchen is a good place for art projects. A kitchen cupboard or closet shelf then becomes a natural place to store the child's art materials. In addition to the basket or tray for a specific activity, it is a good idea to use an acrylic board or a piece of plain cardboard to guard the surface of the child's table. We also suggest a special apron for art activities instead of the apron used for food preparation or housework. As in these other activities, the art apron is not so much protection for the child's clothing as part of the organizing process and serves as a reminder to the child that he is undertaking a special activity.

Above all, it is essential to avoid the vast number of structured "art" materials and projects commercially produced for children. As children get older, this becomes increasingly difficult for parents. After the age of three or four years, children are attracted by "Paint by Number" kits, coloring books, and prescribed models of all sorts, because these do not require the same effort as creating their own ideas for expression through art activities. However, it is experience with this unique inner energy for producing ideas and skill of self-expression that we want the child to have. Instead of buying various kits and premanufactured models to put together, give your child a "making box" for creating his own art projects. Put all manner of items in it with which to make things: empty spools of thread, scraps of material and paper, small scraps of wood, pipe cleaners, bits of wire and string—anything from about the house that with a little imagination could be used for creating something. Add to it often, either from items at home or from a hobby shop. Save a full set of colored pencils and complete watercolor sets until your child is five years old or over. In this way, he will have plenty of time to experiment with shading and mixing of colors before having to use the results of someone else's color palette.

We would also caution against art lessons for young children. What they need instead is the opportunity to participate in the special language of self-expression that artistic endeavor on their own makes possible. There is plenty of time after they have begun elementary school for children to learn the formal techniques of drawing, painting, and sculpting. What they need as young children is parents who serve as good models and access to appropriate materials. Parents need to respect their children's original efforts in art and help them to appreciate the cultural heritage given to us by the best painters, sculptors, and architects of human history.

TOYS AND IMAGINATIVE PLAY

So far, we have talked about communication in human language through our oral, written, and artistic traditions. This combination of traditions gives us a rich heritage of ways to think and learn about our world, and to express ourselves in literature, music, and art. We have discussed that the base of these traditions is a sensorial experience of the real world and that indeed all development for human beings comes from an intense interaction with the things of the environment. We have traced the ways in which we help the infant to have a rich sensorial understanding of his world through hearing and seeing, touching and feeling—first, with mobiles and rattles to develop the eye and the hand, then with real objects followed by their representation in miniature, then with objects matched with pictures, and, finally, by reference to pictures alone.

There is also a secondary path we use to give sensorial symbols of the world to the infant. He uses these symbols too for manipulation and the creation of language and thought. We are referring to traditional toys whose purpose from the adult's point of view is play. In reality, of course, all objects that we give to very young children are for play. Whether we call their activity play or work, young children are always involved in exploring and discovering whatever is around them and using this means to build their own minds.

The selection of toys we make available to our children is as important as what we choose for any other area of their environment. To select wisely, we need to go back to our initial purpose in helping the child in his self-formation. All loving parents want to raise a child to whom the world makes sense, who can think about that world wisely and who loves and respects himself and others. By showing care in the toys you choose for your child, you are showing him that he is important to you. You are sharing what is beautiful and meaningful to you in life. You thereby help your child in turn to look for beauty and logic in the world around him. Parents sometimes forget in the stress of daily living how magnificent, inspiring, and magical the real world actually is to them. Making conscious decisions in what we make available to our infants and young children in every area of life can help us to recapture that awe and appreciation.

We know that infants at birth have an absorbent mind, rather than a reasoning mind. They are not yet capable of abstract thought and the imagination that follows from it. Young children use the first six years of life to gradually develop their potential for these sophisticated and uniquely human capabilities. All objects based on reality, whether man-made or not, are useful to them in this process. A problem occurs for them, however, when the objects given to them for play portray fantasy, or give false information about the world—such as fantasy creatures like "cookie monsters" or a teddy bear that is red. Unfortunately, this difficulty is likely to increase for young children as affluence accrues in the society at large. A walk through a modern toy store gives a ready picture of the magnitude of this obstacle for them.

If the child cannot develop a sound foundation for a reasoning mind, one that can think productively about things, taking in ideas and manipulating these ideas in his mind, by the age of six years, he is handicapped in developing his powers of imagination and abstraction in his elementary school years. Montessori observed that it is between the ages of six and twelve years that children develop two major gifts of human self-formation: reason and imagination. The elementary school child uses these gifts to become an independent social being, capable of dealing with the feelings of self and others. A problem occurs for elementary school children when they spend a large portion of their time with inanimate objects such as computers and electronic games and toys. These objects do not relate back to them with feelings as real beings do. They can treat these objects however they like. No consideration is required. There is no feedback on what it takes to develop caring and responsiveness, as there is when a child interacts with another human being. These objects all tend to replace real interaction between family members and friends, and thus they foster a base for self-centeredness.

Children under three years of age can be tricked into loving something that is not going to love back. Paula remembers the day a neighbor's child deliberately pricked her rubber baby doll in the stomach with a diaper pin, and that it was only then that she realized for the first time that her beloved doll could not actually feel as she could feel. This evolvement to loving only real people and other beings, not material objects, is a natural development inherent in human beings. What is most noble in the human species is our ability to love and care for someone or some creature other than ourselves and thus to embrace the whole of creation. This is a long process of discovery, however, and it requires many experiences of reality. Hence, young children learn that to earn their affection they must not pull the family dog's ears and tail or harass an older sibling.

As for our present culture, fads in toys have come and gone over recent years. The disturbing factors are the direction of these fads and the response of parents to them. Manufacturers of toys, by and large, are self-serving. They have to create a desire in the child (or the adult) for a particular toy. If children needed this toy, manufacturers would not have to convince anyone of its necessity. The problem for the toy industry begins with the fact that children require only a few traditional toys (a doll, stuffed animal, and blocks, for example) to build a strong base for imaginative play. To induce more purchases, toy designers strive to embellish these basic toys. The doll not only talks back, it does what the child tells it to do. The stuffed dog not only barks, it obeys the child's voice commands. There are even toys programmed to a particular child's voice or custom-made to mirror an individual child's unique physical appearance. Adults are intrigued by these elaborations. However, the reality is that they are not sufficiently open ended to enhance the child's ongoing imaginative play.

Parents' response to the plethora of modern toys is also disturbing. Parents in the early half of the twentieth century were primarily concerned with the development of character in their children. They wanted to be certain that their children were ready to cope with adversity, for it was surely coming to them one day whether in personal or national life. The development of character involves self-discipline and often sacrifice of one's own desires for the good of self and others. Montessori education, developed in this historical period, reflects this emphasis on the formation of the child's character. However, parents today are more likely to say their primary wish for their children is that they be happy. In pursuit of this goal they indulge their children, often unconsciously, to a degree that is startling to previous generations. All parents need to remember that true happiness comes through having character and discipline, and living a life of meaningful contribution—not by having and doing whatever you wish.

One way of testing your own response to the cultural messages of today is to determine if you have to provide a "big toy bonanza" at Christmas or birthdays in order not to feel like a "grinch," or if you habitually take weekend trips to the toy store. It is impossible for either child or parent to take care of the resulting superfluity of toys, and soon the house is overrun with them. As one frustrated mother of a two-year-old and a four-year-old said to us, "My children's toys are the bane of my existence!"

As parents and grandparents, we think that we are showing children that we love them by giving them things. In fact such practice, in and of itself, may send them the wrong message. Children may conclude that if people give you things, they love you. If receiving things tells you that you are loved, the next logical step is to measure self-worth by what you have, not by what you are. The reality is that very young children can only truly love one doll, one stuffed animal, and a few toys at a time. This experience provides a basis for adult life where one must learn to cherish one spouse, one family, one life, instead of fantasizing that it is possible to "have it all."

What kind of toys can parents select for their young child that are going to serve as an aid, rather than an obstacle, to his best development? We want any object that we give to the child under the age of three for independent play to enhance our ultimate goal: connection with others and an understanding of his world. We want, then, to avoid toys that represent the fantasy of an adult's mind, instead of building the creative capacities of the child's mind. Unfortunately, toy stores are filled with such items for children: plastic guitars that bear no resemblance to real guitars either by appearance or sound, or "busy boxes" for supposed manipulation by the child but that have unrelated knobs, rotary wheels, buttons to push, bells that ring, and so forth—items you have at home for many days after purchase before you realize that they are supposed to represent a train or a firehouse. Giving children such objects (sometimes even billed as "educational toys") is like giving candy for the child's physical sustenance instead of nutritional food. They have no lasting benefit because they merely entertain and do not involve thinking on the child's part.

Cars and trucks fall into the same category for the child under three years old. He can imitate random sounds and motions with them, hence he makes them go round and round, making "zoom, zoom" noises, but such actions are not helping the child to develop internal order from his world. A teddy bear on the other hand relates to a real animal with a life of its own, capable of feelings and reactions. A cuddly doll represents real beings that can love back. The young child uses it to mimic the actions of those about him: to bathe, to put to sleep, to feed, and to dress and undress repeatedly. This repetitive "play" develops skills for feeding and dressing himself and leads him to further identify with the doll as a symbol of self or other family members.

However, to aid the child's eventual ability to make up a scenario and later to create a plot and story line, with dolls and stuffed animals, the child needs activities that require in-depth thinking. The Montessori activities of practical life described in Chapter 6 provide just such experiences. Cutting carrots requires planning an action that relates to the sequential: that is, it has a beginning, middle, and end, as in a story plot. The child needs to develop in his mind a basis for a story line by acting in reality and figuring out sequentially controlled movements. Thus the practical-life activities, although they involve real experiences with real materials in the real world, have a key role in developing the future imaginative play of the child.

Look for toys for the child under three years old that help him distinguish the real from the unreal, look for order in the world, and understand categories and process. A dollhouse, for example, provides hours of creative play for children over three years old. However, it is also intriguing to children at eighteen months, if you show them how to sort furniture by rooms: beds in the bedroom, table and chairs in the dining room, couch in the living room, and so forth. Realistic models of animals that live today, and that therefore the child can see in real life, provide many opportunities for the young child's play. If you separate them into baskets of jungle animals and domestic animals; all different breeds of dogs; a family of mother, father, and baby of one type of animal; animals that live in North America; animals that live only in the desert; and so forth, you make possible further discoveries for your child by providing keys to the order in his world. When you first show a basket of animals to your child, you can line them up carefully and name each one, using the experience as a language opportunity. Rotate these baskets of animals, depending on your child's interest. You want repetition but be sensitive to when your child might enjoy further knowledge.

Even cars and trucks or blocks are beneficial for children

fifteen months to three years old, if you give some direction and purpose to the activity. Arrange a basket of three identical objects that vary only in color (begin with the primary colors: red, blue, and yellow). Line them up carefully and name the object and its color: "blue car, red car, yellow car." Play a game with your child, naming the cars, and eventually asking for them by name. This is a game where your only goal is sharing your knowledge of the world with your child. In another basket you can put three vehicles of the same color and name them for your child: "car, truck, bus." In another you can subcategorize different types of trucks: a dump truck, fire truck, and tow truck.

Again your only purpose is to give a key to your child for discovering his world. Hence, you can say to your child, "Oh, look there is the tow truck," not "What is this?" As we have mentioned, "What is this?" represents a test of knowledge, not a gift of knowledge from parent to child. Adults are indoctrinated with "testing" from their own school days in regular education. Such testing is entirely inappropriate for young children. Always supply the name for an object yourself: "There is the tow truck" or "Where is the tow truck?" You are making activities with inanimate objects into meaningful experiences for your child by giving him the language for his world. In this way you make possible his further discoveries and you have the joy of sharing your experience of life. Animals share by instinct the preordained skills necessary for the survival of their kind. Human knowledge is different because it must reflect the "time, place, and culture" in which we live. We have to make a conscious effort to give knowledge to our children through language. The principles guiding the process by which we can best do this are to proceed from simple to complex, to use repetition, and to "teach" in short intervals of less than five or ten minutes only.

Wooden blocks are a time-honored toy we can use both to extend the child's knowledge and to encourage him to make discoveries on his own. Whenever possible choose items of wood rather than plastic for young children. Wood offers a diversity of experiences to children: the beautiful detail of its different grains, whether oak or maple; a variety of smells, as in pine or birch; the differing weights of teak versus aspen; and a range of sounds when different woods are struck or tapped. Further, wooden products teach the child respect for the natural world. They must be handled with care if they are to last over time. Wood is a natural product that the world has always offered and hopefully always will. Children need these experiences with objects from the living earth. They serve as reminders of our human responsibilities to the preservation and wise management of the natural world. Plastic, on the other hand, is a man-made product that is virtually indestructible, requiring no special care. Nor does it offer a variety of sensorial experiences to the child. In addition, as human beings constantly develop new materials and technologies, it is unlikely to be part of the world forever.

Set up one basket with an assortment of blocks for general exploration and play. You can arrange a second basket with one of each different shape: prism, cylinder, cone, and so forth. Name and line them up in an orderly fashion. In yet another basket, put two of each shape. Take a triangular prism out and say, "I am going to find the other triangular prism." Line all the shapes up together, two by two. Select just one shape of block, only the prisms, for example. Put six of them in a basket and use them to make a tower or other form.

Even young children can use wooden blocks to create constructions on their own. They need little input from us for this activity. Let them create and build as they choose. However, if you wish, when you pass by, you can say casually, "May I have a turn?" Put out an idea by demonstration, but then it is probably best to move on. Your goal is simply to make your child's play more interesting with options he would lack the knowledge or skill to find on his own. You want to be very careful not to control or force.

There is a tremendous variation in children. Therefore, how much help is just the right amount, not too much or too little, varies tremendously. Creative observation of your child is essential from birth onward. This is the only way to discover who your unique child is and how to adjust yourself to his uniqueness. You have to know your child at the deepest level in order to make the right moves with him, ones that will help and support but not interfere, in both play and work.

Finally, there are toys with a built-in purpose that you can make or purchase for your child from infancy onward. These toys aid specific aspects of the child's self-formation. We discussed a few of these toys that facilitate the child's hand and brain development in Chapter 4. Be very careful in your selection. As we have discussed, a garish plastic puzzle or "busy box" is a poor choice. It might beep when the child punches a knob and a bell might ring when he or she turns a "wheel," but it makes no sense. The child is interested in cause and effect but cannot see it happening here. The bell is hidden from view. There is no reason for the reaction or outcome from his movements. This is mindless "entertainment."

Think instead of the wooden ball that the child drops into a box through a hole in a sliding lid. Such a toy is designed so that the child can begin to fathom exactly what is happening. He can answer his own questions: where did the ball go? what did it hit when it made that sound? why does the lid slide? why won't the lid come off? Meanwhile, he is practicing ever more precise hand movements and sending information to his brain. He grasps the ball and feels its shape and temperature. He aims for the hole in the lid, releases the ball, and hears the sound as it hits the floor of the box. He grasps the knob on the lid, experiencing how it feels as he does so. He moves his arm to the side to open the lid. He releases the knob and grasps the ball. This toy gives knowledge worth learning: namely, reality does not change.

Conversely, what was the point of getting to know about the "busy box train"?—or, for that matter, about fantastic space creatures or unrealistic animals or strange people that are the creations of adults. Even older children re-create the adult's scenario when playing with such toys instead of using their own imaginations. Give young children wooden blocks and replicas of real people and animals so that they are free to create their own stories. When this is done, the imitation and "pretend play" of the very young child gradually evolves into the developed imaginative play of the six-year-old. In such play, children can take a block and imagine that it is a boat. They are able to do this at this older age because they can now hold an image of a boat in their mind. This is why you do not see six-year-olds running around with a boat, chanting "zoom, zoom." Instead, six-year-olds create a place for the boat to dock. They design a harbor and work out a story line. It is at this time that the dollhouse becomes a true vehicle for imaginative play.

However, beware of the too-defined toy for elementary school children: the seventy-nine-dollar Pet Grooming Station for a toy dog, and so on. When compared with the child's caring for his own pet with real supplies, his time with this toy is a meaningless experience. It is important to allow the child to create his own tools for imaginative play. He needs boxes, sheets, pillows, sticks, and household items like paper-towel rolls, rubber bands, and string. We take away the opportunity for children to create for themselves when we give them confining toys and activities. What we have done in our culture is replace the child's creativity with products of a designer's creativity. Children lose confidence in their ability to come up with their own designs because they compare them to the adult's and they do not feel that theirs are as good. There are LEGO sets, for example, to make exact items such as an airplane or space station. The child follows precise directions, much as if he were told how to put together a puzzle. It is a one-time experience for the child. Once he finishes the product, the activity is over. Worst of all, if a single piece happens to get lost in the dismantling that follows, the toy becomes meaningless. The remaining pieces are tossed into a pile of other incomplete sets.

Whether in kits to assemble or as finished products, these fully designed toys exist because we have such abundance, and plastic is so cheap and malleable. We use them to entertain our children when what they need is more experience in creating activities for themselves. The child is attracted to these defined toys because they are designed to catch the undeveloped mind. He begs for them from us and too often we relent, even though we recognize that the child cannot know what is best for himself. Lynn is reminded of the time that she was playing a children's musical tape in preparation for demonstrating what *not* to expose children to, for our parent child course. The tape was an example of the tinny-sounding music and banal lyrics often produced for children's consumption. Her seven-year-old daughter overheard it and said, "I like that music! I hope you will give it to me!"

We cannot protect our children from life, but we can prepare them for life. We can teach our children to respect money and to choose their belongings and possessions with care. How much we can afford is not the issue. The issue is wastefulness and lack of thought about what we are given. Affluence implies responsibility and an understanding that surplus is for sharing with those who are less fortunate.

Of course it will do little good if you provide your child with the toys and materials that facilitate creative play (rather than mere entertainment) if there is no time or space for it. Do not schedule activities, even good ones, for your child every day. A day at home and in the yard is full of adventure for a very young child. Even after the child is in elementary school, one or two scheduled activities a week are sufficient. More than this leaves the child no time of his own for reflection and imaginative thought. Design the child's bedroom or another room in the house with quiet play in mind. Create small spaces within other rooms of the house: quiet nooks in a corner with a basket of blocks or a few stuffed animals, or behind a sofa with a small rocker and a basket of three or four books beside it.

Parents invariably tell us that it is the gifts given by others that make it difficult for them to limit their children's toys. One parent described a backhoe big enough for her four-year-old daughter to ride on, given to her as a birthday present by doting grandparents. There are three options for inappropriate or excessive gifts from grandparents. You can put them in storage, give them away, or take them to the grandparents' house for use on visits there. Give the Michael Olaf catalogue to your parents (or other family members) and tactfully mention that you hope they will use it for their gift selections. In addition to offering only items that are appropriate for young children, this catalogue also briefly describes the child's development at each age. It is therefore helpful in selecting presents from other sources as well. Because your parents may wonder if their grandchild really will find a cleaning or baking set an exciting gift, photograph him happily using these presents and send the picture to them. Explain to your parents that the purpose in giving only one beautiful, high-quality stuffed animal for a Christmas or birthday gift is to encourage imaginative play. When your child is three years old, he will have several of these beloved animals, and you can describe his creative play with them to his grandparents. If all else fails, bring out the grandparents' superfluous presents when they come to visit, explaining that you save them for these special occasions. When they leave, you can put them away again for the next visit. As one parent wisely said to us, " 'When in Rome do as the Romans do,' and when the 'Romans' come to visit, you also 'do as the Romans do'!"

As we help our children along the path to oral and written language, artistic expression, a fully developed imagination, and symbolic play, it is important to remember that it is language that allows us to convey our joy in life. This is the greatest gift that we can give to our children. Through language we share our knowledge of the world and how exciting that world is. We communicate what we care about and what we find interesting and of value in every area of life, whether it be history, science, mathematics, artistic expression, religion, or any other academic or cultural subject. Language is the basis of our intelligence and our civilization. It is the means whereby we share ourselves and our accumulated wisdom with future generations.

NINE

The Developing Will

Of all the major areas of the infant's self-formation—coordinated movement, independence, language and the will—it is the will that is least supported or understood in our present society. Yet, we know that in order to have confidence in ourselves, we need to have control of ourselves. This control extends to our mental lives as well as our physical acts. The child must learn discipline of thought, even as she learns discipline of action.

Civilized societies have always relied upon the discipline of their citizens. Discipline, obedience, and self-control all begin in childhood. Children must develop obedience to legitimate authority as a foundation for adult understanding and acceptance of the expectations of the civilization in which they are born. These expectations range from the simple and straightforward to the deepest commitments of human community: from the fact that the red light means stop and the green light means go, to concern for others and the rule of law, and respect for human freedom and the pursuit of happiness.

This compliance of children with society's "rules of the road," as it were—as well as its deepest values—in no way implies that we should raise children to become complacent and dependent adults. All of our discussion so far reveals that Montessori education supports just the opposite approach to human beings from their birth. Montessori's personal experience with fascism, Nazism, and communism convinced her of the absolute necessity for freedom of thought in all societies. Rigid dogma, whether political or religious, enslaves human beings and inevitably leads to the destruction and decline of human progress. It is because of Montessori's insistence on fostering the ability to think for oneself—and the success of her educational approach in doing so—that both Mussolini and Hitler ordered all Montessori schools in their respective regimes closed in the 1930s. Montessori schools were the only secular educational institutions so designated.

How do we raise children who are in control of self, obedient to adult authority, and who yet grow up to think for themselves? How do we lead them from the "stubborn willfulness" of the child under three years old to the established will and courage required to stay the course in the challenging tasks of adult life? Specifically, how do we help young children in their earliest years of life to develop a capacity for choosing a positive task and then keeping themselves focused on it, oblivious to outer distractions and unmindful of those who would deter them?

Just as the formation of the child's coordinated movement, independence, and language follows from a process of self-formation, so Montessori considered the developing of the child's will to be the result of gradual mental development. The historical concept of "breaking the child's will," still adhered to by many in the first half of the twentieth century, is therefore anathema in Montessori education. It makes no more sense to speak of breaking the child's will than to advocate breaking the child's potential for language development, purposefully thwarting the child's establishment of independence, or deliberately denying the child opportunities to build coordinated movement. Children are not born with a developed will, any more than they are born with the other areas of mature formation. They must develop their will by deliberate effort from their birth. It is a long process, and they require very specific help from their parents and from their environment at each step along the way. If a child does not get this help, her will does not develop. Throughout her childhood she remains driven by her impulses and her whims of the moment. In adulthood she is destined to live a chaotic life devoid of constancy, sense of security, and trust in self and others.

As in other areas of self-construction, our ability to help the child in developing her will depends upon our understanding of the stages of the child's formation. The initial response required for every area of the child's self-formation, including the development of will, is attention to the environment. The child selects a portion of the environment to attend to and excludes all others. In other words, she directs her attention and limits it by a control of self. As we learned in Chapter 2, the infant is born with the potential for such focus. We foster its development by creating an environment favorable to it. In the beginning, this means an environment where the infant is encouraged to concentrate on one stimulus at a time. Hence when the mother is nursing the newborn, she does so in a quiet place. The baby is then able to focus intently upon her mother's face and the process of feeding, instead of being distracted or overstimulated by her surroundings. Similarly, we hang only one mobile at a time over the child-bed, and provide the newborn with time alone to concentrate on her surroundings.

In the first eight to nine months, the baby progresses from an initial dependence on reflexive action to an ability to integrate the information that she is gleaning through this sensorial exploration of the world. Now at nine months, she can form a plan of action such as crawling across the room after a rolling ball and, to a limited extent, even restrict the impulses that interfere with that plan.

It is not until the child is eighteen months old, however, that frontal-lobe formation in her brain makes possible significant control and awareness of self and action. For the first time she is capable of inhibition in a variety of behaviors. For example, she can learn to control her bodily functions as part of toileting awareness. In the right setting, she can even develop restraint before consuming food, and so forth.

At three years old, the child's awareness of self extends to her mental life. She begins to realize that her thoughts are different from those of others. It is not until age four or five years, however, that she develops what cognitive psychologists call a "theory of mind." The child now creates her own narrative, making possible more elaborate play with well-defined, extensive roles for others: for example, a family of mother, father, child, and dog.

Finally, when the child is six years old, her brain is capable of reason and abstract thought. For the first time, she is able to control her behavior, based upon an understanding and appreciation of the desires and thoughts of others. Thus, as we have previously discussed, the dawn of reason and the dawn of the social being occur simultaneously. This slow development of abstract reasoning and of understanding social behavior has strong implications for the adult's response in aiding the child's formation of will in her first six years. It means that the child under six years old has no true understanding of why a certain behavior is inappropriate. Parents cannot give abstract reasons for self-control to their child and expect that she will comprehend them. Instead of reasoning with their child under six years old, parents have to rely on other strategies—specifically, outer control and consequences.

When the baby is very young—up to eight or nine months old—restriction of her own impulses is very primitive; parents have to constantly substitute their attention and energies for the infant's. By eighteen months, as we have learned, the child has developed a limited degree of self-awareness. The parents' role requires just as much vigilance but it shifts to a more supervisory capacity. At three years of age, the child is more completely aware that others are different from herself. Something might hurt her and still not hurt someone else, for example—and vice versa. Adult supervision must continue (although not necessarily as constantly) because the child does not have a developed reason with which to handle new encounters. She cannot reason out for herself the potential danger of a hot stove or a sharp needle, for example, and therefore, she needs protection from them.

Clearly, during the years before age six, children need adults in their lives who will substitute their energy and will for their own, for as yet children have no understanding of their existence and what it ultimately means. The adult's role is to gradually introduce the child to a universe based on order and to the limits of daily life as a finite being living within it.

The importance of a fundamental understanding of universal order cannot be exaggerated. Order in the universe, and a belief that human beings can discover it, is the foundation for all human advancement and civilization. It has freed us from the uncertainty of magical beliefs based on doctrine and dogma. It has brought us from the Middle Ages to the Enlightenment, to an age of global technology and the possibility of unimaginable freedom from human want. It is the basis of human thought, imagination, and will through its connection to sensorial fact. The infant's exploration of the real world of sensorial fact leads her eventually to the real world of abstract thought. She develops a thinking mind and the mental order required for organizing and communicating her thoughts in language. After establishing this order of mind, the creative person can rearrange her thoughts and ideas, and carry them out in concrete acts upon the environment. Hence Einstein establishes a new expression of reality, $E = mc^2$, and the technological age is born. All of this creative adult exploration of the world begins with the initial introduction to the young child of the limits and order to discover within her own environment.

We fulfill our mission of introducing the limits and order of the world by applying the tenets of Montessori's formula for the child's self-formation first discussed in Chapter 1. They consist of the prepared adult, the prepared environment, and freedom with responsibility. With regard to the developing will and its connection to the universal order, what does a "prepared adult" mean? The first assistance we can give to the child is to serve as a model for self-control and order within our own lives. If we are leading an orderly life such actions are natural to us. However, if our lives are chaotic and we habitually feel frazzled and out of control, we need to slow down and take stock of our lives and ourselves. Specifically, we must assess the actions in which we collaborate with our children. Do we gather up toys randomly or with order in our minds, putting all the stuffed animals in one basket and blocks in another, puzzles on the shelf, and books in the basket by the rocker? When we straighten the room together, do we take all the dirty clothes to the hamper and the towel to the bathroom, then line up the shoes in the closet and hang up or put away any clean clothes?

When we are orderly in our daily actions, children experience the disciplined thought that is in our minds. Because our mental order is visible to them, they can incorporate this order for their own use. This reminds us of a twelve-year-old Montessori student who, when the family kitchen was in disarray from chaotic use by other family members, regularly set it to proper order. She did so with seeming ease by approaching the task with organization and direction. Thus, the reward of giving order to the child is ordered thought. Ordered thought can lead to simplifying what may at first appear an overwhelming task and transforming it to a manageable, even enjoyable, one.

Next, let us consider the prepared environment. We know that the child is nourished and made secure by the order of things. Therefore, we need to prepare an environment for the child that demonstrates order and structure in action. Experiences of order in human life create expectations in the infant that, in turn, she can use to build order within her mind and to assist her in developing her will. "What, when, and where" provide the opportunities for these expectations. We want to make clear to the child in her daily life: *what* to expect, *when* to expect it, and *where* to expect it.

What are some experiences of "what and where" for infants and children under the age of three years? Food stays in the kitchen; we eat at a table sitting down instead of wandering the house, cracker in hand (or riding in the car or walking in a public place). We bathe in a bathtub, not the kitchen sink. Urine and feces belong in the toilet or the potty in the bathroom, not in a diaper on a two-year-old child's body. Toys and puzzles do not belong in the kitchen work area. The special toys that are for the living room stay there. They are not dragged all over the house. We sleep in our own beds. Running and loud voices are for outside, and so forth.

Next there is the timing of all this activity: the "when" it is to take place. The infant and young child's schedule consists of mealtimes, naps, activity, and sleep. We also want to build reflective time into the child's day in order to maximize her ability to integrate her sensorial impressions, thereby solidifying her learning. We have also suggested that parents read to their children each night before bed from their earliest months, thus laying a foundation for quiet time and study in the evening hours as a lifetime habit.

It is the consistency of schedule and routines that is essential to the child's understanding of what is expected of her. Her frontal lobes are as yet unformed. Neither her brain nor her language is developed enough to understand changes in routine. Therefore, try to have set times for trips outside the house when your child is to accompany you, whether to the grocery store, to the park for an outing, to attend religious services, or to visit with friends. If your child is spending the morning hours away from home in a Montessori environment or other setting, plan to take her directly home afterward whenever possible and save other events for later in the afternoon. What is it like for a two- or three-year-old child if—instead of predictably having lunch at home each day at noon, followed by a nap or rest—every day is different: not out of necessity (which will sometimes happen), but because of parental ignorance of her true needs? One day the child goes to the park when picked up from school, the next day she goes straight to the grocery store, and the next to a friend's house for lunch, then shopping. On the fourth day, she is back to lunch and a nap at home. The two- and three-year-old child has no understanding of these changes in activities and the reasons for them. If a child likes what happened yesterday, she begs for a repeat of it: "I want to go to the park!" Parents interpret this insistence as willfulness. Yet, the child cannot see why you do not take her to the park or to a friend's house. Similarly, children do not understand that we go to the grocery store only when groceries are needed or that they must wear a coat today because it is cold, whereas yesterday it was warm and they did not need one. Of course, you will not always be able to follow a weekly schedule for trips outside the house. When these times occur, you will help your child's developing sense of security and control of self if you make as much as possible of the excursion routine. Put on her customary coat or sweater. Leave the house in the same manner. Follow the same route. Point out familiar signposts along the way. Do whatever you can that will remind your child of a predictable pattern in her life.

The order of "what, when, and where" in the child's life provides the structure and opportunity for limits and discipline. It is living within these limits and experiencing order through them that develops the child's will. These external limits are needed in each specific instance until the child has internalized them and can control her own behavior.

This is a long process of self-formation for the child. Parents need to take care not to delay it unwittingly by a lack of conviction and firmness. "No" must mean no every time. "No" cannot mean "Ask me again and maybe I will give in." Or "Scream loud enough, hit me, break something, tell me, 'I hate you, you're mean,' embarrass me in a public place or at my in-laws and I might give you what you want." This scenario sounds extreme; yet it is not an uncommon one in parent-child interactions in our society today. As a parent, you need to decide, "What kind of a child do I want?" Children who are allowed to manipulate their parents learn to spend their energy and developing intelligence in this manner. It becomes a habit of mind. Children who encounter conviction and firmness in their parents' setting of limits become people of character who understand life's limitations and responsibilities. In the words of a Montessori trainer of teachers, the adult's role is to "teach children limits with love or the world will teach them without it."

Why is it that so many parents today have trouble following through when they say no to their children? For those of us from an older generation, this observable fact is a puzzle. Certainly our parents and grandparents did not have this problem. It was apparent to us that previous generations acted on the premise that adults were bigger than children—but not for long! There was no time to lose in helping the child develop self-control and an understanding of the limits of civilized life. Our grandparents and parents also were aware of the great power of the adult over the child. Every child wants to please its parents. This is a deep-seated and unconscious need of the child that may well be an evolutionary outcome. Wise parents use this natural attribute of young children to help them adapt to the society in which they are born.

Perhaps the present generation of parents has difficulty saying no to their children and meaning it, because they are not comfortable with the role of legitimate authority in their children's lives. Today's parents grew up in an era when questioning "authority" was not only accepted; it was encouraged. As a result, they represent the first generation of Americans to be uncomfortable becoming that "authority" themselves for the sake of their own children. Further, rather than seeing their role as developing discipline and character in their children, they have been seduced by their culture into focusing on their children's present happiness. As one young parent described it to us, "We live in a culture where happiness is set forth as a main purpose of existence and in which immediacy reigns supreme. Put these two together, and the resulting goal is to make our children happy now, often with little thought to what will make them happy years hence." It may be also that parents today have organized their lives in such a way that they cannot give the energy and attention required for saying no to their children. It is very easy to give in to the expediency of the moment if parents have not taken the time to think through and plan for the limits and routines that are best for their children.

The more routine in the young child's life, the easier life is for both child and parent. This is because, for the child under three years old, the more routine, the more ready acceptance on the child's part. Of course, there are obvious differences in individual children; some children are very passive or "pleasers," while others are "active engagers" who badger for what they want and are often seen as stubborn by their parents. In reality the latter children need more help from the adult in learning to accept limits, just as other children might have more difficulty learning to read, understand mathematics, or get along with others.

Whatever an individual child's personality, however, the reason for the outcome of the rule that the more routine, the more compliance, has to do with the child's brain formation. The child's brain is not ready to accept change in the way the adult brain does. Young children are busily pruning neural synapses and forming "highways" of information in their brain. This is their Sensitive Period for order, and they seek to find order everywhere. We are reminded of a fourteen-month-old who came into our school each morning with his mother while she took his older sister to her classroom. One day he became quite agitated coming down the walk to the school. He kept wailing loudly and pointing to the empty sundial stand in the middle of the walk. His mother explained to us that he got very excited each day when he passed the sundial on its stand. He was upset because this morning he was early and the elementary school children had not yet brought the sundial out to its stand for the day. This is not an atypical response to change in the environment, even a seemingly small detail in it, from a child of this young age. This mother was attentive and alert to her child's reactions. She knew right away what his problem was and could react appropriately, in this case simply to move him past his objection and divert his attention as best she could.

Routines give information to the young child that words cannot. She can hear the words that we give her but they do not bring understanding. Her mother can explain that she is not going to the park because it is cold and rainy. However, she cannot deduce from this information that it is not a good idea to go to the park today because it is not fun in such weather and that, further, she might get sick under such conditions. We have discussed that the child who is accustomed to cold weather insists on wearing a winter coat into summer. Conversely, a child who first becomes aware of his clothing during the summer may insist, "Bobby no coat!" when cold weather begins in the fall. For young children who are not developed enough to understand reasons, it appears that we have arbitrarily changed their world just as they had begun to figure it out. Bobby does not stand there without his coat thinking, "I'm cold. I need a coat." He is only thinking, "I'm cold," and he is not yet able to fathom the resolution. Again, a young child buckled in her seat belt in the back seat of the car is thirsty and says, "I want a drink." Instead of her father helping her with a drink of water as he might at home, he responds, "I'm sorry. I have nothing to give you." Not until the child is closer to five years old is she capable of thinking to herself, "That's right. Daddy has nothing to give me."

We realize that there are reasons that it is difficult for parents to establish a set schedule for their young children. Therefore it is important for parents to understand what it means to their child when routines are altered. When it is necessary to do so, at a minimum, parents need to expend more time and energy in dealing with their child. This is because changes in expectations inevitably create overexcitement, even anxiety in young children.

Finally, we now consider freedom with responsibility for the child. This is difficult territory for every adult. How should we respond to her when she wants to do something that is beyond her capabilities or that she should not do? No matter how carefully we construct the child's environment to meet her needs for formation of coordinated movement, independence, language, and will, her self-centered viewpoint in the first years of life leads her to inevitable frustration and conflict with others. To know how to help in these situations, as in all others that concern the child in self-formation, we begin with what we know of the child's stages in brain development. Thus we develop a different approach for the child at nine months old, nine to eighteen months old, three years old, and after six years old. To differing degrees in all four stages we must substitute our will for the child's will. After children reach age six, we must watch for situations where we need to substitute our reason for the child's reason, and from twelve to twenty-four years, our wisdom and judgment for the newly emerging adult. However, the ways in which we do this should match the child's self-formation.

The optimal time for the concept of limits to begin is before the baby is a competent crawler. In this first nine months, we use the baby's intense desire for exploration to substitute a different object for the one we need to forbid. Because the baby is interested in anything that she can explore with her senses, it is easy to take an object quickly away, put it aside, and replace it with almost any other. We do not, as yet, have to remove the child or object from view.

Sometime after nine months and progressively to twelve months, babies become fully mobile, crawling capably to any object that they wish to explore. Because they still forget easily, a sensorial distraction usually suffices to refocus their attention. However, from twelve to eighteen months a dramatic change occurs: the child appears more willful. It becomes impossible to divert her readily to another object as before. Her brain has developed sufficiently that she can now hold onto the thought of what she wants, even when the object is not in front of her. This is exciting mental formation. It means, however, that our simple strategy of substituting another object is no longer effective. Now we must physically remove either the child or the object from view.

This is a crucial period for the development of the will. How you restrict the child during these six months can either help or hinder her view of self and willingness to work toward discipline and self-control. If your child crawls or walks rapidly away from you, try not to swoop her up from behind into your arms. Instead, go around in front of her and stop her motion by facing her. You are then able to redirect her energies in a decisive and, at the same time, respectful manner. If she is old enough to walk, you can take her firmly by the hand and lead her to a new situation. By redirecting the child in this way, you are showing her that she is not a "lump of clay" to you; she is a developing person. You are respecting her as someone who must one day "turn herself around" and not expect "rescue from behind."

Redirect her behavior every single time that that behavior is inappropriate. Do not think that maybe this once you can let something go. You cannot. The child can only internalize firmness and an understanding of finality and limits in life from your consistency and your confident manner in helping her. A realization that "never means never" grows within her as she approaches adulthood where boundaries and promises to self are vital for self-protection as well as for the protection of others.

Ages eighteen months to three years encompass the period our culture disrespectfully labels "the terrible twos." Perhaps adults think of this new period of self-formation in such derogatory terms because we are so unprepared for it. Parents have no idea why their young children who once were comparatively cooperative suddenly seem so impossible, and they are confused about what to do next. The problem for the adult is that the child now not only holds an idea of an object in her mind, she can continue to think about it—and she can continue to think about it for some time. The more developed the child's mind becomes, the longer she can keep up her mental rehearsal.

What are we to do? We need to help the child refocus herself by substituting diversion of thought for diversion of object. Because she can now remember her thoughts, our new strategy must be to help her to think about something else. It is essential to understand that we are not talking about a "reasoning session" with the child. Trying to reason with the child at this age in the way that we might with anyone over age six is a classic mistake of adults. Discussing all the reasons why a child under three years old cannot have something that she badly wants simply cements her obsession with it. A child's desire increases with every repetition of thought about it. The sight of her grandmother's shining antique teapot remains in mind all the while you are explaining why she must not touch it—all your child is thinking is "teapot, teapot, shining teapot!"

If the child can no longer be distracted by new sensorial exploration, and yet is not ready to reason, is there any other new brain formation that we can use to help us? There is. The major new self-formation of the child in this period is the development of language. We can add language to the object or situation that we are using to redirect the child's focus and guide her to think about something else. There are at least two ways that we can use language for this purpose. We can give the child a choice of activities or objects, and we can use description to focus the child on what is in front of her. These two strategies can best be presented through anecdotes. These are from situations we have observed in our Young Children's Community. Therefore, the specific details are not necessarily practical for the home, but the principles involved remain the same and are applicable in all circumstances.

One morning an eighteen-month-old we were observing at school decided that she did not want to use the potty; to be precise she had just said in a definite tone, "No, no potty." The teacher knew both from the time interval involved and from observing the child's present body language that it was important that she do so right then. The teacher responded in an equally definite but unchallenging voice, "Would you like to use the blue potty or the pink potty?" (Notice that the choice is between two alternatives only. In most situations, limitation to two choices is a key to successful response by a child of eighteen months.) By responding in this firm but unthreatening manner, the teacher was helping the child focus on the question asked of her and her own thinking about it. Children like to think at this age. Because we think in words, this means that they are thinking through language. This child's eighteen-month-old mind is as busy exploring mentally, "Which one do I want to use?" as her infant mind was previously obsessed with the sensorial exploration of an object. By now she has forgotten that she did not want to use the potty at all.

The goal is to get the child's focus away from the objection she is making and on to another thought. Children at this stage like to hear themselves object. By using choice, we distract them from their initial objection. Do not let them get stuck there by falling into a negotiation trap: "You need to go potty. It's been an hour. Be a good girl. Do it for mommy," or worse still, "Go to the potty and I'll give you M&M's." Keep it simple. A child of eighteen months does not have the will to move her thoughts off her objection without help that is clear and directive.

Description is also a way of using language to refocus young children's attention and help them move past their own objection. One morning a child new to the Young Children's Community was protesting as his father said goodbye to him at the door. The teacher led him directly but in an unhurried manner to the bowl of goldfish. In an interested but soothing voice she explained slowly, "Oh, look at the fish. Those are his black fins." She paused for a moment. "See how they wave in the water. See his mouth move. He needs to eat. I'll show you how to feed him." This combination of directing attention to detail and inviting subsequent action is similar to the points of interest used by Montessori teachers during an activity of practical life.* Both are strategies to refocus thinking and engage the mind in directing the body in activity. They take the child out of the past and into full attention to the moment. For success in redirecting a child through description, you must select an object or activity that is truly interesting to her. Living things are thus a natural choice.

One other point to consider in this anecdote is the ease with which the child can forget even his parents when they are no longer present. It happens, of course, because young children have no real concept of time. They do internalize order, however. Thus this child in the Young Children's Community began to cry again three hours later, as soon as he saw his classmates begin to

_____

*See Chapter 6.

put on their coats. Then he knew his father would come for him soon and, subsequently, he was reminded of his father. The interesting fish was forgotten until the next day. Parents need to understand this ability of children to live in the present in a way that the adult cannot. It is possible to divert children from any thought of their parents when they are not present, and if they can forget about their parents, they can forget anything. It might help you to remember this the next time your child seems to want something so badly and is protesting vehemently because she cannot have her own way.

Another point to remember when using language to help redirect children is not to expect immediacy in compliance. We have to wait a few moments for a response, perhaps even repeating our words. We know that the child's brain has half the neural speed of the adult's until approximately age twelve years. It may be necessary to repeat our words two or three times very patiently and with no threat in our voice. Thus the teacher in the Young Children's Community says to a child who has come out from using the potty with no pants on, "Karen, you need your pants." A half-minute later: "Get your pants and put them on." Instead, Karen sits down on the floor next to the teacher. "Stand up," says the teacher. She helps Karen get to her feet and gently turns her toward the bathroom. She repeats again, "You need to put your pants on." This time Karen responds and moves off toward the bathroom.

Again the essential point is to allow no combativeness in tone during such an encounter. If we add a challenging note to our voices, an emotional response is touched off in the child and overwhelms whatever willpower she has managed to develop. Emotions reside in the area of the brain next to memory. This is why emotion attached to learning cements a memory so firmly. Thus, members of Paula's generation remember exactly where they were and what they were doing when Pearl Harbor was attacked. Lynn's generation has parallel memories of the assassination of John F. Kennedy. The role of emotion in establishing memory is the reason we remember what is interesting to us during the process of learning in school and readily forget what is boring, no matter how thoroughly memorized for the moment the latter material might be.

When choice and description through language do not work to refocus the child's thinking or the child otherwise will not obey, the adult needs to follow through in a direct way. Pick the child up and move on: take her away from the candy at the checkout counter, put her pants on, put her in the car and promptly leave for school, and so on. It is important not to wait until you are angry to take such controlling action. You are bigger than your child. You know that the situation is going to end with your objective achieved, one way or the other. Knowing that the desired outcome for your child is assured, you are freed from feeling anxious and insecure.

Nor should parents feel guilty when they set limits on their child's behavior. Knowledge of the child's formation of the will helps us to know if we are asking too much of her. Because we are realistic in our expectations of the child's behavior, we do not become micromanagers, overcontrolling and demanding obedience with the child's every move. We realize that the possibility of the child's obedience changes at each age as a result of brain development. Hence, we can think of obedience as coming in three stages. From twelve to eighteen months old, the child understands but cannot carry through without a good deal of adult help. From eighteen months to three years old, she can understand the adult's request and can sometimes obey without help. At about three years old, the child reaches the level of development where she can consistently obey, but may still choose not to.

These stages to obedience mirror the child's development

from a being with an unconscious mind at birth, to a child with a conscious mind at age three years. The child's formation of a conscious will in this three-year period is the reason for Montessori's judgment that "school" could begin for the child at this time. Children are capable of obedience if they so choose. They can push in their chairs, return material to the shelf, handle things carefully, and carry out all the other behaviors necessary for a civilized community of others.

To illustrate how the adult follows the stages of the child's obedience, consider a child of fourteen months at mealtime. The adult realizes that if he does not want the child to begin eating whenever she chooses, he must pick the food up and move it out of her reach. With food in front of her, the child can only think, "I want that food." She cannot yet continue her thought to "But I'll have to stop myself until the blessing." At eighteen months old, the child is able to get to this way of thinking, if the setting is right—for example, in the Young Children's Community where she has the reminder of order and routine, in addition to the help of the teacher and other children as models. It is not until the child is three years old, however, that the adult can say, "No, you may not eat yet," and expect her to comply willingly and consistently with the request to wait.

Because children are three years old upon entering the Montessori Children's House, teachers expect compliance when they say no to the child whose behavior is inappropriate. However, knowing that "work" is the key to the child's self-formation in every area of development, teachers move directly to connect the child to the environment through a positive focused activity. In fact, they strive to connect the child to the environment before a negative behavior can appear. For example, when a relatively new or young child comes into class in the morning, the teacher might say, "Put on your apron." After the child does so, the teacher might continue: "Take this tray," and, finally, add,

"Put it here." The next thing the child knows, she is happily absorbed in washing a table.

Teachers are able to bring about this positive outcome with apparent ease because the human tendencies—exploration, orientation, order, abstraction, manipulation, repetition, and perfection—are constantly at work within the child. Teachers have allied themselves with these universal actions of human beings by setting the proper environment for children this age and acting to engage them in work. Their activity requires effort, will, and focus. At its completion, they feel relaxed and satisfied. After a short interval, they regroup and this time choose an activity without adult help. The cycle of self-formation through focused activity continues. Coordinated movement, independence, language, and will are enhanced and the child's developing intelligence proceeds apace with her years.

This is the indirect preparation for academic learning that makes it possible for a child in the Montessori Children's House to learn to write and read, to use the decimal system in mathematical operations, to memorize facts of addition and the countries of Asia—all by the age of six and a half years. Such a foundation for learning in the first six to seven years of the child's life does not just "happen." It is established through the thoughtful responses of the parents at home and the teacher in the Montessori Young Children's Community. When parents come on a tour-visit of Forest Bluff School, they invariably ask, "What do you do about discipline?" We think they ask this question because they assume that disciplinary actions are necessary to keep the children so intent on their work and respectful of each other and of the materials they are using—yet these children are obviously enjoying themselves.

What have we done to achieve such a remarkable result? We explain that we are meeting the children's needs in their self-formation. The teachers understand these needs and prepare the environment for the children accordingly. They then give to each child as much freedom within the classroom as she can handle with responsibility. Once the children become involved in concentrated work in such a setting, discipline takes care of itself. When teachers, for whatever reason, cannot get a child to respond independently to the environment, they take freedom from the child by requiring her to stay temporarily with them. By keeping her close to them, they can substitute their discipline and control for the child's. In addition, the child becomes aware of whatever the teacher is doing at the moment. Most often she sees the teacher giving a lesson to another child, or group of children, and ultimately becomes interested in working again.

Children whose lives are filled with the overstimulation and entertainment of television, computer games, and endless plastic toys inside the home, and an action-packed daily schedule of events outside of it, have trouble developing the concentration required for forming the will and thus a disciplined approach to learning. Too often today we allow our adult idea of "fun" to encroach on the lives of young children. We forget that books were once the major entertainment of children. When John and Abigail Adams, Thomas Jefferson, and, in a later period, Abraham Lincoln were children, reading books was a luxury and a welcome opportunity to use the mind instead of laboring physically with the body. They grew into adults who valued their libraries most of all their possessions. To help our children become worthy citizens of our country, we need to recapture an understanding of what activities aid the development of will and focus in early life.

Our goal is a teachable child who is able to collaborate with the adult in discovering the world. We must work toward the infant's participation with us from the beginning of life. We show the baby an action in slow motion and invite her collaboration: "Here is your sweater. I'm putting it over your head. Give me your arm. Here it is," and so forth. As we have discussed in all our actions of practical life and personal care with the child, this combination of action and language develops into collaboration and a concept of "my turn, your turn." Repetition and practice of each new experience results in learning.

For much of the time, however, because the child is unformed, the parent must substitute his own energy and will for those of the child. For this role, the adult must have the confidence necessary for good leadership. The parent can use a gentle voice when saying "I will help you" to the child. However, everything in the adult's manner and tone must leave no doubt as to the outcome of each situation. The adult's words and actions, as a part of the structure of the child's environment, are as real as its physical elements; they must reflect authority.

Natural leaders act as if they know what they are doing. Who would follow someone across a flooded river if he said, "Well, I do not know if you can make it. Probably you can but that river is really deep. Maybe you should wait or maybe you should go?" and so on. When parents convey such hesitation and lack of conviction in their parental role, children begin to act as if they were in charge, not their parents. As these children grow older, they behave as if the world has come to an end when they do not get what they want in life.

One thing is clear. Although we must have an expectation that the child can act within the limits that we set, we also need to remember that obedience represents an internal decision on the child's part. The child often exhibits fussiness, irritability, and discomfort in the process of making this decision. Our goal is not to eliminate this struggle from the child's life. It is to keep this struggle manageable.

Unfortunately, assisting the child in developing her will is not an easy task in our present society. American culture today is ambivalent in its attitude toward authority in general and toward parental authority in particular. Movies and television shows, for example, routinely depict children as more capable than their parents. These unrealistic messages encourage an unhealthy bravado in children and a belief in their own superiority. When they become adolescents, they find that these false beliefs result in insecurity, fear, and a sense of inferiority, as they discover the reality that they are far less prepared to deal with life than they were encouraged to believe.

Parents can make life much easier for their children and themselves by following the example of a mother in one of our parent child classes. This mother of a two-year-old daughter and a five-year-old son had described to us some of the problems she was having with her children, particularly her son. We suggested that she attend an upcoming public lecture that several schools and colleges in our community were sponsoring. The topic was the discipline of children, and the speaker was John Rosemond, author of *Six Point Plan for Raising Happy Healthy Children* (Kansas City, Mo.: Andrews and McMeel, Universal Press Syndicate, 1989). The day following the lecture, she left a message for us at school: "I am adamant! No more negotiating! I am assuming the posture and attitude of a mother in control!"

What is the result for the young child when parents accept their own responsibility to teach her about limits and the universal order supporting human existence? It means that the child has the opportunity to develop control of self. Difficulties and challenges will come, as they do in every life, but now she will have developed her inner strength for dealing with them. She can accept the world as a finite place and that we are all finite beings within it. She can face the final limit for each of us—the end of life itself on earth—with courage, optimism, and a zest for the journey. Above all, control of self frees your child to seek meaning and fulfillment in life through service and love of others and of the natural world that sustains us each day of our lives.

TEN | Conclusion

We have traced the child's progress from a seemingly helpless newborn to an independently functioning three-year-old, capable of purposeful movement, language, and a controlled will. We have suggested ways to aid this remarkable feat of the child's self-construction based on universal principles of human development first discovered by the intuitive observations of a woman medical scientist of the early twentieth century and now substantiated by research studies in education and behavioral science. These include the Sensitive Periods and the absorbent mind of the child in the early years of life. We have identified Montessori's educational formula of the prepared adult, the prepared environment, and freedom with responsibility, and explained its reliance on the human tendencies—exploration, orientation, order, abstraction, imagination, manipulation, repetition, exactness, control of error, perfection, and communication—for successful implementation.

As to the settings in which the practical guidelines that we have given are successfully applied, they vary widely. For example, in some of our school families, the traditional gender roles of mother and father are reversed. The mother works every day outside the home, often traveling out of town and working late into the evenings. Rather than hiring someone outside the family, the father has elected to take primary responsibility for the children and the management of the home. We find that these fathers are as capable as mothers in understanding the principles behind our specific suggestions in the raising of their children.

Again, in some of our families the mother works outside the home three to five days a week, and it is necessary to find a non-family member to care for the children during this time. In such situations, parents can hire sitters to come to the house. This solution works out well if you take the time to explain not only what you want the sitter to do, but why. A sitter whom you help to understand the new role Montessori identified as "educator," not "servant," to the newborn finds the expanded responsibilities in caring for your child more interesting and rewarding than mere babysitting—just as you, the parents, do.

One of our mothers was not in a position to hire a sitter at home five days a week, yet needed to return to work full-time after her six-week baby leave. She found a quality setting for her child in another family's home—in this case, a family where the mother was already familiar with Montessori principles and implemented them in her home with her own three children, ages six months, three years, and five years. This age-spread of her own children made bringing a new baby into the home optimal for all concerned. The "sitter-mother" could give sufficient attention to her own children while caring for an infant, thus adding much-needed income for her family; our mother found a ready-made Montessori "daytime family" for her newborn.

If you are a working parent and an institutional setting is your best option, look for one that most closely follows the principles that we have discussed. For example, is the atmosphere calm and peaceful for children? Is the environment orderly, uncluttered, and beautiful in its simplicity? Do the children have materials for purposeful activities, and are they suited to each child's stage of development in independence, personal care, and care of the environment? Are physical movement and the development of coordination encouraged? Are the children exposed to good language: oral, written, and symbolic, such as artistic and musical expression? Is the formation of the will aided through encouragement and respect for the children's concentration on their individual activities? Are the expectations for the children's behavior sufficiently demanding, yet appropriate to their stage of development? Is there a two-to-three-year age range in the children and is the adult-to-child ratio optimal? (We suggest one adult for two children under twelve months, one for three children under eighteen months, and one for six children if the children are nearly evenly spaced between eighteen months and three years.)

We live in an historical period of revolutionary change in regard to an understanding of human infants and the role of the adults caring for them. Montessori foresaw these changes and viewed them as opportunities, not only for the freedom of women and their ultimate place in society, but for the advancement of men and the betterment of children as well. It was never a perfect solution for mothers to be isolated from adult companionship all day long, each in their own homes or apartments, with no opportunity to contribute to the larger society, dependent upon their husband's return in the evening for relief from their twenty-four-hour-a-day duties. Each family must find its own solution to the challenge of caring for their children in an optimal way, whether at home with a parent or in another setting.

What has not changed is the energy and commitment that we must give to this task. As in every era since human life began, to raise children well from their birth requires sacrifice, patience, flexibility, and wisdom on the part of the adults. To illustrate this truth and to give you a sense of what it is like in a home setting to follow the guidelines we have suggested in this book, we will tell you the story of Patricia and Andrew. They were first-time parents and their son, Charlie, was almost six months old. Patricia began attending the parent child course when she was pregnant, and from the start, Andrew was also very interested in what she was learning. Andrew was a completely involved father, and whenever he was at home, he helped to care for his son much of the time. As Patricia told us: "It is so much easier when Andrew is there, and we are collaborating and making decisions together about Charlie."

We have chosen Patricia and Andrew here from among our parent child course parents because of their grasp of the principles involved in raising a child well and their commitment to following through on practical details in a reasonable way. Most importantly, they understood the role of observation in determining what their son needed. For example, they did not rush to pick Charlie up every time he cried. Rather, they waited to observe him and tried their best to discover what seemed to be behind his crying, before responding. In large part, because of this reflective approach, Charlie was developing into a baby who could spend long periods of time alone, needing the constant supervision of his parents, of course, but otherwise happily engaged in working to develop himself and in exploring the world about him. He smiled appealingly at everyone who passed by and was happy to be picked up and played with at any time. He was not, however, typically demanding of such attention.

We have learned these things about Charlie by visiting him in his home over a period of time. What most impressed us about these visits with Charlie was his obvious contentment and, at the same time, the intensity and concentration with which he explored his environment wherever he happened to be. In our last visit, Patricia explained that as a newborn of several weeks, Charlie had focused intently on his black-and-white mobile as the currents of air in his room shifted its pieces ever so slightly. After a few weeks, he was equally absorbed in lifting his head from his position on his stomach, or side, to view himself and the figures of his mobile in passing, as reflected in the wall mirror by his child-bed. She said, "It was remarkable to see that a baby is capable of concentrating from birth. I think we helped, too, by being very quiet around him, and we didn't interrupt his gaze, waving things in his face or distracting him in other ways. He lived basically in two rooms—our room and his. For the first month we didn't interfere with his natural ability to 'concentrate' on his environment. We did not have a lot of visitors—he really saw only three people consistently—and we didn't take him anywhere. He seemed very content, calm, and secure in his room. It seems to have been enough for him to have just one room to become very alert to, to try to 'soak it in.'"

We remarked that we had noticed in our visits how active Charlie was with his body, including his arms and hands, and how hard he was working for coordination. Patricia told us that from the very beginning they put rattles in his hand. First, they gave him the newborn's rattle. He would use his reflexive grasp to hold it an instant before dropping it. They added two more rattles—a smooth natural wood, crescent-shaped one to grasp with the whole hand and one of natural wood rings to hold with his fingers. Patricia continued, "He did not seem terribly interested in his rattles. He would get them to his mouth and then drop them until he was about three and a half months. But by four months it was 'rattle mania' and he was active with them all the time. By five months he would reach, grasp, shake, and hold them with two hands. He was more interested in color now so we exchanged his earlier three rattles for three new ones made of wood and painted in different colors. He has one with interlocking triangles, another consisting of rings, and a third one that combines rings and spheres. I bought all of them from baby catalogues and stores. He has them in his mouth a lot but he also likes to listen to the sound when he hits them against the wooden floor."

When we mentioned the obvious strength in Charlie's arms, back, and legs, Patricia told us that from the beginning he could lift his face from one side to the other. Before he was three months old, he could roll from his stomach over onto his back, but it wasn't until he was four and a half months old that he could roll consistently back again to his stomach. "From birth, we put him on his stomach all his waking hours except, of course, those times in the early weeks when we wanted him to be on his back, watching his mobile. By two months he could push up on his arms and hold his head for several moments at a time.

"He could slither a good distance very early on. It is amazing how much babies move about when they are allowed to. By two months old he got himself all the way to the middle of his room a few times. It usually happened when he was alone in his room. At four months he was doing this as many as three times a week. Now at five and a half months he is really inching all over, and getting up on his knees and rocking, too. At first he was enjoying this latest new conquest but now he gets frustrated because he can't move forward.

"That is something interesting that we noticed; he goes through periods of frustration and crying each time that he develops a new ability. He cried when lifting his head the first weeks, for example, then it eased. When he first got up on his knees, he cried a lot for a week, when he was actually pushing himself up. It was amazing to watch him; he would scream out with the physical effort—actually, not really a scream but a throaty roar-like grunting sound. But we didn't pick him up right away when these stressful moments happened. We would let him continue his efforts until it became clear that he had worked as hard as he could and was exhausted. Then we would intervene because he seemed not to know how to stop himself. We would lift him up, giving him a change of scene or taking him to bed if it was time for a nap. These transition stages would only last a few days, then he would move on with ease and he would squeal with delight each time he accomplished his latest triumph. Right now he is starting to crawl so he is fussing a lot.

"If he has been awake one to three hours, we know that his

fussing is also a clue that he's getting tired. He is always on the floor and free to move about so he is very active when he's awake. Sometimes he is ready to go down again after only one and a half hours. His fussing tells us that pretty soon it will be time for a nap and that he will go right to sleep for two hours or so. When he is going through a "growth spurt," he is also likely to fuss when he's settling down to sleep. He'll cry pretty hard sometimes. If we don't interfere and just let him be, within five minutes he will suddenly fall into a deep sleep on his own."

We asked Patricia about being a first-time mother and, looking back on the experience now, what seemed most difficult about it. After a moment's reflection, she replied, "The different kinds of crying. Sometimes Charlie's crying really bothers me; sometimes I can shut it out. It is how and why he is crying that makes the difference. If he is crying and fussing to go to sleep or if he is fed and dry and seems only to be frustrated because he is trying to move toward a toy on the floor, even if he is really loud, it doesn't bother me. If he is fussing and it is that 'I want something from you' cry, then it is like a knife going in. Even if someone else is trying to take care of him, I can't shut that crying off. It is like an alarm going off.

"It is already five and a half months since Charlie was born. It's strange how fast time is going. I learned so much in the course— what to do at each stage, month by month. Six months seemed like such a long time then, if all you had to do was take care of a baby. Then you wake up one day and you think, 'Oh, where did all those months go? Did I do all that I should have done? Did I get the rattles out?' When you are a mother, you are not thinking clearly. I have such a warped sense of time now; my lifestyle is so totally different.

"I can't imagine what it would be like with more children. I only have one child, and I have all the information at my fingertips—memorized, really—yet, I still feel so unclear. I still need review. It is very much 'learn as you do.' It is like playing tennis and stopping in mid-stroke. You look back to see how you are doing. But you can't really tell, because you don't know the conclusion. If something *was* wrong with your baby—wow—any *hint* of something wrong, it would be that much more terrifying!

"I have set up the weaning table now because Charlie is already better at sitting in the chair and it's time for him to have some tasting experiences. I've gotten him in there almost every day. The problem is that it hasn't been the same time every day. I know that would be optimal. But there are some days when I'm still figuring out his feeding schedule. I have the same problem with his bath. We were doing better and then we went on vacation. It is just really hard to make something happen at the same time every day. I would have thought of all things, the schedule would have been the easiest. I'm a schedule sort of person. Even when I go to a really relaxing place for a vacation, I have a schedule in my mind: 'First, I will go for a swim, then eat breakfast and read for a while.' Of course, I do have to follow the baby. A second baby in the family just gets taken in the car, regardless, because the older child has to be in school. For the second baby, that is the schedule they have been offered and that is the schedule they are going to live by. With the first baby, if they have had you up all night and they will sleep until nine in the morning, you are not going to get him up earlier to keep him on a schedule because you are trying to take care of yourself, too.

"What I notice is that families that only have two children sometimes try to overcontrol. When the third child arrives, they have, to a certain extent, become more flexible. Where they were almost too concerned about the oldest child, they now relax a bit. They see that their oldest child is actually functioning and so they relax. They really hit their stride as parents. I can see it on the faces of the other parents in the course when they bring their children to school in the morning. It's as if they are saying, 'Okay, I'm a mother now' or 'I'm a father.'

"For my part, things are definitely settling down now. At

almost six months, Charlie is much more aware of routine and luckily that is happening at the same time that I'm getting it more together. I was a pretty confident and secure first-time mother. I knew to put my marriage first and I was convinced and determined about the knowledge of what to do with our baby. Yet, in these early months, I doubted myself far too easily. I would let myself be influenced by just one conversation, thinking to myself, 'Maybe I should be doing things differently.' I can't imagine what a less secure, less determined person with less information and less support—for example, with a husband who might actually make things more difficult—would feel like. That must really be a nightmare. I feel so fortunate."

Since Patricia did not return to work full-time soon after Charlie was born, we asked her how she felt about changing her lifestyle so radically. She replied, "At thirty-two, I was really happy. I had learned how to have good relationships with people. I loved my job and I was very successful in it. After the baby was born, the combination of hormonal changes and sleep deprivation made me feel like a mixed-up teenager again. I couldn't control my life. I wanted things I wasn't allowed to have. People even had to drive me places. I don't know which is better or worse: being forced to go back to work, back to the life that you knew, or having to stay at home where all day long you have to adjust to an entirely new life. It's a shock to be a fulltime mother. I remember a co-worker commenting on her surprise that a full-time mother of four children from ages two to eight would want help in her house five mornings a week. "She doesn't have anything to do but take care of her children. Why does she need help with that?" she said. At this point in time, I have to say that I can't imagine what the mornings are like for a mother getting all those children off to school at once.

"I just thought that I'd be able to control things a little bit better in those first months. It was so hard just to get to the bathroom or get something for myself to eat or to brush my hair: things that you don't even realize you are doing when you are alone. I would keep thinking, 'It would be nice to go to the bathroom now but I'll just get Charlie to sleep first.' It really helped when Andrew was home so I could ask him to help. It might be so that I could do something small like change my clothes—not to go somewhere, but because it would help to feel clean and fresh for a change. It is better now. At six months I'm trying to decide what I can work back into my schedule for myself. I've had to let go of things that I cared so much about before and that's hard. But I'm very lucky because I have choices. I can only fit in one other thing for a few hours a day but I could get a sitter and go back to work part-time or use that time to exercise and do community service work. I wonder if, for these few years, it would be enough just to cook, garden, sew, and do laundry. It seems that few of us these days consider people happy who make that choice. Yet, I think Montessori had a point in balancing the physical with the intellectual. There is something that nurtures the spirit, something relaxing and satisfying, about using your body in conjunction with your mind, like the children in a Montessori classroom.

"As to the intellectual challenge of being a mother at home with a little baby, I am finding that a nice surprise. Boring it is not! I think this is a direct result of having taken the parent child course. You are given a lot of information but you have to think creatively to make the model work for you. You have to have a good understanding of the purpose behind the child-bed or the weaning table, for example, because there are going to be times when you have to be flexible. You will have to come up with a creative response and you will have to determine if your solution really meets its intended purpose.

"When we went on vacation recently, we couldn't childproof a whole room for Charlie. There was a setup that seemed pretty natural for adaptation, though. There was a glassed-in porch off of our bedroom where, lying on our bed, we could still see where he was sleeping. That way we could tell if we were meeting the purpose of the child-bed: to provide a large surface on which the baby can move freely. We took a bunch of large wool blankets and put a sheet on top with pillows all round so he couldn't roll into the glass wall. This new situation actually gave us an opportunity to understand why Charlie was going off of his child-bed all the time now. He was flipping around while he was totally asleep. In the small space of a crib, he would have had to stay in the same position or keep bumping up against the crib every time he rolled from side to side. Because he has always been in the child-bed, he now rolls all over the place when he's asleep. He is developing his ability to move even while he sleeps. An open surface on the floor with pillows is fine for sleeping when you are not at home, then. We just made sure the pillows were heavy and stiff (like most couch pillows) so that they held the edges of the blankets down, and that the space was very large. It was probably six feet by six feet.

"The visual field that the child-bed makes possible is not as key at six months. A newborn must see, so a proper child-bed with the wall mirror next to it is important. He has to build that visual map of his room that he is going to move out into. By the time that he is six months old and moving readily, it isn't quite so terrible that the pillows block some of his vision. Charlie could also see above the pillows and was very entertained by the trees outside, their pine needles shimmering in the sunlight. It was fascinating to be able to watch him unobserved. I was so surprised to see that he is comfortable sleeping with his arms and legs flung out, lying on his back. I think that I am leaving him all cozy and snuggled up to sleep. Yet, he is all contorted in various positions within minutes.

"One thing I've learned is that this is all a process. Things are constantly changing. You can't be a person who thinks she can make it totally safe for her baby forever. Parents get into those catalogues and think they can make the entire world safe for their child. But the child changes every few weeks. Last week Charlie began pushing up on his arms, tipping over and banging his head on the floor. I realized that I could still put him down on the hard floor and read next to him, or continue whatever I am doing, if I first put down a flat pillow from the couch on each side of his head. If he does flip over, his head will hit the pillow, not the hard floor. Of course, this is only going to work temporarily. In a few weeks, there will be something new to figure out.

"These six months have been hard but we are rewarded now with a baby who seems secure and comfortable, even when he is away from home. He is very social and engaging with his constant smiles—a truly calm, happy baby. It's becoming more and more fun every week now."

We had a talk with Andrew next. As we listened to his comments, we became even more aware of the advantages of a fully active and participating father in the raising of children and the development of a marriage. Andrew's involvement from his wife's pregnancy, labor, and delivery to the first weeks afterward was a key factor in his son's successful development to that date. Paula remembers that these opportunities for fathers to participate in their children's births and first weeks of life are new developments in our culture. Of all the revolutionary changes in Western society in recent years, recognition and respect for the responsibilities of fathers in the child's earliest years is among the most important.

First, we asked Andrew what it was like, as a first-time father, to raise his son by Montessori guidelines. He replied, "I didn't feel forced to go against any instinct. It seemed to make sense to me. Logical ideas became the foundation. There are these working parts: bed, mobiles, mirror. They are set up to allow the child's development. These are the physical parts of the room; then there is an emotional commitment. The focus is on the child and building a family. I don't even see the physical parts when I enter the room, say, to change his diaper. I don't think, 'I'm getting my son on the floor bed.' I just start changing his diaper. Incidentally, his bed has advantages for me, too. I'm over six feet tall but we can lie on it together when I'm exhausted!

"I really like things not being cluttered and that we've kept it simple. The benefit of making the choices up front is that we don't have to think about all those decisions anymore. You're not suddenly transforming your home with all those crazy things. Our home has a Shaker-like simplicity. We understand the essence of what's required in the absolute for our son—diapering, feeding, sleeping, playing—and we have provided for it. We didn't have to bring more complexity into our lives.

"I don't feel like we're a 'Montessori house.' We're just two committed parents following a common-sense-based approach to raising a child. I'm happy to be consistent with it. I feel like I am just raising my child. Patricia and I want peace and calm in our home and to do it together. We think of what is best in the long run for our son and we balance what is best for us, too. Our marriage is our first focus. It sets the tone. We're just getting up to speed [as parents] now that it's been almost six months. We're providing what is best for our son's development—peace and calm and keeping things loving, practical and simple. I think of my son as joining our family, not the reverse."

When we asked Andrew about his son's delivery and the first weeks after his birth, he responded, "We had decided on a natural birth and I was going to be a big part of that. We took a birthing course together. I was going to be actively involved as the 'husband-coach.' I learned about the relaxing techniques and working through the first stage of labor and then the second stage and the delivery. So we had planned for this husband-wife process. I was excited about that and I knew it was a nice comfort for Patricia. I kept my travel schedule to a minimum from two weeks before her due date. I also took two weeks off of work after the baby was born. It was important to me to be there to support my wife in the first days after delivery and make sure things were do-able for her.

"The birth was harder than most. Our son is a big baby and the second stage took two and a half hours so it was a challenge. It took a real team effort to bring him into the world. The first days afterwards are somewhat of a blur. The doctor wanted Patricia in bed for two weeks so I was taking one hundred percent care of our son. Actually, it was more like ninety-five to five, I guess, because Patricia was breast-feeding. To tell you the truth, though, I was really more focused on my wife, her emotional well-being and safety, and being certain that she was comfortable. For some reason, I never worried about the baby. Once his breathing was established after delivery and I could see that he was healthy, it didn't dawn on me that anything could go wrong. Right from the start, I always felt comfortable holding him and doing everything for him. Maybe seeing his tough birth made me see how strong he was. I felt really close to my wife, having lived through this experience with her and it was almost like the baby was just a part of this process: its goal or culmination. The baby wasn't neglected but Patricia was on the top of my mind.

"I describe those first days as a 'blur' because I was up all the time and very need-focused, whether it was for the baby or Patricia. I was so tired that I just wanted to get done with whatever needed doing. Things settled down after three or four days and I got some sleep. Patricia was feeling better and we could catch our breath. That's when I first had the luxury of looking at our son and realizing how incredible he was."

We asked Andrew what he considered the biggest challenges now. He said, "I'm mostly out of town because I'm the primary breadwinner, so maintaining closeness with my wife and son is paramount to me. I always have a small folding picture frame in my pocket with pictures of my wife and son in it [even though he is dressed in 'at-home' relaxing clothes, Andrew pulls the frame out of his pants' pocket and shows us their pictures]. Also it helps to have the cell phone and e-mail. Whenever I do get home, it's like jumping onto a moving merry-go-round and trying not to stop the ride. I have to get into the flow and right back into where my son was in his schedule.

"Another challenge is the change in activity. We have a quieter lifestyle now, although I can't say we ever 'raced around' to have fun. For a treat now, we might order food from a restaurant and watch a video at home, instead of going out. When you are a parent, you have to forget about yourself. You can't just go and read the paper. I don't play my sports with as much rigor or for as long as I used to. I might start them early in the morning so I can get back to relieve Patricia or if I go out at mid-day, I'm certain that I get back in time for us to do something together. I'm at peace with these changes. I've given a little but I've gotten a lot in return.

"As to what comes next, I feel we have a good understanding of what needs to be done. But I don't look on the things we learned in Montessori as a checklist. We've been given goals, not absolutes, to follow. We won't always be doing things well and getting an A+. We'll have to observe and evaluate what we're doing, as if we were good 'scientists.' It is the spirit of Montessori, not the letter that is important to me. So many people want that 'bullet' or 'pill' that will fix the problem. They just want someone to tell them what to do. The problem is there is no 'cookie-cutter' approach to raising a child, whether you are talking about the child-bed or cloth diapers. If you are going to improvise, though, the change has to meet the objectives you and your wife have established together.

"I'll give you an example. We had decided originally that Patricia would breast-feed for nine months. However, at five months she was pretty miserable with recurring breast infections and really tired. It didn't help that Charlie cut two teeth—really sharp ones—at this time, too. We decided to substitute formula for his midmorning and midafternoon feedings. Almost immediately, Patricia began to feel better. The good thing about this plan is that it still ensures that our son is getting plenty of breast milk and the experience of nursing with his mother but, at the same time, Patricia is relieved of providing one hundred percent of his nourishment. Our plan now is for her to complete weaning from the breast about eight months or so. It's not the nine months of nursing that we had originally planned on but it's a reasonable substitute.

"When we need a new plan to rebalance things like this, it is really important to me to be in the loop with the decision. I'm not leading the discussion; maybe I'm not the CEO. But I'm needed to help meet the ultimate objectives: a peaceful home and an environment to live and grow in. And when I come in the house, I always look for my wife. Too often, the father comes home and looks for the children first, not the wife. The baby follows the marriage. There has to be a solid relationship between the parents. That's the basis for being a good father."

It was clear from both Patricia's and Andrew's comments that they had a good working relationship with each other and a marriage based on love and respect. They were collaborating well with their first child, and were successful in meeting his needs in his first months of life. But what about parents who have multiple children and are attempting to follow Montessori guidelines? Patricia alluded to the difficulties she imagined arising for these families. How do they really fare? By way of illustration, we relay the following anecdote told to us by two young parents, Karen and John, who are presently taking our parent child course.

Their story is about the same mother whose comments began the Preface of this book and helped inspire us to write it. It took place just six days after the mother, Sarah, and her husband, Tom, had had their third baby. Their two older children—Edith, who was six years old, and Todd, who was four years old—started in the parent child classes as newborns and are now students at our school.

On a warm June evening, Karen and John, knowing how much they had appreciated it when their friends had brought them meals after their own baby had been born just a few months earlier, decided to drop a dinner off for Sarah and Tom's family. It was a little before five-thirty. Tom who had been playing with Edith and Todd in the back yard greeted them at the door. When she heard Karen and John arrive, Sarah called from the bedroom, "Oh, please stay and eat with us. I'm just finishing nursing the baby." Tom added enthusiastically, "Yes, come and sit down with us. We'll set up a picnic in the yard." Karen said, "Are you sure?" She was afraid that this was all overwhelming for the older two children. It was a spur-of-the-moment situation and perhaps one that could turn into a "free-for-all" of wild behavior. After all, there was a new baby in the house and one would expect that siblings might be asking for additional attention for themselves, not to share their parents with visitors at the end of the day. In addition, Karen and John had brought their four-month-old son with them, adding to the excitement and novelty for the children. However, Karen and John did stay after all because Sarah and Tom were so insistent.

While the adults were carrying food out to the picnic table, the children carried their own small table—one child on each end—out into the back yard from the kitchen. They then went back for their child-size chairs and, finally, they set their own places to eat, bringing their own dishes and utensils from a small cupboard in the kitchen. When all was ready, they ran about the yard, collecting peonies off the bushes and putting them in two glasses, one for the adults' table and one for their own small table. Amazingly, they did all of this very quietly on their own, and Karen realized afterward that she was barely aware of all their activity. During dinner, the children ate contentedly at their own table while the adults ate at theirs.

After the children had finished eating, they cleared their own places, taking the dishes into the kitchen—again all on their own and without anyone saying anything to them. Todd then began to "garden," contentedly digging in the dirt. Edith sat down to watch Karen's baby who was on a blanket spread on the grass. The baby at four months was spending his "picnic time" on his stomach, pushing up on his arms and lifting his head, very alert and engaged by this new back yard environment. Eventually, Edith joined Todd investigating all the flowers and bushes in the yard, and they then began to run and play with their dog, throwing his ball for him. When it was seven o'clock, Tom called the children into the house to take their baths, and get ready for bed.

On the ride home, Karen and John commented on the evening: how truly remarkable the children were in their self-sufficiency and ability to entertain themselves, even without toys or planned activities. As a result, the adults could have a relaxing evening of conversation and companionship with each other and, at the same time, the joy of having their children with them, "working," picnicking, and playing in the yard.

The experiences of these couples, and similar ones relayed to us by others, help to show that parents following the practical guidelines we have outlined find their lives and the lives of their children running more smoothly. This is our goal. If, however, you are not finding this to be the case in your own experience, it may be that you are trying too hard to follow exactly every idea we have given. Our intention is not to create a checklist for raising a child. As Patricia's and Andrew's comments earlier in this chapter make clear, it is the principles behind the practical detail that you must concentrate on understanding. If you then observe your child carefully, you can apply these principles to a variety of situations.

The key tool for applying principle to reality successfully is always observation of the child. Yet, observation is a great challenge for adults in aiding children in their self-formation. Why should this be so? As we have learned, helping children in their development always involves choosing a right moment and a right object or activity to present to them. *How* to show something to the child is the easy part. *How to* steps are easily demonstrated and presented as a checklist in any educational course, whether for parents or teachers. Taking the time and making the effort to observe the child, and thus discovering what to introduce and when to intervene is difficult.

Observing is not watching. To use Andrew's terminology, to observe is to think like a "scientist": to be completely open to what you are seeing with no preconceived ideas in mind. Therefore, when we observe children, we cannot project what we are thinking onto them. We cannot assume that when a two-month-old baby keeps lifting his head over and over, and sees the design on the pillow in front of his eyes, what he wants is to get to that pillow. He may just be absorbing its pattern or just lifting his head in order to strengthen his neck and back, and the pillow just happens to be in his line of vision.

If we observe as a scientist does, we not only learn children's needs and what we can give them that meets those needs, we learn what we need to take away from them or to stop doing for them, as well. In other words, we become aware of the obstacles to their development. We begin to see that by too readily giving to the five-month-old baby the rattle that he is struggling for, we are taking away an opportunity for manageable struggle. If, at a year and a half, he is trying to fit a cube into the lid of the sorting box, we need to wait until he is close to the point of becoming too frustrated or of giving up, before we intervene to help. When a two-year-old spills water down his chin while drinking with a glass, we need to observe which part of the process is going wrong. When we can see why he is spilling, we can do the one thing that will help him. Taking all challenge away—giving him a "sippy" cup instead of letting him continue his efforts with the glass, for example—presents an obstacle to his development.

Look, then think: "What is the one thing that I want to do to help?" Your aim is to give the least amount of help necessary and to give it at just the right moment. This means that when you are with your child, you need to stand back at least some of the time. It is not necessary to be constantly interacting with him. If you are sitting and reading a magazine, put it down for a while just to watch your child and gather information. What is he doing with his hands, his fingers? What are his legs and back doing? How hard is he working? For example, when he is a year and a half and trying to get dressed in the morning, watch to see what he is doing on his own. Think whether what you are about to do is really going to be of help to him, and so forth, throughout the day. Observe, think, act. By following this pattern, you can best guarantee that your actions result in collaboration with your child for his benefit, not an undermining of your child's efforts for self-formation.

It was by following this path of observation, reflection, and collaboration with the child that Montessori discovered the purpose of human childhood and how to assist it. But it was her respect for the child that originally set her on this path, and it is respect for the child that will enable us to embark upon it, too. We discovered in our visits that this was certainly the case for Patricia and Andrew. Listen to Patricia's words from our last visit to Charlie's house. This incident occurred when a friend of Charlie's grandmother stopped by to see him. He was playing contentedly on the living-room floor, exploring a colorful wooden rattle and occasionally rolling over and getting up on his knees, rocking back and forth, smiling and making sounds of delight. His visitor smiled, too, and said, "He's so adorable. I'd want to keep picking him up. Don't you want to do that?" Patricia looked thoughtful for a moment. Then she answered, "Yes, but I try not to. It's really out of respect. I respect what he is doing. He's working really hard to develop himself almost all of the time."

Human life is precious and special, and respecting it is essential to human happiness and progress. Only by respecting human beings can we discover our role in creation and how best to prepare ourselves for it. Particularly, we need to have reverence for the child and his task of self-formation. The child's is truly a monumental assignment, not repeated by any other species. He has to build a "complete human being" capable of making a contribution to the world as an adult, indeed to change that world for the better. To do this the child must struggle to raise himself to a spiritual level. It is certainly possible for human beings to live on an animal level. We engage in the same acts: eating (nursing), sleeping, mating, grooming, sheltering ourselves, and relating in groups. Historically, we vary in our success in fulfilling our destiny as a spiritual species. In the struggle for physical survival, we have often neglected our higher needs.

Today we are conscious of the physical needs of human existence, but we are also aware of the challenges to the human spirit in our daily lives. We struggle to deal with the heightened level of activity that results from a constant barrage of instantaneous technological information from every corner of the globe. The speed with which we live, too often leads to complicated, stressful lives and a deep feeling of emptiness and spiritual dryness. To help the child become a "complete human being," capable of thriving in this challenging new time, it is essential that we learn all we can about his task of self-formation and how to aid it. To reach this goal, we must observe the child, collaborate with him, and respect his self-formation.

Over a hundred years ago Montessori began her quest for "discovering" the child. She identified children's need for respect from adults and collaboration with them. Because she recognized that their need for collaboration begins at birth, she realized the importance of parents' having knowledge of childhood's planes of development and the special energies and needs of each one. We hope the information we have given in this book about Montessori's discoveries of childhood helps to make the first three years of your child's life more joyous and rewarding for you both.

Acknowledgments

We thank all Montessori Teacher Trainers worldwide for their dedicated work on behalf of children and the development of Montessori education. We are particularly grateful to our Primary Course trainers, Margaret Stephenson, Elizabeth Hall, and Hildegard Solzbacher, and to Lynn's Assistant-to-Infancy Course trainers, Silvana Montanaro and Judi Orion. Paula was also fortunate in attending Elementary Course lectures given by Margaret Stephenson and Allyn Travis. Mario Montessori, Jr., Mario Montessori III, Amsterdam, the Netherlands; Camillo Grazzini, Bergamo, Italy; Marsilia Palocci, Perugia, Italy; Maria Teresa Vidales, Mexico City; and Margot Waltuch, New York City, also greatly contributed to our understanding of Montessori education and influenced the direction of our teaching and writing. Renilde Montessori, President of the Association Montessori Inernationale (AMI), Amsterdam, the Netherlands, and Virginia McHugh Goodwin, Executive Director, AMI/USA, Rochester, New York, were invaluable sources of encouragement and advice. We thank David Kahn, Executive Director, North American Teachers' Association (NAMTA), for the regional workshops with contemporary psychologists and researchers.

For practical assistance in producing this book, we appreciate the expert secretarial assistance of Cynthia Grieshop and the wise comments and enthusiasm for this project of our editors, Rahel Lerner and Altie Karper, at Schocken Books. Karin Olsen Campia is responsible for the excellent photographs of the children. We are grateful to Judi Orion, Silvana Montanaro, and AMI for permission to reprint the Time Line of Development accompanying the text. We could not manage professional careers without the assistance and dedication of Margaret Alvarez in running our households. We thank her for giving so much to us and to our families.

For making possible an ever-deepening understanding of children and how to help their development, we thank our colleagues and the parents and children of Forest Bluff School. Our daily journey with each one of them gives the greatest purpose and meaning to life. To our children, grandchildren, sons-in-law, brothers-in-law, nieces and nephews, bless you for your readiness to help with every kind of assistance throughout the writing of this book. You are the most generous, supportive, talented, and companionable of families. Thank you for bringing joy to us every day of our lives.

Bibliography

Baumrind, Diana. "Rearing Competent Children." In William Damon, ed., *Child Development Today and Tomorrow.* San Francisco, Calif.: Jossey-Bass, 1989.

Csikszentmihalyi, Mihaly, Ph.D. *Flow.* New York: Harper and Row, 1990.

————. *Finding Flow.* New York: Basic Books, 1997.

————. *Becoming Adult.* New York: Basic Books, 2000.

Eliot, Lise, Ph.D. *What's Going On In There?* New York: Bantam Books, 1999.

Greenspan, Stanley I., M.D. *The Growth of the Mind.* Reading, Mass.: Perseus Books, 1997.

Hunter, James Davison. *The Death of Character.* New York: Basic Books, 2000.

Kubey, Robert, and Mihaly Csikszentmihalyi. "Television Addiction Is No Mere Metaphor." *Scientific American* 286, no. 2 (February 2002).

Lillard, Angeline, Ph.D. *Montessori: The Science Behind the Genius.* New York: Oxford University Press, forthcoming.

Lillard, Paula Polk. *Montessori: A Modern Approach.* New York: Schocken Books, 1990.

Montessori, Maria. "Lecture on Movement by Dr. Montessori, London, 1946." In *Communications* 1 (2001), journal of the Association Montessori Internationale (AMI), 161 Koninginneweg, 1075 CN Amsterdam, the Netherlands.

Rathunde, Kevin, Ph.D. "Montessori Education and Optimal

Experience." In *NAMTA Journal* 26, no. 1 (Winter 2001), journal of The North American Montessori Teachers' Association, 13693 Butternut Road, Burton, Ohio 44021.

Weissbluth, Marc, M.D. *Healthy Sleep Habits, Happy Child.* New York: Ballantine Books, 1987.

Index

About the Authors

Paula Polk Lillard and her daughter Lynn Lillard Jessen cofounded the Forest Bluff School in Lake Bluff, Illinois, a Montessori school for children from preschool through the eighth grade. Paula is the director of the school, and she and Lynn teach the parent child course, a workshop for parents on using Montessori methods with infants from birth to age three years. They live in Lake Forest, Illinois.